Metropolitan Planning in India

Metropolitan Planning in India

Based on the National Urban Policy Framework

Nirmala
Assistant Professor, Department of Architecture
Deenbandhu Chhotu Ram University of Science and Technology

Satpal
Associate Professor, Department of Architecture
Deenbandhu Chhotu Ram University of Science and Technology

Shanika
Research Scholar, Department of Architecture
Deenbandhu Chhotu Ram University of Science and Technology

FeelFirst Publishing LLP
4381/4 Ansari Road, Daryaganj,
New Delhi 110002, India

Publisher: Amarjyoti Dutta
Acquisitions Editor: Ankush Kumar Manhas
Development Editors: Ilina Pagay, Debosmita Guin
Digital Platform and Media Lead: Rishav Kakati
Marketing Director: Annie Hazarika

ISBN-13: 978-93-49919-48-8
ISBN-10: 93-49919-48-6
ISBN-13 (ePub): 978-93-49919-42-6
ISBN-13 (uPDF): 978-93-49919-62-4

Typeset in by Bharati Composers.
Cover designed by Syed Dilshad Ali.
Printed and bound in India.

Contents

List of Maps

Preface

The rapid urbanization and expansion of metropolitan regions in India present both tremendous opportunities and complex challenges. As cities grow and evolve, they become the primary drivers of economic growth, technological innovation, and cultural transformation. However, this urbanization is not without its hurdles. Strained infrastructure, fragmented governance, environmental degradation, and social inequality are just a few of the issues that have emerged in the wake of India's metropolitanization.

This book, *Metropolitan Planning in India: Based on the National Urban Policy Framework*, seeks to explore these challenges and offer a comprehensive analysis of metropolitan planning in the Indian context. It brings together both theoretical insights and practical solutions, emphasizing the role of the National Urban Policy Framework (NUPF) as a guiding force for sustainable and inclusive urban development.

Through a detailed exploration of urban growth, governance models, and spatial planning strategies, this work aims to contribute to the ongoing discourse on urban sustainability. It draws from global best practices, comparing them with India's unique urban challenges and proposing pathways for improvement. With an emphasis on case studies, the book aims to provide a grounded understanding of how metropolitan regions in India can navigate the complexities of urbanization while remaining resilient, inclusive, and sustainable.

In embarking on this exploration, we are driven by the belief that well-planned metropolitan regions are not only essential for economic prosperity but also for the creation of socially just and environmentally responsible urban spaces. By addressing the diverse challenges of governance, infrastructure, and resource management, we can ensure that India's growing cities remain not only economic powerhouses but also liveable, equitable, and resilient spaces for all.

This book is the culmination of years of research, observations, and case study analyses in the field of urban planning and metropolitan governance. We hope that it will inspire further research, encourage innovative planning practices, and ultimately contribute to the creation of more sustainable and inclusive metropolitan futures.

Acknowledgements

We would like to express our sincere gratitude to all those who have supported us throughout the development of this book.

Our deepest appreciation goes to the various academic institutions, research organizations, and urban planning bodies whose publications, resources, and expertise have provided valuable insights and guidance in shaping the content and theoretical framework of this work.

We are also grateful to our colleagues, peers, and professionals in the field of urban planning for their thoughtful feedback, constructive criticism, and engaging discussions, all of which have significantly enriched the depth of this book.

Additionally, we would like to acknowledge the contributions of the many urban planners, policymakers, and practitioners whose case studies and practical experiences have helped to ground the theoretical concepts discussed in this book in real-world urban planning and development challenges.

Finally, we wish to thank the readers and future scholars who will engage with this work, hoping it provides meaningful perspectives and contributes to the ongoing dialogue in the field of metropolitan planning and urban development.

Nirmala
Satpal
Shanika

CHAPTER

1

Introduction

1.1 Background and Context

Metropolitan regions serve as the economic, social, and political nerve centres of modern nations. They act as engines of economic growth, fostering technological innovation, trade expansion, and employment generation. The shift from predominantly agrarian economies to urban-centred economic models has led to a global increase in metropolitan regions, shaping the economic and spatial fabric of countries. This trend is particularly pronounced in India, where rapid urbanization, industrial expansion, and infrastructural developments have led to the emergence of several metropolitan hubs (Bhagat, 2014). However, while urbanization has historically been associated with progress and development, it also brings forth unprecedented governance, environmental, and infrastructural challenges.

Urbanization in India has followed a complex trajectory, shaped by historical patterns, economic shifts, and policy frameworks. Unlike many developed nations where urbanization was a gradual process, India has witnessed an accelerated and often unregulated urban expansion (Kundu, Pandey, & Sharma, 2019). The post-independence era saw major policy shifts, with the government focusing on industrialization, urban expansion, and planned economic growth. However, despite numerous Five-Year Plans, economic policies, and urban development programs, metropolitan growth remained largely uncoordinated, leading to severe infrastructural and governance issues (Chatterjee & Chattopadhyay, 2020).

By the early 21st century, Indian cities had begun experiencing exponential growth, driven by technological advancements, economic liberalization, and rural-to-urban migration. Cities like Delhi, Mumbai, Bengaluru, and Kolkata emerged as major urban centres, attracting large-scale migration from rural regions (Seta, Sen, Biswas, & Khare, 2017). However, this rapid growth has not been without consequences. The lack of integrated urban policies and weak metropolitan governance structures has resulted in severe traffic congestion, housing shortages, environmental degradation, and strained public services (Nazim, 2022).

The governance of metropolitan areas remains highly fragmented, with multiple agencies overseeing different aspects of urban management. In cities like Mumbai and Delhi, overlapping jurisdictions between municipal corporations, development authorities, and state governments have created bureaucratic bottlenecks, leading to inefficiencies in policy implementation and infrastructure development (Gandhi & Pethe, 2017). Recognizing these challenges, the Indian government has introduced several policy frameworks and urban planning initiatives to streamline metropolitan governance. One of the most significant developments in this regard is the National Urban Policy Framework (NUPF), introduced in 2018 and refined in 2020 (Ministry of Housing and Urban Affairs, 2020).

1.1.1 Urbanization Trends and Challenges in India

Urbanization in India is occurring at an unprecedented rate, with projections suggesting that over 50% of the country's population will reside in urban areas by 2050 (NITI Aayog, 2021b). The growth of metropolitan regions has been driven by industrialization, economic diversification, and improved connectivity. However, this expansion has also led to several challenges. The rapid influx of people into metropolitan areas has placed immense pressure on transportation networks, housing supply, and public utilities. Cities like Mumbai and Bengaluru face severe traffic congestion, inadequate public transport, and inefficient waste management systems (Chatterjee & Chattopadhyay, 2020). The demand for affordable housing has skyrocketed, leading to rising property prices, expansion of informal settlements (slums), and encroachments on environmentally sensitive areas. Metropolitan areas have struggled to implement effective zoning regulations and land-use planning (Gandhi & Pethe, 2017).

Environmental concerns have also become a pressing issue. Urban expansion has led to deforestation, loss of green spaces, water scarcity, and increased pollution levels. Delhi and other large metropolitan regions consistently rank among the world's most polluted cities, highlighting the need for environmentally sustainable urban policies (Nazim, 2022). Additionally, a major barrier to effective metropolitan planning is the lack of coordination between various administrative bodies. Multiple agencies often oversee urban management without clear delineation of responsibilities, leading to bureaucratic inefficiencies and delays in decision-making (Gandhi & Pethe, 2017). While metropolitan areas drive economic growth, they also exacerbate income inequalities and social exclusion. The rise of gated communities, informal settlements, and unequal access to basic services has resulted in spatial segregation (Bhagat, 2014).

To address these challenges, the Indian government has developed various policy responses, urban planning strategies, and institutional reforms aimed at fostering sustainable and inclusive urban development.

1.1.2 The Need for a Comprehensive Urban Policy Framework

Recognizing the pressing need for a structured approach to urbanization, the Government of India introduced the National Urban Policy Framework (NUPF) as a strategic document to guide metropolitan growth (Ministry of Housing and Urban Affairs, 2020). The NUPF aligns with global best practices and integrates principles from international urban policies to develop a sustainable and inclusive approach to metropolitan governance and planning (UN-Habitat, 2016). The framework establishes a structured urban development roadmap that aligns with India's economic and demographic realities while enhancing metropolitan governance through institutional restructuring and capacity-building initiatives.

By promoting sustainable land-use planning, the NUPF aims to balance urban expansion with environmental conservation while improving urban infrastructure and service delivery to enhance the quality of life for urban residents. The framework also emphasizes social inclusion and participatory governance, ensuring that local communities play a significant role in decision-making processes. By integrating these goals into urban policy and governance frameworks, India aims to create resilient and future-ready metropolitan regions that can effectively accommodate growing populations while maintaining economic, social, and environmental balance (Revi, 2016).

1.1.3 Future Prospects for Metropolitan Development

India's transition to an urban-majority nation is inevitable. The success of metropolitan regions in the future will depend on the ability to implement adaptive governance mechanisms, invest in smart infrastructure, and integrate sustainable planning practices (Aayog, 2021). The adoption of smart city technologies, such as AI-driven urban planning, real-time data analytics, and Internet of Things (IoT)-based smart grids, will play a crucial role in optimizing metropolitan infrastructure (Biswas & Maurya, 2018). Additionally, increased collaboration between government agencies, private sector investors, and urban planners will be critical for financing and executing large-scale urban projects (Chatterjee & Chattopadhyay, 2020).

Climate-resilient urban planning will also be essential. Integrating green urban policies, renewable energy adoption, and climate-adaptive infrastructure will help mitigate the impacts of climate change on metropolitan regions (Nazim,

2022). Moving towards decentralized governance models, where municipal governance is strengthened, community-driven planning is encouraged, and participatory urban decision-making is prioritized, will enhance urban resilience and inclusivity (Gandhi & Pethe, 2017).

The background and context of metropolitan development in India highlight both the immense potential and the critical challenges facing urban regions today. As India urbanizes at a rapid pace, it is imperative to develop strategic policy interventions, governance innovations, and sustainable urban planning frameworks. The following chapters will provide an in-depth exploration of urbanization trends, policy frameworks, case studies, and recommendations for strengthening metropolitan governance in India.

1.2 NUPF and Its Relevance to Metropolitan Planning

India's urban planning landscape has historically been governed by fragmented, state-driven frameworks that often lack integration across sectors and scales. Recognising the need for a cohesive national vision, the Ministry of Housing and Urban Affairs (MoHUA) introduced the National Urban Policy Framework (NUPF) in 2018 as a guiding document to structure urban growth and governance in a sustainable, inclusive, and future-oriented manner. Although not a statutory document, NUPF offers a critical reference point for aligning local and regional urban plans with national development goals.

The NUPF is structured around 10 transformative levers—such as urban governance, planning and managing urban growth, housing, infrastructure, mobility, sustainability, and economic development—and underpinned by 16 core principles, including subsidiarity, participatory planning, inclusiveness, resilience, and equity. These principles aim to foster coordinated urban development that is responsive to the unique needs of India's diverse urban systems, including metropolitan and mega-urban regions.

In the context of metropolitan planning, the NUPF serves as a valuable normative and operational framework. It calls for regional spatial strategies, institutional strengthening of Metropolitan Planning Committees (MPCs), and long-term visioning based on functional urban areas. The framework explicitly highlights the need to address challenges such as fragmented governance, inadequate metropolitan data, environmental degradation, and social exclusion—challenges that are deeply embedded in India's current metropolitan governance fabric.

The NUPF's emphasis on multi-level governance, functional urban units, and strategic regional planning aligns well with the imperatives of metropolitanization in India. Its relevance becomes even more pronounced in the post-COVID era, where the importance of regional coordination, resilience-building, and inclusive infrastructure has become central to urban sustainability. Furthermore, its alignment with global agendas such as the Sustainable Development Goals (especially SDG 11) makes it a key enabler for integrated metropolitan futures.

In this book, the NUPF serves not only as a reference framework but also as a lens to analyse case studies, assess governance challenges, and propose future-ready solutions for India's metropolitan regions.

1.3 Objectives

The primary objective of this book is to explore the evolving dynamics of metropolitanization in India through a multi-dimensional lens that bridges theory, policy, governance, and practice. As India's metropolitan regions continue to expand in both size and complexity, there is an urgent need to understand how planning systems, institutional frameworks, and socio-economic conditions interact to shape urban futures.

This book aims to fulfil the following core objectives:

1. To critically examine the phenomenon of metropolitanization in India, tracing its historical evolution, spatial patterns, and socio-political implications.
2. To analyse the role of the National Urban Policy Framework (NUPF) in guiding metropolitan planning and governance across multiple levels and jurisdictions.
3. To investigate the institutional structures and planning mechanisms currently governing India's metropolitan regions, with a focus on gaps, overlaps, and opportunities for reform.
4. To document and evaluate case studies of metropolitan regions, drawing comparative insights from both Indian and global examples to highlight best practices and contextual challenges.
5. To propose a strategic framework for sustainable and inclusive metropolitan futures, informed by contemporary planning theories, participatory governance models, and global development agendas such as SDG 11 and the New Urban Agenda.
6. To contribute to the discourse on regional urbanization by situating metropolitanization within broader debates on city-region linkages, functional urban areas, and the rural-urban continuum.

These objectives together seek to address the pressing question: *How can India's metropolitan regions be planned and governed to ensure sustainability, inclusion, and resilience in the face of future urban transformations?*

1.4 Focus on Case Studies and NUPF Framework

This book places significant emphasis on the role of case studies as a means of critically examining the real-world functioning of metropolitan regions in India. Through detailed and contextual analyses of selected metropolitan areas, the book highlights not only the diversity of spatial forms and governance mechanisms but also the common challenges they face, such as institutional fragmentation, infrastructure deficits, and social exclusion. These case studies function as both empirical illustrations and diagnostic tools, helping to bridge the gap between normative frameworks and on-ground realities.

Each case study is examined through the analytical lens of the National Urban Policy Framework (NUPF). The NUPF's ten functional levers and sixteen guiding principles offer a structured yet flexible matrix through which metropolitan systems can be assessed. These levers—ranging from planning, housing, mobility, and infrastructure to economic development, inclusiveness, and sustainability—provide an integrated framework to evaluate both the strengths and limitations of existing metropolitan planning models.

By aligning the case studies with the NUPF framework, the book seeks to:

- Understand how metropolitan regions are responding to NUPF's vision and principles in practice.
- Evaluate institutional alignment or divergence with key levers such as decentralized governance, participatory planning, and climate resilience.
- Identify spatial, governance, and policy gaps that hinder the operationalization of integrated metropolitan planning.
- Explore opportunities for innovation, reform, and localization of national policy directives within diverse metropolitan contexts.

The selected case studies not only illustrate the current state of metropolitanization in India but also reflect broader global transitions, such as the rise of functional urban regions, the turn toward data-driven governance, and the push for socially just urban systems. Through this grounded focus, the book aims to provide insights that are both academically rigorous and policy-relevant.

1.5 Methodology

The methodology adopted in this book is interdisciplinary and qualitative, combining policy analysis, case study research, theoretical exploration, and document-based inquiry. It draws upon planning theory, urban studies, regional development frameworks, and public policy analysis to build a comprehensive understanding of metropolitanization in the Indian context.

The study is structured around the following methodological components:

1. Analytical Framework Based on the NUPF: The National Urban Policy Framework (2018) serves as the central analytical lens. Its ten levers—ranging from planning and governance to infrastructure, sustainability, and inclusiveness—are used to evaluate metropolitan regions and case studies. The framework also offers normative principles to assess alignment with national goals and global development agendas.
2. Case Study Approach: A comparative case study method is employed to examine specific metropolitan regions in India. These cases are selected to represent varied spatial forms, governance systems, and socio-economic conditions. The case studies are contextualized using secondary data, planning documents, academic literature, and reports from urban institutions such as MoHUA, NIUA, NITI Aayog, and UN-Habitat.
3. Document Review and Policy Analysis: The book relies heavily on an in-depth review of open-access and government-published documents, including URDPFI Guidelines (2014), the Habitat III National Report (2016), NIUA and NITI Aayog publications, and municipal development plans. These are analysed to extract institutional, spatial, and policy insights relevant to metropolitan planning.
4. Theoretical Grounding: Planning theories such as the Right to the City (Lefebvre-1968), Collaborative Planning (Healey-1997), Urban Political Ecology (Heynen, Kaika and Swyngedouw 2006), Resilience Theory (Holling-1973), and Glocal Urbanism (Brenner & Schmid-2005a) are employed to interpret the dynamics of urban governance, spatial inequality, and ecological sustainability in metropolitan areas.
5. Descriptive and Analytical Synthesis: Each chapter is structured to blend descriptive detail with analytical insight. While the book outlines the historical and institutional evolution of metropolitanization, it also critically engages with gaps, contradictions, and emerging possibilities within India's planning ecosystem.

This methodological approach ensures that the book remains grounded in policy realities while contributing to theoretical and academic debates in the field of urban and regional planning.

1.6 Structure of the Book

This book is structured to provide a comprehensive and integrated understanding of metropolitan planning in India, addressing both foundational concepts and future strategies. It begins by setting the stage with the broad context of urban growth, the system of cities, and the evolving nature of metropolitan regions. This provides the necessary backdrop for understanding the complexities of metropolitanization and the need for a robust planning framework.

The book then delves into the National Urban Policy Framework (NUPF), the key guiding framework for metropolitan planning in India. NUPF offers the guiding principles and actionable levers needed to align urban growth with national objectives, which are critically explored in the book.

Following this theoretical grounding, the book shifts focus to the practical side of metropolitan planning by examining urban development plans, policies, and programs that shape the metropolitan landscape in India. These planning tools, while effective in some cases, also face numerous challenges in implementation. A closer look at the challenges these policies encounter sets the stage for the core analysis of metropolitanization—a process that directly shapes the governance structures, spatial development, and socio-economic impacts of urban areas.

With the theoretical and policy groundwork established, the book moves into case studies of metropolitan areas, providing real-world examples to illustrate the practical application of planning frameworks and policies. These case studies not only highlight successes but also critically examine challenges, offering insights into the barriers that metropolitan regions face in achieving sustainable and inclusive development.

The final chapters transition into a comparative analysis that draws on international experiences, comparing Indian metropolitan regions with global best practices. This section identifies opportunities for improvement, synthesising lessons from both India and abroad to propose a way forward for improving metropolitan planning and governance.

The book concludes with a visionary look at the future, focusing on building sustainable and inclusive metropolitan futures. By integrating the insights gained throughout the book, this final section offers a strategic framework to navigate the complexities of metropolitan governance, ensuring that urbanization remains inclusive, resilient, and sustainable.

CHAPTER

2

Urban Growth, System of Cities, and City-Region

2.1 Origins and Evolution of Urbanization

2.1.1 Historical Background: From Settlements to Cities

The origins of urbanization are deeply embedded in the story of human civilization. The transition from nomadic to sedentary lifestyles laid the foundation for the formation of early settlements, which, over time, evolved into complex urban societies. The rise of agriculture around 10,000 years ago enabled food surpluses, leading to population concentration and the establishment of governance systems, economic exchange, and cultural activities. The world's earliest cities, such as Uruk in Mesopotamia, Mohenjo-daro in the Indus Valley, and Thebes in Ancient Egypt, served as hubs of innovation, religious practice, and political authority. These cities demonstrated sophisticated planning, from grid-based layouts and public sanitation to monumental architecture and institutional governance (Fields 2009) (McGranahan, Tacoli, & Satterthwaite 2006)

In the Indian context, urbanization has a distinct historical trajectory. The Harappan civilization (c. 2600–1900 BCE) presents one of the earliest examples of urban planning, with cities like Mohenjo-daro and Harappa exhibiting broad streets, drainage systems, and standardized brick architecture—features that highlight the technological and administrative sophistication of early Indian urbanism. Urban growth continued through the Mauryan and Gupta periods, marked by administrative capitals like Pataliputra and Ujjain, which became important nodes for trade, culture, and political activity. Medieval Indian cities, shaped by Islamic architectural and spatial principles, introduced new urban forms such as walled cities, narrow alleys, and market-centred growth (Ramachandran, 1989) (MoHUA 2014).

The British colonial era ushered in a new wave of urban restructuring. Colonial urbanization was primarily extractive and administrative in nature, focusing on port cities and cantonments. Cities such as Bombay (Mumbai),

Calcutta (Kolkata), and Madras (Chennai) were developed as strategic trade and military outposts, leading to the emergence of a new urban hierarchy aligned with British imperial interests. Segregated urban planning, which divided cities into 'native' and 'European' quarters, characterized this period and laid the foundation for many of the spatial and infrastructural inequalities that persist today (Watson, 2009; Solecki & Leichenko, 2006).

2.1.2 Phases of Urban Growth in India and Globally

Globally, the trajectory of urbanization took a dramatic turn during the Industrial Revolution. Between the late 18th and early 20th centuries, cities became engines of economic growth, population agglomeration, and social transformation. With industrialization came factories, railways, mass housing, and urban labour markets. Urbanization during this era was marked by the migration of rural populations into rapidly expanding urban centres in search of employment and improved living conditions, although many faced exploitation, overcrowded housing, and poor sanitation (Guénard & Giraud, 2014).

Urban growth patterns differed between the Global North and South. While European and American cities expanded based on industrial economies and state-backed infrastructure, many cities in Asia, Africa, and Latin America experienced urbanization through different processes—often as a result of postcolonial state formation, informal economic growth, and population pressure without corresponding economic capacity or governance structures (World Resources Institute 2021). Consequently, the urban poor in the Global South often face exclusion from basic services and formal planning mechanisms, leading to the rise of slums and informal economies.

In India, urban growth can be divided into three broad phases. The first phase includes ancient and medieval cities, which grew organically around trade routes, rivers, or administrative capitals. These cities were often compact, walkable, and formed around core institutions like temples, markets, or palaces. The second phase, under colonial rule, introduced modern planning principles but also fostered inequality through spatial segregation and prioritization of imperial infrastructure. The third phase began with India's independence in 1947 and was initially characterized by planned development under the state. The Nehruvian era saw the establishment of new capital cities like Chandigarh, designed by international planners to reflect modernist ideals of order, functionality, and progress (Kim, 2012; URDPFI Guidelines, 2015).

The liberalization of the Indian economy in the 1990s marked a fourth and most transformative phase of urban growth. This period witnessed the rise of new economic sectors such as information technology, telecommunications, and finance. Cities like Bengaluru, Hyderabad, and Gurgaon emerged as global service centres, attracting skilled migration, private investment, and massive real estate development. Simultaneously, there was a spatial decentralization of urban functions, with growing importance given to satellite towns, peri-urban regions, and special economic zones (SEZs) (IWMI, 2021; NIUA, 2021a). However, this growth has also exacerbated inequality, strained urban infrastructure, and intensified land conflicts, particularly in the periphery.

2.1.3 Industrialization, Liberalization, and Urban Transformation

Urban transformation in the modern era is being shaped by a wide array of forces—economic, environmental, technological, and institutional. The traditional monocentric model of cities is increasingly being replaced by polycentric and corridor-based models, where interconnected cities form regional economic clusters. The Delhi-Mumbai Industrial Corridor (DMIC) and similar megaprojects are examples of this shift, where spatial planning is oriented toward regional connectivity, logistics, and transnational investment (MoUD 2012; MoHUA 2014).

Indian cities today are confronted with the dual challenge of sustaining economic growth while ensuring environmental sustainability. Rapid expansion of the built environment, conversion of agricultural land, depletion of natural resources, and increased waste generation have raised concerns about ecological balance. The concept of the "urban ecosystem" offers a framework to understand cities as complex entities that depend on energy, material inputs, and waste outputs, interacting with natural systems at multiple scales (McDonald et al., 2014; Solecki & Leichenko, 2006).

The liberalization era has also witnessed the increasing role of private developers, public-private partnerships (PPPs), and international funding agencies in shaping urban form and infrastructure. This has brought about architectural and planning experimentation but also created highly unequal access to land, services, and opportunities. Informality remains widespread in Indian cities—both in terms of housing and employment—challenging the capacity of formal governance systems to manage urbanization inclusively (Watson, 2009).

Urbanization today no longer respects jurisdictional boundaries. The growth of city-regions—functional urban areas that include core cities, peri-urban areas, and rural linkages—requires a shift in planning paradigms. These regions are shaped not only by spatial proximity but also by economic, ecological, and social interdependencies. Traditional urban planning tools must be updated to address these complex dynamics, as acknowledged in India's URDPFI Guidelines (2014), which emphasize inclusive, regional, and integrated approaches to planning.

This ongoing transformation is also influenced by the rising discourse on climate change, resilience, and sustainability. Urban planners are now being challenged to create cities that are both efficient and equitable, economically vibrant and ecologically sound. These pressures make it imperative for urbanization to be treated not merely as a demographic process but as a multidimensional challenge that cuts across scales, disciplines, and governance levels (Mills, G., & Tarasova, O, 2021; BRICS, 2019).

2.2 Understanding Urban Growth

2.2.1 Key Drivers of Urban Growth

Urban growth is a multi-causal phenomenon that unfolds through the complex interaction of demographic trends, economic transitions, technological advancements, political decisions, and environmental shifts. At its core, the process of urban growth reflects the evolving relationship between people and space—how populations cluster in response to opportunity, infrastructure, and governance. Historically, urbanization has been driven by agricultural surplus and trade; however, in the post-industrial era, the primary driver has been economic restructuring—from manufacturing and heavy industries to knowledge economies and service-based sectors (Fields, 2009; BRICS, 2019).

In the Indian context, economic liberalization has played a decisive role in intensifying urban growth. The shift towards a market-driven economy during the 1990s resulted in massive inflows of foreign direct investment (FDI), expansion of the IT and service sectors, and the globalization of Indian cities. Urban centres such as Bengaluru, Hyderabad, and Gurugram experienced exponential growth not only in population but also in infrastructure development and real estate demand (Kim, 2012; MoHUA, 2014). Additionally, state-led policies, such as the development of industrial corridors and special economic zones, have acted as spatial catalysts for concentrated urban expansion.

Infrastructure availability—particularly in transportation, communication, electricity, and water supply—has also influenced patterns of urban growth. Investment in expressways, metro systems, and international airports has redefined connectivity and accessibility, leading to the emergence of new urban nodes and corridors (MoHUA, 2015c). Equally influential is governance: decentralization policies, urban local body reforms, and the Jawaharlal Nehru National Urban Renewal Mission (JnNURM) created both the institutional and financial architecture to support city growth, though with varying degrees of success (McGranahan et al., 2006; Solecki & Leichenko, 2006).

2.2.2 Role of Migration and Natural Increase

Two key demographic processes—natural increase and rural-to-urban migration—underpin population growth in urban areas. Natural increase, defined as the excess of births over deaths, is often the predominant contributor to urban growth in developing countries. In India, for example, the urban natural increase rate has remained high due to improvements in healthcare, declining mortality, and a young age structure in cities (SDSN 2021).

However, migration—especially rural-to-urban migration—continues to reshape the urban demographic landscape. Push factors such as agrarian distress, limited employment in rural areas, and declining land productivity compel rural populations to seek better livelihoods in cities. Simultaneously, urban pull factors like diversified job markets, educational institutions, and healthcare services attract migrants across state and district boundaries (IWMI 2021). Seasonal and circular migration is also significant, especially in construction, manufacturing, and informal economies, although such movements often remain unrecorded in official datasets.

India's urbanization has also been shaped by intra-metropolitan migration, where people move from the urban core to peripheral zones in search of affordable housing or employment. This shift, driven in part by real estate speculation and displacement from inner cities, has expanded the boundaries of cities and created vast peri-urban belts with hybrid characteristics of both urban and rural life (NIUA, 2021). These areas, often lacking in formal planning and governance, present both opportunities and challenges for inclusive urban development.

2.2.3 Urban Growth Patterns: Horizontal vs. Vertical Expansion

Urban growth manifests in two principal spatial patterns—horizontal (outward) expansion and vertical (upward) densification. Horizontal expansion, or urban sprawl, refers to the outward extension of cities into adjacent rural areas. This form of growth is particularly visible in Indian metropolitan regions such as Delhi-NCR, Bengaluru, and Pune, where suburbanization and ribbon development along highways have reshaped the urban morphology (MoHUA, 2014; MoUD, 2012). While horizontal growth accommodates population pressure, it often comes at the cost of agricultural land, forests, wetlands, and ecological buffers, leading to resource depletion and habitat fragmentation (McDonald et al., 2014).

Vertical expansion, by contrast, involves the intensification of land use through multi-storey construction and compact development. High-rise housing, commercial towers, and transit-oriented developments are typical examples. Cities like Mumbai have historically followed this model due to geographic constraints and land scarcity. Although vertical growth can improve land use efficiency, it also creates pressure on infrastructure systems and challenges related to light, ventilation, and social equity (Watson, 2009).

In practice, Indian cities exhibit a combination of both growth patterns—often without cohesive spatial planning. This fragmented growth has led to traffic congestion, inadequate service delivery, and the proliferation of informal settlements. Moreover, the speculative real estate market has skewed urban expansion towards profit-driven rather than need-based development, further marginalizing low-income groups from access to affordable housing and urban amenities (Watson 2009).

2.2.4 Cities as Ecosystems: Energy, Resource Flow, and Urban Metabolism

Viewing cities as ecosystems allows us to conceptualize urban areas not merely as built environments, but as dynamic systems that consume, transform, and exchange energy, materials, and information. Urban metabolism—the analysis of material and energy flows within cities—provides insights into how resources are extracted, utilized, and disposed of within the urban system. This lens is particularly important in an age where cities account for more than 70% of global energy consumption and greenhouse gas emissions (McDonald et al., 2014; Solecki & Leichenko, 2006).

In Indian cities, energy consumption patterns are highly stratified. While elite households and commercial sectors rely on uninterrupted electricity, air-conditioning, and private vehicles, low-income populations face shortages, pollution, and infrastructural neglect. Water scarcity, solid waste mismanagement, and declining green cover are becoming endemic in rapidly growing urban areas. Moreover, most Indian cities lack robust data on their material and ecological footprints, hampering effective environmental governance (Mills, G., & Tarasova, O., 2021).

A systems view of urban growth also emphasizes the interdependence of ecological and social systems. For example, the degradation of wetlands in peri-urban zones not only reduces biodiversity but also diminishes the ecosystem services that urban populations rely on—such as flood control, water purification, and microclimate regulation (McDonald et al., 2014). Similarly, energy-inefficient buildings and transportation systems contribute to urban heat islands, public health crises, and carbon emissions. These trends necessitate a paradigm shift in urban planning—towards circular economies, renewable energy integration, and climate-sensitive infrastructure (Solecki & Leichenko, 2006; URDPFI, 2014).

Understanding urban growth, therefore, requires not just population and spatial analysis, but also ecological intelligence. As cities continue to expand, their resilience and sustainability will depend on how well they balance growth with environmental stewardship, social justice, and institutional innovation.

2.3 The System of Cities

2.3.1 Definition and Concept of City Systems

The term "system of cities" refers to the spatial and functional arrangement of urban settlements that operate in relation to each other across regional and national scales. Rather than existing in isolation, cities form networks of economic, cultural, administrative, and infrastructural linkages, which together shape the urban structure of a country. This interlinked nature of cities—connected by flows of people, goods, services, capital, and information—makes urban systems a key framework for understanding national development strategies (Fields, 2009; MUD, 2012).

Historically, the study of city systems emerged from central place theory and location theory in geography, which analysed how cities are distributed spatially to serve surrounding populations. In modern planning, however, the system of cities is not only defined by size and location, but also by their specialization, economic functions, connectivity, and roles within larger governance structures (MoHUA, 2015). A well-functioning urban system is characterized by complementarity rather than competition between cities of different scales. It allows for functional specialization, economic efficiency, and more equitable distribution of infrastructure and opportunities.

India's urban system has evolved through multiple stages—rooted in ancient trade and pilgrimage routes, reorganized through colonial administrative hierarchies, and transformed in the post-liberalization era. While older cities developed organically along rivers, coastlines, and cultural nodes, modern cities have emerged through policy-driven mechanisms such as industrial corridors and new township schemes (IWMI, 2021).

2.3.2 City Tiers and Classification in the Indian Context

India's urban system is stratified through a formal hierarchy based on population size and functional role. India officially classifies its cities based on population size and economic functions, resulting in a multi-tiered hierarchy. According to the Census of India, the urban classification includes statutory towns, census towns, and urban agglomerations. These are further grouped into city categories such as Tier I (metros with over 1 million people), Tier II (cities with 100,000 to 1 million population), and Tier III and IV towns (under 100,000). This classification informs not only government policies but also private investment decisions, infrastructure allocation, and program eligibility.

The Ministry of Housing and Urban Affairs (MoHUA) (2014) **URDPFI Guidelines** offer a standard classification of towns and cities into six categories:

- **Class I**: Cities with a population of **100,000 and above**
- **Class II**: Towns with a population between **50,000 and 99,999**
- **Class III**: Towns with a population between **20,000 and 49,999**
- **Class IV**: Towns with a population between **10,000 and 19,999**
- **Class V**: Towns with a population between **5,000 and 9,999**
- **Class VI**: Towns with a population less than **5,000**

Further, within the Class I category, Million-Plus Cities (Metropolises) are often distinguished as a separate class due to their size and complexity. These include India's largest urban agglomerations—Delhi, Mumbai, Kolkata, Chennai, Bengaluru, and Hyderabad—which have developed significant regional influence.

Tier I cities such as Delhi, Mumbai, Kolkata, Bengaluru, and Chennai dominate economic and political discourse. They are recipients of large-scale investment, attract international corporations, and house advanced infrastructure and institutions. Tier II cities like Lucknow, Bhopal, Coimbatore, and Surat are emerging as growth centres due to lower costs, increasing connectivity, and state-level urban missions. Tier III and IV towns, while often neglected in national discourse, perform critical functions in linking rural hinterlands with regional economies, and in many cases serve as nodal points for agrarian markets, small-scale manufacturing, and localized service economies (MoHUA, 2014; McGranahan et al., 2006).

This classification is important not only for demographic analysis but also for guiding planning strategies, infrastructure provisioning, fiscal transfers, and programmatic funding. For example, centrally sponsored schemes like AMRUT and Smart Cities Mission consider population thresholds and class-based criteria for city selection and resource allocation (MoHUA, 2014).

Yet this hierarchy also reveals deep spatial disparities. While Class I cities are usually hubs of investment, employment, and innovation, lower-class towns often suffer from weak infrastructure, limited planning capacity, and underinvestment. Addressing this imbalance requires more integrated regional planning and equitable urban development strategies.

2.3.3 Functional Roles of Cities (Administrative, Economic, Cultural)

Cities perform multiple functions beyond housing populations—they are administrative centres, engines of economic production, cultural landscapes, and hubs of knowledge. In India, the administrative role of cities is deeply rooted in the colonial legacy, which concentrated governance institutions in select urban centres. State capitals, district headquarters, and cantonment towns were designed to serve specific bureaucratic and military functions, a trend that continues today (Watson, V., 2009).

Economically, cities contribute over two-thirds of India's GDP, despite occupying less than 3% of its land area (SDSN, 2021). Metros and Tier I cities dominate in services, finance, and trade, while industrial production and logistics have expanded into Tier II and III cities through policy incentives and industrial estates. Economic clustering has led to the development of specialized zones—such as Bengaluru for IT, Surat for diamonds, and Ludhiana for textiles—demonstrating the functional differentiation of the urban system.

Culturally, Indian cities are repositories of heritage, religion, language diversity, and art. Cities like Varanasi, Jaipur, and Kochi are not just economic spaces but also centres of historical significance, tourism, and spiritual practice. This cultural dimension contributes to city branding, tourism-led economies, and the protection of intangible heritage. Urban spaces, therefore, must be viewed not only through the lens of development but also as living embodiments of regional identity and memory (Fields, 2009).

2.3.4 Interdependence Among Cities: Hierarchies and Networks

No city functions in isolation. Inter-city interdependence arises from the flows of goods, services, capital, information, and people. Larger cities depend on smaller towns and rural areas for food, raw materials, and labour. Conversely, small and medium towns rely on larger cities for specialized services such as healthcare, higher education, administrative services, and markets (MoHUA, 2014). This interdependence has grown stronger in the era of digitization, improved connectivity, and integrated infrastructure systems.

India's cities also exist within economic hierarchies—where certain metros act as primate cities, disproportionately concentrating wealth, power, and influence. This can result in spatial imbalance and rural-urban migration pressures. However, improved networks—such as national highways, rail corridors, and digital connectivity—can reduce overdependence on primate cities and facilitate regional integration.

Urban agglomerations like Mumbai Metropolitan Region (MMR) and National Capital Region (NCR) exemplify this interconnectedness. They comprise core cities and surrounding municipalities, industrial townships, and rural settlements that function as a single economic and spatial unit. Within these regions, flows of labour, goods, and infrastructure bind multiple jurisdictions, necessitating coordinated planning and governance (Kim, 2012; NIUA, 2021).

2.3.5 Urban Corridors and Regional Development

One of the most significant spatial trends in India's urban system has been the emergence of urban corridors—linear zones of development connecting multiple cities through transport infrastructure and economic functions. Examples include the Delhi-Mumbai Industrial Corridor (DMIC), the Bengaluru-Chennai Industrial Corridor (BCIC), and the Amritsar-Kolkata Industrial Corridor (AKIC). These corridors are designed to enhance regional productivity, reduce urban-rural divides, and attract foreign and domestic investment.

Urban corridors foster a new form of city growth—multi-nodal, polycentric, and functionally integrated. They facilitate agglomeration economies, encourage clustering of industries, and support regional innovation ecosystems (IIHS, 2012). However, they also raise concerns regarding exclusion, environmental degradation, and displacement if not managed with inclusivity and sustainability in mind (McDonald et al., 2014).

In many cases, smaller towns along these corridors experience secondary urbanization effects, including rising land prices, new housing demand, and infrastructural expansion. Yet without adequate planning support, these gains may be uneven. Effective corridor development requires integrated planning approaches that address land use, infrastructure investment, governance alignment, and social equity (MoHUA, 2015).

In conclusion, the system of cities in India is dynamic and layered, marked by diversity in scale, function, and interrelation. Understanding this system—its structure, flows, and disparities—is essential to shaping national urban strategies that are equitable, resilient, and future-ready.

2.4 Human Settlement Planning

2.4.1 Key Concepts in Human Settlement Planning

Human settlement planning is a multidisciplinary process that integrates spatial, economic, social, and environmental considerations to guide the development and transformation of human habitats. At its core, it is about ensuring that land, resources, and services are distributed and managed in a manner that enhances the quality of life while promoting sustainability, equity, and efficiency. Human settlements encompass a continuum from rural villages to megacities, and planning seeks to organize these spaces through rational land use, infrastructure networks, housing provision, and institutional frameworks (MoHUA, 2014).

The concept evolved to address the challenges of uncoordinated urban growth, poor infrastructure, environmental degradation, and spatial inequality. It recognizes that human settlements are not isolated units but part of a broader ecosystem of interdependent social, economic, and spatial processes.

According to the URDPFI Guidelines, human settlement planning should promote compact, inclusive, resource-efficient, and sustainable development while safeguarding ecological resources, conserving heritage, and enabling participatory governance.

Human settlement planning also emphasizes integrated development, meaning the coordinated growth of housing, transport, water supply, sanitation, education, employment zones, and recreation. The goal is not merely to create urban forms but to support functioning societies where infrastructure, land use, and people align harmoniously. In recent decades, settlement planning has expanded its scope to incorporate disaster risk reduction, climate resilience, gender sensitivity, and livelihood security—particularly in the context of rapidly urbanizing and vulnerable peri-urban regions (Mills, G., & Tarasova, O., 2021; Solecki & Leichenko, 2006).

2.4.2 Evolution of Planning Approaches in Urban India

The evolution of planning in India reflects changing state ideologies, global influences, and socio-economic priorities. In the post-independence period, urban planning was seen primarily as a state-led activity focused on spatial control, land use regulation, and infrastructure provisioning. The early decades of planning adopted the British legacy of rigid master planning—a technocratic approach that emphasized zoning, static projections, and centralized governance (Watson, V., 2009).

This era gave rise to planned cities like Chandigarh and Gandhinagar, which became symbols of modernity and administrative control. Planning institutions like the Town and Country Planning Organisation (TCPO), Development Authorities, and Housing Boards were established to regulate land and infrastructure delivery. However, many of these plans remained disconnected from socio-economic realities, particularly in informal settlements and smaller towns (McGranahan et al., 2006).

The 1970s and 1980s saw a modest shift with the introduction of integrated urban development plans, focusing on area-level infrastructure, slum improvement, and land pooling mechanisms. Yet urban planning remained limited to major cities, with smaller towns receiving little attention. Planning was also hampered by overlapping jurisdictions, slow bureaucracies, and weak enforcement mechanisms (MoHUA, 2014).

The post-liberalization period from the 1990s brought market-oriented reforms and new planning paradigms. Structural changes in the economy—particularly the growth of the service sector, rise of the real estate market, and emergence of global capital flows—demanded more flexible and dynamic planning instruments. Policies such as the National Urban Housing and

Habitat Policy (NUHHP), Smart Cities Mission, and AMRUT signalled a transition toward performance-based planning, public-private partnerships, and infrastructure-centric development (Kim, 2012; BRICS, 2019).

Notably, planning has also become more multi-scalar and participatory in approach. There is increasing recognition of the interdependence between cities, towns, and rural settlements. Integrated development plans and regional spatial strategies have been introduced to balance the needs of core urban areas with peripheral and hinterland settlements. Contemporary planning approaches also highlight the role of community participation, gender inclusion, and livelihood security, especially in the context of informal settlements, resettlement colonies, and peri-urban zones (MUD, 2021; SDSN, 2021).

2.4.3 Tools and Instruments in Settlement Planning

India's planning framework utilizes a range of tools and instruments to organize urban and regional growth. The most conventional is the Master Plan, which provides a long-term spatial vision for a city, detailing land use zoning, transportation networks, housing, and infrastructure provision. While master plans offer structure, they have often been criticized for being outdated, overly rigid, and disconnected from on-ground realities (MoHUA, 2014).

To address these limitations, several reform-oriented instruments have been introduced. Development Plans and Zonal Plans offer more localized implementation strategies. Town Planning Schemes (TPS), especially in Gujarat and Maharashtra, allow for land pooling and readjustment mechanisms where landowners voluntarily contribute parcels for public infrastructure and receive reconstituted plots. TPS is considered a successful model of land readjustment in Indian planning practice (McDonald et al., 2014).

Another critical tool is the Urban and Regional Development Plans Formulation and Implementation (URDPFI) Guidelines, which offer a comprehensive framework for preparing, implementing, and monitoring development plans. The 2014 revision of these guidelines emphasized sustainability, inclusivity, public participation, and use of geospatial technologies in planning. URDPFI introduced new planning typologies such as Local Area Plans (LAPs), Special Area Plans, and City Development Plans (CDPs) to bridge the gap between macro planning and micro-level interventions.

With the rise of technology, Geographic Information Systems (GIS) and Remote Sensing have become crucial for data-driven planning and spatial analysis. These tools allow planners to monitor land use changes, infrastructure gaps, and environmental degradation with accuracy and timeliness (Mills, G., & Tarasova, O, 2021). Urban planning has also started incorporating Environmental

Impact Assessments (EIA) and Social Impact Assessments (SIA) to evaluate the implications of projects on ecosystems and communities.

Finally, participatory planning tools—such as stakeholder workshops, community mapping, and public hearings—are becoming more mainstream, particularly under the Smart Cities and AMRUT frameworks. These aim to democratize the planning process, giving voice to marginalized communities and enhancing the responsiveness of urban governance.

In sum, the evolution of human settlement planning in India reflects a gradual shift from rigid, top-down systems to more inclusive, flexible, and responsive frameworks. Yet challenges remain in terms of capacity, coordination, and integration across scales. As cities and towns continue to grow and transform, there is an urgent need for adaptable planning approaches that bridge the formal-informal divide, promote regional balance, and integrate environmental resilience into the DNA of urban development.

2.5 Urban Resources and Development

2.5.1 Key Urban Resources (Land, Water, Energy, Housing, Mobility)

Urban areas are resource-intensive systems that depend on a steady and equitable supply of key resources to function efficiently. As cities grow in population and spatial extent, the demand for land, water, energy, housing, and mobility increases exponentially. These resources form the basic foundation upon which urban economies, infrastructure, and social systems operate.

Land is perhaps the most contested resource in urban India. Rapid urban expansion, speculation, and unregulated development have contributed to escalating land prices, land fragmentation, and displacement of vulnerable populations. Much of urban development occurs on former agricultural land, common land, and ecological zones, often bypassing formal planning regulations. The lack of a transparent and efficient land market, coupled with weak enforcement of zoning and building norms, has resulted in a pattern of spatial inequality and fragmentation (MoHUA, 2014; Watson, V, 2009). Land acquisition for public infrastructure and real estate projects often generates conflict and marginalizes low-income groups who lack secure tenure or legal recognition (McDonald et al., 2014).

Water is another critical urban resource, yet Indian cities face severe shortages, contamination, and inequitable access. Surface and groundwater sources are overexploited, and water infrastructure is aging, underfunded, and poorly maintained. Urban residents often rely on tanker supply, borewells, and informal vendors, especially in peripheral and informal settlements.

Water governance is further complicated by fragmented responsibilities across municipal, state, and parastatal agencies, leading to inefficiencies and service gaps (IWMI, 2021). Climate change has further exacerbated urban water stress, with irregular monsoons, declining recharge zones, and urban flooding becoming increasingly frequent.

Energy access and efficiency are foundational to modern urban life, influencing everything from household well-being to industrial productivity. Indian cities exhibit wide disparities in energy consumption and access. While affluent households and commercial centres benefit from uninterrupted supply and renewable alternatives, low-income communities often face erratic supply, unsafe connections, and limited affordability. Urban transportation systems, building stock, and informal markets are typically energy-inefficient, contributing to high emissions and vulnerability to supply shocks (Solecki & Leichenko, 2006; Mills, G., & Tarasova, O., 2021). As cities aspire to become climate-resilient and low-carbon, mainstreaming clean energy and energy efficiency into planning is becoming essential.

Housing remains a fundamental yet unresolved challenge. Despite various national missions, including the Pradhan Mantri Awas Yojana (PMAY), a significant proportion of urban residents live in inadequate, overcrowded, and informal housing. Slums, unauthorized colonies, and peri-urban settlements absorb much of the urban poor and migrant populations, often in precarious conditions without tenure security, basic services, or social integration (Watson, V, 2009; SDSN, 2021). While formal housing markets cater to middle and upper classes, there is a persistent shortage of affordable housing. The commodification of housing as an investment asset has widened class divisions and contributed to spatial segregation.

Urban mobility—both motorized and non-motorized—is crucial for economic productivity, social inclusion, and environmental sustainability. Indian cities face chronic congestion, air pollution, inadequate public transport, and poor last-mile connectivity. Car-centric infrastructure continues to dominate investment patterns, often at the expense of pedestrians, cyclists, and public transport users. Although initiatives such as metro rail systems, bus rapid transit (BRT), and electric vehicles have gained momentum, their coverage, affordability, and inclusivity remain limited (MoHUA, 2014; BRICS, 2019). Moreover, the absence of integrated transport and land use planning has led to fragmented urban form, travel inefficiencies, and exclusion of low-income commuters.

2.5.2 Infrastructure, Services, and Liveability

The quality and distribution of urban infrastructure directly influence a city's liveability, productivity, and equity. Infrastructure includes not only physical assets such as roads, bridges, sewerage, and water supply systems, but also social infrastructure like schools, healthcare, public spaces, and safety systems. In India, infrastructural deficits are visible across sectors and city classes, with smaller towns often worse off in terms of coverage, quality, and financing capacity (McGranahan et al., 2006).

Liveability is affected by the extent to which infrastructure and services are responsive to residents' needs, especially in marginalized communities. Issues such as waterlogging, solid waste accumulation, traffic bottlenecks, and air and noise pollution are everyday realities for urban dwellers. These problems are not merely technical but rooted in governance and political economy—poor coordination among agencies, limited municipal capacity, and insufficient public investment are recurring barriers to improving infrastructure delivery (MoHUA, 2014).

The rise of private provision in sectors such as water, electricity, and solid waste has raised questions about affordability, equity, and accountability. In many cases, privatization has led to improved efficiency, but also to exclusion of those unable to pay or access services. Informal and community-based infrastructure provisioning continues to play a vital role in bridging these gaps, particularly in low-income and peripheral areas (NIUA, 2021).

Infrastructure planning must increasingly respond to emerging risks and opportunities—from climate change adaptation and disaster risk reduction to digital infrastructure and smart technologies. Concepts such as nature-based solutions, blue-green infrastructure, and climate-resilient urban services are beginning to reshape how infrastructure is conceived, funded, and maintained (McDonald et al., 2014; Mills, G., & Tarasova, O., 2021).

2.5.3 Impact of Urban Growth on Regional and National Development

Urban growth is closely linked to the overall development trajectory of a country. Cities are not just engines of economic output but also platforms for innovation, social mobility, and cultural expression. In India, urban areas contribute more than two-thirds of the national GDP, house over a third of the population, and act as nodes of international trade, capital flows, and knowledge exchange (SDSN, 2021). The clustering of people, firms, and institutions in urban areas generates agglomeration economies—efficiencies that arise from proximity, shared services, and networked infrastructure.

However, the impact of urban growth on development is not uniformly positive. Without careful planning and inclusive policies, urban expansion can deepen inequality, displace communities, strain ecosystems, and exacerbate regional imbalances. While metros grow rapidly and attract most public and private investment, many smaller towns and rural regions are left behind, contributing to migratory pressure and spatial disparities (MoHUA, 2014; IWMI, 2021). This unbalanced growth challenges the long-term sustainability of the urban system and calls for more deliberate efforts to foster polycentric development and regional equity.

Urban development also shapes national-level policy in terms of housing, energy, transport, education, health, and employment. Therefore, the quality and inclusiveness of urban governance directly impact broader development outcomes. Investment in urban infrastructure, services, and planning must be aligned with sustainable development goals (SDGs), climate targets, and equity principles if cities are to serve as catalysts of national progress rather than sites of exclusion and crisis (Mills, G., & Tarasova, O., 2021; Solecki & Leichenko, 2006).

In this context, recognizing urban resources as not merely inputs to be consumed but as systems to be sustained becomes critical. Effective urban development hinges on the management, distribution, and regeneration of these resources through inclusive, data-informed, and forward-looking strategies.

2.6 Introduction to City-Regions

2.6.1 Concept and Historical Evolution

The concept of the city-region represents a paradigmatic shift in how urbanization is understood and governed. Traditionally, cities were viewed as discrete, bounded entities—defined by municipal borders and administratively contained systems. However, contemporary urbanization patterns have shown that urban influence extends far beyond these boundaries, giving rise to broader spatial formations characterized by complex interdependencies between urban cores and their surrounding rural or semi-urban areas. These are termed city-regions.

The roots of the city-region concept can be traced back to early 20th-century urban geography and regional planning, particularly the works of scholars like Patrick Geddes, who emphasized the interconnection between cities and their hinterlands as vital for sustainable development. Geddes introduced the idea that urban settlements cannot be understood in isolation but are part of a larger bio-social continuum shaped by natural, economic, and cultural flows (Fields, 2009). Later theories, including regional spatial economics and the notion of functional urban regions, further refined the concept by focusing on the commuting patterns, economic exchanges, and service provision networks that define the reach of urban cores into their peripheries (McGranahan et al., 2006).

In post-industrial societies, the boundaries between urban and rural have become increasingly blurred. Urban expansion, improved mobility, digital connectivity, and infrastructure development have created spatial forms that are neither wholly urban nor rural, but hybrids—a defining feature of city-regions. These formations are often polycentric, containing multiple settlements that are functionally interlinked rather than anchored solely to a dominant urban core (MUD, 2012). This evolution has challenged traditional planning approaches and demanded new frameworks for governance and resource management.

2.6.2 Importance in Planning and Governance

City-regions are of immense importance in planning because they represent the real geographies of people's lives—where they live, work, access services, and engage with institutions. Planning at the level of the city-region allows for integrated strategies that consider land use, mobility, housing, employment, environmental conservation, and disaster risk across administrative boundaries. Without this level of coordination, spatial disparities, duplication of infrastructure, and resource inefficiencies become prevalent.

In the Indian context, the city-region concept is increasingly relevant given the scale and nature of urban growth. Cities such as Delhi, Bengaluru, and Hyderabad are no longer contained within their municipal limits. Their peripheries have become dynamic zones of transformation where agricultural land is converted into real estate, traditional villages become urbanized, and governance struggles to keep pace with physical and demographic change (IWMI, 2021; MoHUA, 2014).

City-regions also pose unique governance challenges. Multiple jurisdictions, overlapping authorities, and institutional fragmentation can hamper effective coordination. For example, the Delhi National Capital Region includes multiple municipal corporations, development authorities, and state governments, each with different priorities and planning capacities. This often leads to policy misalignment and service delivery gaps (Kim, 2012; MoHUA, 2014).

Recognizing these challenges, planning frameworks now emphasize the need for metropolitan and regional plans, cross-jurisdictional governance mechanisms, and participatory planning. The URDPFI Guidelines recommend Integrated Development Plans and City-Region Plans that focus on the balanced development of both urban and rural areas within a shared spatial framework. These approaches promote infrastructure integration, land use compatibility, and shared economic development goals (MoHUA, 2014; Mills, G., & Tarasova, O., 2021).

2.6.3 Global Models and Indian Context

Globally, city-region models have been instrumental in shaping regional development policies. In Europe, the concept of functional urban areas (FUAs) has been adopted to guide regional planning, based on data from commuting zones, labour markets, and service areas. The OECD and EU have used these models to promote spatial cohesion and balanced development across urban-rural gradients (SDSN, 2021).

In East Asia, city-region planning has taken shape through the formation of mega-urban regions like the Pearl River Delta in China, where integrated infrastructure, regional transport networks, and coordinated economic strategies have generated high productivity and innovation. These examples show how functional interdependencies can be institutionalized through regional planning frameworks and investment mechanisms (McDonald et al., 2014).

In the Indian context, city-region thinking is gradually being embedded into national planning strategies, though not always explicitly. The Smart Cities Mission, AMRUT, and industrial corridor projects like the DMIC inherently involve multi-jurisdictional planning, even if not formally designated as city-regions. The NCR Planning Board and the Mumbai Metropolitan Region Development Authority (MMRDA) are examples of regional governance bodies that manage development across city-regions, albeit with limited powers and varying effectiveness (MoHUA, 2014).

However, challenges remain. Many regional institutions lack legal backing, financial autonomy, and adequate human resources. Moreover, political fragmentation and bureaucratic silos continue to hinder integrated planning. There is also a conceptual gap in mainstream planning education and practice, which tends to focus on city-centric or sectoral interventions rather than regional systems (Watson, V., 2009).

Despite these challenges, the importance of city-regions is increasingly acknowledged in discourses around sustainability, resilience, and equity. They are seen not only as engines of economic growth but also as laboratories for testing governance innovation, participatory planning, and ecological balance. As urban and rural areas become more functionally integrated, embracing the city-region as the unit of planning is both necessary and urgent for achieving long-term development goals.

2.7 Fringe and Peri-Urban Areas

2.7.1 Definitions and Conceptual Clarification

The fringe and peri-urban areas represent dynamic spatial zones where the urban and rural intersect, blur, and often collide. These transitional areas are neither fully urban nor rural, but rather contain mixed land uses, evolving economic patterns, and fragmented governance. The fringe typically refers to the immediate edges of built-up urban areas, while the peri-urban extends beyond the fringe, incorporating a broader region influenced by the city's growth and functionality. Though often used interchangeably, the terms have distinct implications in spatial planning and development policy (MoHUA, 2014; IWMI, 2021).

Peri-urban areas are characterized by rapid land-use change, where agricultural landscapes are converted into residential colonies, industrial estates, and informal settlements. These zones absorb much of the urban sprawl resulting from population growth, migration, and real estate expansion. Their significance lies in the crucial services they provide to urban cores—such as food, labour, waste sinks, and land—while also being sites of ecological and social vulnerability (McGranahan et al., 2006).

Conceptually, peri-urbanism challenges the traditional dichotomy between urban and rural by highlighting their functional interdependence. It reflects a continuum rather than a binary, where settlement typologies, economic activities, and governance mechanisms are fluid and overlapping. This complexity demands new frameworks of analysis and planning that are spatially inclusive and adaptive to change (IWMI, 2021).

2.7.2 Morphological, Socio-Economic, and Functional Characteristics

Peri-urban areas exhibit a **morphological patchwork**—with gated housing societies adjacent to informal slums, industrial sheds beside agricultural fields, and highways intersecting traditional village lanes. This heterogeneity results from speculative urban expansion, lack of coherent zoning, and reactive planning. Morphologically, these spaces often lack the dense urban form of core cities, but experience intensifying development pressure, land fragmentation, and declining green cover (NIUA, 2021).

Socio-economically, peri-urban populations are diverse, including original rural inhabitants, migrant labourers, real estate investors, and displaced urban poor. The economic base is equally varied, combining agriculture, informal enterprises, real estate construction, small-scale manufacturing, and service work. This mix creates both opportunity and tension. On the one hand, peri-urban regions offer lower land and housing costs, enabling industrial and housing expansion. On the other, they often suffer from job insecurity, land conflict, and inadequate public services (Mills, G., & Tarasova, O., 2021).

Functionally, peri-urban zones are deeply tied to the city. They act as labour catchments, waste disposal zones, commuter belts, and logistical hubs. Many low-income workers commute daily from peri-urban settlements to urban centres, while the city relies on peri-urban agricultural produce, water, and construction materials. This asymmetry in resource flow often results in environmental degradation and unequal benefit-sharing, making peri-urban areas highly contested and politically marginal (MoHUA, 2014; McDonald et al., 2014).

2.7.3 Informality, Encroachment, and Governance Challenges

One of the defining features of fringe and peri-urban areas is the prevalence of informality—in housing, employment, service delivery, and even governance. Unplanned layouts, unauthorized colonies, and slums proliferate in these areas due to poor enforcement of land use regulations, speculative land markets, and institutional gaps. The lack of clear legal titles and absence of planning approval processes make these settlements vulnerable to eviction, underinvestment, and exploitation (Watson, V., 2009).

Encroachment onto common lands, wetlands, and forest patches is common, often sanctioned informally through political patronage or left unchecked due to administrative neglect. In some cases, large-scale infrastructure and industrial projects are established on peri-urban lands without adequate environmental or social safeguards, resulting in displacement and loss of livelihoods for original rural residents (IWMI, 2021; Fields, 2009).

Governance in these areas is especially problematic. Administrative responsibility is often split between urban municipal corporations and rural panchayats, neither of which is adequately equipped to handle the unique challenges of peri-urban spaces. Development authorities may prepare land use plans, but implementation is weak and contested. Moreover, the voices of peri-urban residents—particularly women, migrants, and the poor—are often excluded from formal planning processes, perpetuating cycles of marginalization (MoHUA, 2014).

Efforts to improve governance in peri-urban areas have included proposals for special planning zones, transitional governance bodies, and metropolitan regional planning. However, these measures remain largely pilot-driven and ad hoc. A more strategic and inclusive approach is needed—one that recognizes peri-urban regions as legitimate planning spaces with unique needs, rather than temporary or peripheral zones awaiting absorption into the city.

In sum, the fringe and peri-urban areas are both the product and pressure points of urban growth. They represent critical geographies where ecological systems, social claims, and economic forces intersect—making them essential to any discussion on sustainable and equitable urban futures.

2.8 City–Region Linkages

2.8.1 Types of Linkages (Economic, Social, Ecological, Institutional)

City-regions are defined not only by their physical extent but by the flows and relationships that bind their components together. These linkages—economic, social, ecological, and institutional—are the lifeblood of regional integration and balanced development. Understanding these diverse and intersecting connections is key to recognizing how urban cores and their surrounding areas co-evolve.

Economic linkages are among the most visible and measurable. Urban centres rely heavily on their peri-urban and rural hinterlands for essential goods such as food, water, raw materials, and labour. Conversely, surrounding settlements depend on cities for access to markets, employment, credit systems, and technology. For example, agricultural produce from rural areas is transported daily to urban markets, while manufactured goods and financial services from cities penetrate rural consumption patterns (McGranahan et al., 2006; MoHUA, 2014). Informal supply chains, transport corridors, and labour migration also constitute important components of economic integration.

Social linkages manifest through familial ties, cultural exchanges, seasonal migration, and shared institutions. Rural families often send members to cities for employment or education, maintaining strong ties to their home communities. Urban residents may retain social and emotional connections to rural areas, particularly during festivals, agricultural cycles, or in times of crisis. The persistence of dual residence and remittance flows highlights the social continuity that underpins regional systems (IWMI, 2021; Fields, 2009).

Ecological linkages underscore the interconnectedness of urban and rural environmental systems. Cities draw on their hinterlands for water, energy, waste absorption, food production, and biodiversity conservation. Wetlands in peri-urban zones absorb floodwaters, forests regulate air and temperature, and rural ecosystems support regional climate stability. However, urban expansion often disrupts these ecological flows—encroaching on natural assets, increasing pollution, and severing landscape connectivity (McDonald et al., 2014; Solecki & Leichenko, 2006).

Institutional linkages pertain to governance mechanisms, service delivery frameworks, and administrative coordination across jurisdictions. Effective city-region planning requires cooperation between municipalities, panchayats, development authorities, and state-level bodies. Yet in India, institutional fragmentation is common. Different agencies operate with misaligned mandates, limited data sharing, and overlapping functions—resulting in planning gaps and policy incoherence (MoHUA, 2014; Mills, G., & Tarasova, O., 2021). Strengthening these institutional linkages is fundamental to enabling integrated and inclusive regional development.

2.8.2 Rural–Urban Continuum and Spatial Relationships

The conventional rural–urban binary is increasingly inadequate to describe the lived realities and spatial dynamics of contemporary India. Instead, a **rural–urban continuum** better captures the gradations of settlement, function, and identity that define regional landscapes. This continuum includes everything from compact urban cores to low-density suburbs, informal fringe settlements, industrial townships, and agrarian villages with urban characteristics.

This spatial fluidity results from both planned and unplanned processes. Infrastructure investment, mobility improvements, and the spread of communication technologies have blurred the boundaries between rural and urban zones. Simultaneously, population growth, real estate speculation, and *industrialization* have generated hybrid spaces where rural and urban functions coexist and overlap (NIUA, 2021; MoHUA, 2014).

Spatial relationships within the continuum are characterized by mutual dependence. While rural areas contribute land, labour, and food, urban zones offer access to higher-order services, markets, and employment. These flows are sustained through transportation networks, commuting patterns, and supply chains. For instance, daily migration from peripheral settlements into cities enables the functioning of the urban economy, even as these commuters live in jurisdictions with lower levels of public services and weaker institutions (Kim, 2012; IWMI, 2021).

Recognizing and planning for this continuum requires flexible zoning, multi-scalar governance, and infrastructure that serves trans-boundary regions. It also requires a shift in mindset—acknowledging that rural and urban areas are not mutually exclusive categories but points along a dynamic developmental spectrum (Watson, V., 2009; SDSN, 2021).

2.8.3 Impacts of Weak/Strong Linkages on Development

The quality and strength of city-region linkages can significantly influence regional equity, ecological resilience, and economic competitiveness. Strong linkages—characterized by efficient infrastructure, inclusive governance, and well-managed resource flows—tend to support balanced growth, service delivery, and integration of peripheral areas into urban opportunity structures. Such integration reduces migratory stress on core cities, improves rural incomes, and supports spatial equity (MoHUA, 2014; McDonald et al., 2014).

By contrast, weak or broken linkages produce fragmentation and exclusion. Peri-urban areas may lack access to basic services, be governed by disconnected authorities, and face environmental degradation due to unchecked urban sprawl. This leads to social tension, rising inequality, and inefficient land use. Informal settlements proliferate, ecological systems are compromised, and rural areas remain underdeveloped even as urban regions prosper (Fields, 2009; Mills, G., & Tarasova, O., 2021).

In practice, weak linkages often result from institutional silos, poor regional data systems, and narrow policy approaches that treat cities and villages as separate silos. Development planning that ignores the city-region scale may achieve gains in isolated sectors but fail to address systemic challenges such as migration, resource depletion, and environmental vulnerability (IWMI, 2021).

Strengthening city-region linkages requires integrated regional planning, participatory governance, and adaptive institutional structures. Investments in physical infrastructure (roads, transit, utilities), human capital (education, healthcare), and digital networks can create synergistic growth. Equally important are mechanisms for collaborative governance across jurisdictions, such as joint planning boards, metropolitan commissions, and shared fiscal tools (MoHUA, 2014; SDSN, 2021).

Ultimately, city-region linkages determine whether urbanization becomes a force for inclusion and resilience—or a driver of inequality and conflict. Recognizing, sustaining, and strategically managing these linkages is central to achieving equitable and sustainable urban development.

2.9 Planning for the City-Region

2.9.1 Integrated Regional Planning Approaches

Effective planning for city-regions requires approaches that transcend the traditional boundaries of municipal jurisdictions. The complexity of spatial, economic, and ecological interactions across urban and rural areas makes it necessary to adopt **integrated regional planning**—a strategic, multi-scalar process that considers land use, infrastructure, environment, and socio-economic development in a coordinated manner.

In India, integrated planning has remained an aspirational goal rather than a widespread practice. Most urban plans are confined to city limits, while rural development schemes follow separate administrative frameworks. This division undermines the ability to manage issues that are inherently regional—such as commuting patterns, watershed management, transport corridors, housing affordability, and environmental protection (MoHUA, 2014; Mills, G., & Tarasova, O., 2021).

The URDPFI Guidelines strongly advocate for a tiered planning framework, which includes Metropolitan Region Plans, Development Plans, and Local Area Plans, all coordinated through an overarching vision. These documents stress the need for interdepartmental collaboration, data integration, and convergence of sectoral investments to prevent duplication and address service delivery gaps. A truly integrated approach incorporates demographic projections, environmental assessments, and socio-spatial analysis to guide future growth in a balanced and inclusive manner.

Globally, integrated regional planning has been institutionalized in several countries through functional urban areas, regional growth management strategies, and metropolitan governance bodies. These models prioritize spatial coherence and sustainability across administrative lines. While India has taken initial steps—such as NCR Planning Board and regional development authorities—most lack the legal authority, financial capacity, or political will to coordinate across diverse institutions (Kim, 2012; SDSN, 2021).

2.9.2 Urban–Rural Partnerships and Infrastructure Integration

One of the core strategies for city-region planning is fostering urban–rural partnerships. These partnerships are essential for realizing the interdependence between cities and their hinterlands—linking production and consumption, labour markets, service delivery, and environmental flows. Instead of viewing urban expansion as encroachment on rural territory, planning frameworks must acknowledge and facilitate mutually beneficial relationships.

Infrastructure plays a key role in connecting urban and rural systems. Investments in transportation, energy, water supply, digital connectivity, and logistics can dramatically improve the accessibility and productivity of rural settlements while reducing pressure on urban cores. For example, expanding regional bus services, freight corridors, and internet access enables labour mobility, market access, and service delivery across the urban–rural continuum (MoHUA, 2014; McDonald et al., 2014).

Integrated infrastructure planning must also recognize differential capacities. While urban centres may have robust public utilities and governance systems, rural and peri-urban areas often rely on informal or underfunded services. Joint planning mechanisms—such as metropolitan infrastructure funds, pooled budgets, or shared asset management platforms—can help address these asymmetries and promote co-financing models for shared regional infrastructure (IWMI, 2021; NIUA, 2021).

The Smart Cities Mission and AMRUT have initiated some forms of urban–rural integration, but their implementation often remains limited to city-level infrastructure. For city-regions to succeed, partnerships must be embedded not only in infrastructure projects but also in institutional relationships, policy alignment, and participatory mechanisms (Mills, G., & Tarasova, O., 2021).

2.9.3 Incrementalism and Community-Led Regional Development

While regional master plans and infrastructure investments are essential, large-scale top-down strategies alone cannot address the diversity and complexity of city-regions. Incrementalism—defined as a phased, adaptive approach to planning that builds on local needs and capacities—is critical for achieving inclusive regional development. This is especially important in peri-urban areas, where land tenure is often unclear, institutions are weak, and communities are highly heterogeneous (Watson, V., 2009; MoHUA, 2014).

Incremental planning allows for flexible interventions—such as community upgrading, participatory mapping, micro-infrastructure, and livelihood support—that gradually transform unplanned settlements into sustainable neighbourhoods. These interventions often originate from the ground up, driven by community-based organizations, NGOs, and local institutions. The cumulative effect of such actions can lead to large-scale change while respecting local contexts and avoiding displacement (Fields, 2009; McDonald et al., 2014).

Community-led regional development has also gained traction as a response to the governance vacuum in fringe and peri-urban spaces. Participatory budgeting, cooperative housing, self-help infrastructure, and inclusive land readjustment schemes empower residents to play an active role in shaping their environments. These initiatives also build trust between authorities and communities—an essential ingredient for long-term development (Mills, G., & Tarasova, O., 2021; IWMI, 2021).

While incremental and community-led strategies cannot replace formal regional planning, they serve as vital complements. Their success depends on enabling policies, technical support, and institutional flexibility to bridge the gap between informal practices and formal systems. Planning for city-regions, therefore, must balance visionary regional strategies with grounded, participatory, and context-sensitive actions.

2.10 Spatial Forms and Typologies of Cities

2.10.1 Compact vs. Dispersed Cities

Urban form plays a pivotal role in shaping the efficiency, equity, and environmental sustainability of cities. One of the foundational distinctions in spatial typologies is between compact cities and dispersed cities. Compact cities are characterized by high population densities, mixed land uses, and efficient public transport systems. They encourage walkability, reduce travel distances, and minimize land consumption. Dispersed or sprawling cities, on the other hand, expand horizontally, often into peri-urban and rural areas, leading to lower densities, segregated land uses, and increased reliance on private vehicles (MoHUA, 2014; McGranahan et al., 2006).

Compact urban development has long been championed for its environmental and social benefits. By minimizing the use of land and infrastructure per capita, compact cities can reduce energy consumption, carbon emissions, and infrastructure costs. They also enable greater access to services, facilitate social interaction, and promote a more vibrant urban life. Many European cities—including Barcelona, Amsterdam, and Copenhagen—exemplify the advantages of compactness through integrated land use and transport planning (McDonald et al., 2014).

In India, however, the reality is more complex. While city centres tend to be dense, much of the recent growth has been dispersed, especially in Tier I and II cities. Suburban developments, gated communities, special economic zones, and informal colonies have proliferated along highways and city peripheries, often beyond the purview of statutory plans. These patterns are driven by land markets, real estate speculation, and infrastructure gaps in core cities. As a result, even when density is achieved, it is not always planned, serviced, or equitable (IWMI, 2021).

Dispersed development poses several challenges—longer commute times, traffic congestion, environmental degradation, and greater per capita infrastructure costs. Yet it remains the dominant trend in Indian metropolitan areas due to institutional weaknesses, fragmented planning, and the failure to implement density-supportive policies. Promoting compactness requires a shift in planning priorities—focusing on mixed-use zoning, transit-oriented development (TOD), affordable housing, and green infrastructure (MoHUA, 2014; Mills, G., & Tarasova, O., 2021).

2.10.2 Monocentric vs. Polycentric Urban Structures

Another important dimension of spatial form is the distinction between monocentric and polycentric cities. A monocentric city is one in which a single core—typically the historical or commercial centre—dominates economic activity, employment, and decision-making. By contrast, a polycentric city is structured around multiple centres or nodes that are relatively independent but interlinked through infrastructure, economy, and governance.

Monocentric cities are efficient in terms of centralized infrastructure and services, but they often suffer from congestion, overburdened facilities, and social polarization. Urban growth in such cities tends to concentrate wealth, investment, and political influence in a limited area, leaving peripheral regions underdeveloped. For example, central Mumbai or Delhi's Lutyens zone exemplifies this concentration of resources (Watson, V., 2009).

Polycentric structures, on the other hand, offer several advantages. By distributing functions across multiple centres—such as employment hubs, administrative units, cultural districts, and transport terminals—polycentric cities reduce the pressure on any single node. This fosters regional balance, enhances resilience, and allows for more inclusive and diversified urban development. Cities such as London, Tokyo, and Berlin have adopted polycentric strategies to accommodate growth without undermining liveability (McDonald et al., 2014; MUD, 2012).

In India, polycentricity is emerging organically, particularly in metropolitan regions. The National Capital Region (NCR), Mumbai Metropolitan Region (MMR), and Bengaluru are evolving into polycentric formations with multiple urban nodes—each with distinct functions and governance setups. However, without coordinated planning and investment, polycentric growth can also deepen fragmentation, with certain nodes flourishing while others remain neglected. Implementing polycentric strategies requires spatial coordination, inter-jurisdictional governance, and a shared vision for regional development (MoHUA, 2014).

2.10.3 Form and Function in Urban Design

Beyond structural typologies, the form and function of cities are deeply embedded in their spatial design, land use configurations, and socio-cultural patterns. Urban form is not merely a physical layout but a reflection of planning ideologies, economic structures, political priorities, and historical processes. The physical organisation of streets, public spaces, building types, and neighbourhoods determines how people interact with their environment and with each other.

Functional zoning has long dominated modernist urban planning, separating land uses into distinct zones for residential, commercial, industrial, and institutional purposes. While this can offer clarity and control, it often results in spatial segregation, long commute distances, and exclusionary urban landscapes. Mixed-use development, by contrast, allows for overlapping functions within the same spatial footprint, enabling more vibrant, accessible, and efficient cities (MoHUA, 2014).

Urban design also influences environmental performance. For instance, grid layouts may support better ventilation and walkability, while radial or hierarchical designs may be more suited for administrative functions. The integration of green infrastructure—such as urban forests, parks, bioswales, and green roofs—enhances liveability and ecological resilience. Design features such as building orientation, street shading, and public plazas play a critical role in climate adaptation and social inclusion (McDonald et al., 2014; Mills, G., & Tarasova, O, 2021).

In the Indian context, formal urban design is often outpaced by informal growth and speculative development. Yet vernacular urban forms—such as courtyards, stepwells, chowks, and mohallas—offer rich insights into climate-responsive, community-oriented design. Recognizing and integrating such indigenous knowledge systems into contemporary planning can contribute to more context-sensitive and sustainable urban development (Fields, 2009; IWMI, 2021).

Ultimately, the form and typology of a city are not merely aesthetic or technical choices—they shape and reflect the lived experiences, resource use patterns, and development trajectories of urban systems. As India navigates the dual pressures of urban expansion and climate change, a renewed focus on spatial form, typology, and design becomes indispensable for creating inclusive, efficient, and sustainable city-regions.

2.11 Governance of City-Regions

2.11.1 Institutional Actors and Jurisdictional Complexities

The governance of city-regions involves a constellation of institutional actors, each with varying degrees of authority, capacity, and accountability. These include municipal corporations, panchayati raj institutions, development authorities, regional boards, parastatals, and state-level departments—often operating in parallel, with overlapping functions and fragmented mandates. In such a complex environment, the coordination required for cohesive and equitable planning becomes extremely challenging (MoHUA, 2014; Mills, G., & Tarasova, O, 2021).

City-regions are inherently multi-jurisdictional in nature. They encompass urban cores, expanding suburbs, industrial nodes, peri-urban villages, and ecologically sensitive areas. These territories may fall under different administrative units, governed by separate elected bodies and bureaucratic hierarchies. For instance, a metropolitan region may span multiple municipal bodies—each with its own budget, planning process, and priorities—while the surrounding villages may fall under rural governance frameworks such as gram panchayats or zila parishads (IWMI, 2021).

At the same time, state governments exercise significant control over urban planning, infrastructure, and finance. Development authorities, industrial boards, and infrastructure corporations—often set up under state legislation—play dominant roles in land acquisition, zoning, and investment decisions. These bodies are typically not accountable to local governments, reducing the autonomy of municipalities and bypassing democratic processes (Fields, 2009; McGranahan et al., 2006). The result is a highly layered institutional landscape where decision-making is centralized, fragmented, and often opaque.

2.11.2 Urban Local Bodies and Rural Governance Overlaps

A unique governance challenge in city-regions is the institutional divide between urban local bodies (ULBs) and rural governance institutions. As cities expand into adjoining rural areas, the resulting peri-urban and fringe zones are governed by rural panchayats, even though their socio-economic and spatial realities have become urban in character. This misalignment results in regulatory gaps, inadequate service delivery, and the absence of integrated land use planning (MoHUA, 2014; IWMI, 2021).

Urban local bodies are expected to manage infrastructure, sanitation, water supply, housing, and transportation. However, their jurisdiction ends at municipal boundaries. Areas beyond these limits, even when functionally part of the city, fall under rural institutions that lack technical capacity, financial resources, and legal authority to address complex urban challenges. For example, issues like construction approvals, sewage treatment, and road connectivity may fall into a grey zone where no agency takes full responsibility (Mills, G., & Tarasova, O, 2021; IWMI, 2021).

Moreover, urban expansion often displaces rural populations and traditional governance structures without integrating them into new institutional setups. Discrepancies in taxation, electoral representation, and service entitlements create a sense of exclusion among peri-urban residents. Meanwhile, municipalities often avoid formal annexation of these areas to escape the financial and administrative burden of upgrading services or legalizing informal development (Watson, V., 2009).

Efforts to bridge this urban–rural divide include calls for integrated planning bodies, shared service agreements, and the expansion of municipal limits. However, such transitions are politically sensitive and administratively cumbersome. Without enabling legal frameworks and fiscal incentives, the governance overlap continues to persist, leaving large parts of the city-region unregulated and underserved (MoHUA, 2014).

2.11.3 Challenges in Coordinated City-Region Governance

The governance of city-regions is marked by three interrelated challenges: fragmentation, informality, and lack of accountability. Fragmentation occurs not just in administrative boundaries but also in sectoral functions. Water supply may be managed by one agency, housing by another, and transport by a third—none of which are institutionally bound to coordinate or share data. This leads to policy incoherence, overlapping investments, and uneven spatial outcomes (McDonald et al., 2014).

Informality in governance refers to the growing influence of non-statutory actors—such as private developers, informal service providers, and political intermediaries—in shaping urban development. In the absence of clear rules, these actors often dictate the form and function of urban expansion through negotiations, loopholes, and parallel systems. This undermines long-term planning, weakens regulatory enforcement, and skews urban development in favour of elite interests (Fields, 2009; Watson, V., 2009).

Accountability deficits emerge when institutions operate without public oversight or participatory mechanisms. Metropolitan Planning Committees (MPCs), envisioned under the 74th Constitutional Amendment, remain largely ineffective or non-functional in most Indian cities. Regional development authorities often function autonomously, without transparency or local representation. Citizens and local communities have limited voice in shaping regional infrastructure, land use, or investment priorities (MoHUA, 2014; Mills, G., & Tarasova, O, 2021).

Overcoming these governance challenges requires legal reform, institutional innovation, and participatory frameworks. Strengthening the role of elected local bodies, mandating inter-jurisdictional coordination, and decentralizing planning authority are critical. Equally important is capacity building—ensuring that institutions at all levels have the skills, data, and tools to manage complex regional dynamics.

Governance of city-regions is ultimately about managing diversity—of interests, institutions, and spaces. It requires a shift from fragmented, top-down models to collaborative, transparent, and accountable systems that reflect the lived realities of interconnected urban and rural regions. Only then can city-regions serve as engines of equitable and sustainable development.

2.12 Urban–Rural Transformation and Continuum

2.12.1 Beyond the Binary: Spectrum of Settlement Types

Urban and rural areas have traditionally been viewed as distinct categories, separated by physical form, economic function, and administrative governance. However, contemporary settlement patterns increasingly challenge this binary. Across India and much of the global South, the emergence of intermediate settlements—such as census towns, peri-urban villages, industrial hamlets, and satellite townships—illustrates that rural and urban are no longer mutually exclusive but rather exist on a spectrum (MoHUA, 2014; IWMI, 2021).

These hybrid spaces demonstrate characteristics of both rural and urban areas. They may retain agricultural landscapes but also host urban infrastructure and services; they may follow panchayati raj governance systems yet function as dormitory towns for nearby cities. Such zones do not fit easily within standard planning classifications or policy frameworks. As a result, they are often overlooked in both urban and rural development programs, creating regulatory and developmental vacuums (Mills, G., & Tarasova, O, 2021; IWMI, 2021).

The transformation of rural areas into urban settlements is also not uniform. It can be incremental or sudden, formal or informal, planned or organic. Processes such as real estate speculation, highway-led development, infrastructure extension, and administrative reclassification play a significant role in shaping this continuum. The lack of recognition of this spatial diversity often results in ineffective planning and missed opportunities for strategic regional integration (Watson, 2009; Fields, 2009).

2.12.2 Functional Integration of Urban and Rural Economies

Urban–rural transformation is not only about spatial change—it is deeply rooted in economic interdependence. Rural areas are critical suppliers of food, water, labour, raw materials, and ecosystem services, while cities serve as markets, innovation hubs, and service providers. The integration of these two systems forms the backbone of regional economies.

This functional integration has intensified with improved transport and communication networks, digital platforms, and the rise of value chains that span across the rural–urban divide. Agricultural goods are now linked to urban retail through cold chains, logistics hubs, and processing centres. Rural labour supports construction, domestic work, and service industries in cities. Conversely, urban investments in infrastructure, education, and health have transformative impacts on surrounding rural communities (McGranahan et al., 2006; MoHUA, 2014).

The challenge lies in ensuring that this integration is equitable and sustainable. Often, the flow of benefits is skewed toward urban centres, while rural areas face land alienation, environmental stress, and social disruption. Policies that facilitate joint economic planning, promote rural entrepreneurship, invest in rural infrastructure, and ensure fair market access can help bridge this gap. The National Rurban Mission, for instance, seeks to create clusters that blend urban amenities with rural livelihoods, recognizing the potential of integrated development (SDSN, 2021).

2.12.3 Migration, Mobility, and Hybrid Spaces

One of the most tangible manifestations of urban–rural transformation is mobility—the movement of people across the continuum. Seasonal migration, circular migration, daily commuting, and long-term relocation are common strategies through which individuals and households navigate livelihood opportunities and social obligations. Migrants often maintain ties to both their origin and destination, creating multi-nodal life patterns that span across rural and urban spaces (IWMI, 2021; McDonald et al., 2014).

These movements contribute to the formation of hybrid spaces—both physical and social. Informal settlements on the urban fringe are often populated by migrants who bring with them rural social networks and cultural practices. Simultaneously, returning migrants invest in housing, education, and businesses in their home villages, bringing urban influences into rural settings. Such flows complicate notions of identity, place, and development, creating dynamic spaces of negotiation, innovation, and resilience (Fields, 2009).

However, policy responses to migration and hybridization remain inadequate. Migrant workers face exclusion from urban welfare programs due to lack of documentation or tenure. Rural planning ignores the temporary densification caused by returning migrants or new commuter populations. Urban planning rarely accounts for informal rental housing or the needs of transient populations. Recognizing mobility as a central component of urban–rural transformation is critical for inclusive planning (Mills, G., & Tarasova, O, 2021; MoHUA, 2014).

In conclusion, the urban–rural continuum is not a transitional phase but a stable and growing reality in India's development landscape. Planning and governance must evolve to embrace this complexity, moving beyond rigid categories and toward flexible, integrated, and responsive frameworks. Only then can the full potential of interconnected human settlements be harnessed for sustainable and equitable growth.

CHAPTER

3

Urban Development Plans, Policies, and Programs

Urban development in India is guided by a complex but structured framework of statutory plans, strategic policies, and national programs aimed at facilitating orderly, inclusive, and sustainable urban growth. These instruments not only define the spatial configuration of cities and towns but also steer infrastructure development, environmental conservation, social equity, and economic productivity. The formulation and implementation of urban development plans in India is primarily governed by state-level town and country planning legislations, supported by national policy directives and centrally sponsored schemes (MoHUA, 2015; MoHUA, 2023).

The growing pace of urbanization—projected to reach nearly 600 million urban residents by 2031—poses significant challenges in terms of housing, sanitation, mobility, resilience, and urban governance (UN 2016). In response, the Government of India has launched a series of missions such as AMRUT, Smart Cities Mission, PMAY-U, and SBM to provide institutional and financial support for achieving desired service levels and infrastructure standards (MoUD 2016b; MoHUA 2023).

This chapter presents an integrated view of the various types of urban development plans in India, the tools and strategies that guide their implementation, key national policies shaping urban transformation, and their cumulative impact on metropolitan and mega cities. It draws upon the URDPFI Guidelines, NUPF principles, mission-specific guidelines, and national reports to explore the structure, content, objectives, and evolving nature of urban planning and governance in India.

3.1 Plans for Urban Areas

Urban areas in India are planned and regulated through a multi-tiered hierarchy of spatial development plans that serve different geographical scales and planning timeframes. These plans are categorized broadly into statutory and non-statutory instruments, each playing a distinct role in shaping the built environment, guiding land use, provisioning infrastructure, and enabling coordinated development. The planning system follows a top-down yet increasingly participatory approach, integrating long-term regional visions with short-term localized actions (MoHUA 2015).

The key statutory plans include the Master Plan, Development Plan, Zonal Plan, and Town Planning Scheme (TPS). These are supplemented by Spatial Development Plans, Detailed Project Reports (DPRs), and sector-specific plans such as the Comprehensive Mobility Plan (CMP) and City Sanitation Plan (CSP). The emergence of Smart City Plans and area-based development proposals under national programs has added a new dimension to urban planning by incorporating digital technologies, sustainability frameworks, and community-led development (MoUD 2015).

According to the URDPFI Guidelines (2015b), spatial plans should be prepared based on a clear understanding of regional dynamics, settlement hierarchy, land suitability, infrastructure capacity, and social needs. They must be aligned with broader policy goals including inclusivity, environmental sustainability, and economic viability. Moreover, planning today demands the integration of GIS tools, climate resilience frameworks, and digital data systems to ensure accuracy, transparency, and accountability (MoHUA, 2022; NIUA, 2021b).

The following subsections explore each of these plans in detail, beginning with the Master Plan, which serves as the foundational vision for urban development and land use regulation.

3.1.1 Master Plan

The Master Plan is the fundamental statutory instrument guiding the spatial development and land use regulation of urban areas in India. It serves as a vision document that outlines the long-term development trajectory of a city, typically spanning 20 to 25 years, with the objective of promoting balanced, inclusive, and sustainable urban growth. Prepared under the relevant State Town and Country Planning Acts, the Master Plan integrates demographic forecasts, economic projections, environmental considerations, infrastructure needs, and social development goals into a coherent spatial framework (MoHUA 2015).

A Master Plan comprises key components such as existing land use analysis, projected population and employment trends, land suitability assessment, zoning proposals, infrastructure networks, environmental management strategies, and implementation mechanisms. It delineates zones for residential, commercial, industrial, recreational, and institutional uses, supported by transport, water supply, sanitation, solid waste, and social infrastructure planning (MoHUA

2015, 2023). The URDPFI Guidelines also advocate the inclusion of sustainability principles, disaster risk reduction, and Service Level Benchmarks (SLBs) in modern Master Plans, aligning with India's commitments to the Sustainable Development Goals (SDGs) and the New Urban Agenda (UN 2016).

The preparation of a Master Plan follows a systematic process that includes surveys, base map preparation, stakeholder consultations, spatial and sectoral analysis, formulation of development proposals, legal vetting, public display for objections and suggestions, and final approval by competent authorities (MoHUA 2015). As per the 74th Constitutional Amendment Act (1992), Urban Local Bodies (ULBs) are empowered to prepare plans for economic development and social justice, including Master Plans, thereby decentralising urban planning functions (GoI 1992).

Despite their statutory status, Master Plans in India face criticism for being overly rigid, time-consuming, and often disconnected from ground realities. Challenges include outdated data, weak implementation frameworks, lack of coordination between departments, and limited participation of citizens and marginalized communities (MoUD 2016a). Moreover, the plans often fail to incorporate peri-urban and fringe areas effectively, resulting in unplanned urban sprawl and infrastructural stress on core city areas (UN 2016; NIUA 2022).

In response to these limitations, the URDPFI Guidelines (2014) propose a more dynamic and responsive planning system, where the Master Plan is integrated with short-term Action Plans, Local Area Plans (LAPs), and Special Purpose Plans. Emphasis is also laid on incorporating tools like Geographic Information Systems (GIS), spatial analytics, climate risk assessment, and digital data platforms to make Master Plans more robust, responsive, and spatially accurate (NIUA 2022; MoHUA 2015).

In the context of metropolitan areas, the Master Plan is also a coordination tool across multiple jurisdictions and agencies. For example, in the National Capital Region (NCR), the Delhi Master Plan is aligned with the regional vision laid out by the National Capital Region Planning Board, ensuring integration with regional transport corridors, housing strategies, and environmental buffers (MoHUA 2023, 2015).

Furthermore, the effectiveness of a Master Plan depends not only on its formulation but also on institutional capacity, financing mechanisms, public participation, and periodic review. The integration of participatory planning methods and transparency in plan preparation and approval processes are vital for democratic urban governance (NIUA 2021; MoHUA 2015). The need to shift from land use-centric to people-centric planning is being recognized in India's evolving planning practices, especially in initiatives like AMRUT, PMAY, and Smart Cities Mission that encourage convergence and flexibility (MoHUA 2023).

Table 3.1 Simplified Structure of the Master Plan Preparation Process

Stage	Activities		
Base Map Preparation	Initial data collection	Surveying and mapping	
Visioning and Objective Setting	Stakeholder consultations	Identifying growth patterns and trends	
Land Use Zoning and Allocatior	Delineating residential, commercial, industrial, and recreational areas	Assessing land availability and suitability	
Infrastructure and Connectivity Planning	Transportation networks	Water supply, sanitation, drainage systems	Utility services
Master Plan Drafting	Integrating all components into a draft master plan	Reviewing land use patterns, zoning, and infrastructure plans	
Public Consultation and Feedback	Community engagement and discussions	Modifying the plan based on feedback	
Finalization of Master Plan	Final adjustments and revisions	Approval by relevant authorities	
Implementation and Monitoring	Actionable steps for implementation	Continuous monitoring and revisions	

Source: *adapted from URDPFI Vol I, (MoHUA 2015)*

3.1.2 Development Plan

A Development Plan is a comprehensive blueprint that provides spatial and sectoral proposals for the development of a town or city over a specified horizon period, typically 10 to 20 years. It is more detailed than the Master Plan and often acts as an intermediate instrument to translate long-term visions into actionable strategies at the city or municipal level (MoHUA 2015).

Prepared under state planning acts, Development Plans include zoning regulations, land use proposals, infrastructure projects, social and environmental infrastructure provisioning, transportation systems, and implementation phasing. They focus on resource mobilization, urban renewal, housing provision, slum upgrading, and improving urban services (MoHUA 2015; MoUD 2016a).

While the Master Plan sets the overarching vision, the Development Plan focuses on realising that vision through spatial demarcations, institutional mechanisms, and project identification. It integrates financial planning with spatial strategies, often guiding the preparation of sectoral plans like Comprehensive Mobility Plans and Local Area Plans (MoHUA 2015).

Development Plans are crucial in high-growth and fringe areas, where rapid urbanization creates pressure on land and services. They help control unplanned sprawl, enable equitable development, and ensure the integration of informal areas into the urban fabric (UN-Habitat). However, implementation challenges remain, including land acquisition bottlenecks, overlapping jurisdictions, and limited coordination among urban agencies.

3.1.3 Zonal Plan

A Zonal Plan is a spatial plan prepared at a finer scale to operationalize the Master Plan and Development Plan within designated zones or sectors of a city. It acts as a bridge between city-level visions and site-specific implementation by detailing land use distribution, infrastructure layouts, development control norms, and regulations within a defined zone (MoHUA 2015).

Each Zonal Plan typically corresponds to a ward, sector, or planning unit within the urban area. These plans identify plots for residential, commercial, industrial, recreational, and public uses, and indicate alignment of roads, green buffers, public utilities, and social infrastructure. Zoning regulations in these plans help govern permissible uses, building heights, floor area ratios, and open space requirements (MoHUA 2015; MoUD 2016a).

In the context of large cities like Delhi or Mumbai, Zonal Plans are key instruments for managing local-level growth, addressing redevelopment needs, and guiding infrastructure investment. They also play a critical role in coordinating with Special Area Plans, heritage precincts, and environment-sensitive zones (Habitat III 2016).

Prepared by development authorities or municipal corporations, Zonal Plans ensure micro-level planning coherence with city-wide objectives. However, their success depends on timely preparation, public participation, legal enforcement, and regular updating to reflect evolving needs (NIUA 2021b).

3.1.4 Town Planning Scheme (TPS)

The Town Planning Scheme (TPS) is a land readjustment mechanism primarily used to reorganize fragmented land parcels and provide planned infrastructure in growing urban and peri-urban areas. Widely adopted in Gujarat and increasingly used in other states, TPS enables equitable development by pooling privately owned land, reserving portions for public infrastructure, and returning reconstituted plots to landowners with improved access and value (MoHUA 2015).

Unlike traditional land acquisition models, TPS offers a participatory and negotiable approach where landowners contribute land voluntarily in exchange for serviced plots. The scheme allocates land for roads, open spaces, schools, sanitation, and utilities while retaining fairness through reallocation and compensation principles (MoHUA 2015).

TPS is particularly effective in rapidly urbanising fringe areas where acquisition is either costly or politically sensitive. It supports structured urban growth, facilitates infrastructure development in anticipation of future demand, and aligns with strategic spatial plans like the Development Plan or Master Plan (MoHUA 2023).

Challenges to TPS implementation include legal complexities, delayed approvals, and coordination between planning agencies and revenue departments. However, with appropriate legal backing and stakeholder engagement, TPS presents a scalable and efficient tool for inclusive urban expansion (UN 2016; MoHUA 2016).

3.1.5 Spatial Development Plan (SDP)

The Spatial Development Plan (SDP) is a non-statutory yet strategic document that outlines a spatial vision for broader regions such as metropolitan areas, city-regions, or industrial corridors. It provides an overarching framework for integrating land use with economic, environmental, and mobility strategies, especially in cases where multiple jurisdictions are involved or where statutory planning tools are absent or delayed (MoHUA 2015).

Unlike Master Plans or Development Plans, SDPs are not legally enforceable but serve as guiding instruments to align infrastructure investments, environmental safeguards, and spatial growth patterns. They are often prepared by metropolitan development authorities, regional planning boards, or special purpose vehicles under national programs (MoHUA 2015; MoUD 2016).

SDPs help visualize spatial futures over a horizon of 20–30 years, focusing on land suitability, regional connectivity, ecological sensitivity, economic nodes, and risk zones. In India, examples include the Delhi–Mumbai Industrial Corridor (DMIC) Concept Plan and the National Capital Region Plan, which provide a broad spatial framework for coordinated regional development (MoHUA 2023).

These plans are instrumental for identifying growth centres, logistics hubs, transport corridors, and investment zones while safeguarding environmentally sensitive areas. When linked effectively with statutory plans, SDPs strengthen regional planning and promote equitable and resilient urbanization (UN 2016; MoHUA 2022).

3.1.6 Detailed Project Report (DPR)

A Detailed Project Report (DPR) is a comprehensive technical, financial, and institutional document that outlines the feasibility, design, and execution plan for specific urban infrastructure projects. It acts as the final blueprint used for project appraisal, funding approval, and implementation, and is often a prerequisite for accessing central or state-level funding under schemes such as AMRUT, Smart Cities Mission, and SBM (MoHUA 2023; MoHUA 2016).

DPRs are typically prepared by urban local bodies, parastatal agencies, or consultants, and include details such as project justification, technical design, cost estimates, stakeholder analysis, environmental impact, implementation schedule, and risk mitigation strategies. They cover sectors like water supply, sewerage, mobility, solid waste management, housing, and drainage (MoHUA 2015).

The preparation of DPRs follows guidelines issued by nodal ministries, ensuring standardization in terms of technical specifications, financial structuring, public-private partnership models, and performance indicators (Smart City Guidelines, 2015). In many cases, DPRs also integrate sustainability and climate resilience components, aligning with national commitments to green infrastructure (MoHUA 2022).

DPRs serve as an operational link between planning and implementation, translating spatial visions into executable projects. However, challenges include poor quality of baseline data, lack of technical capacity at the ULB level, and delays in approval processes. Strengthening institutional frameworks and providing capacity-building support for DPR formulation remain key to ensuring efficient urban service delivery (NIUA 2021; MoUD 2016a).

3.1.7 Comprehensive Mobility Plan (CMP)

A Comprehensive Mobility Plan (CMP) is a strategic transport planning document prepared at the city level to ensure safe, efficient, and sustainable mobility for all. The CMP aims to address both current and future travel demands by integrating land use planning with transport infrastructure, focusing on promoting public transport, non-motorized transport (NMT), and inclusive access (MoUD 2014; MoHUA 2015).

Guided by the principles of the National Urban Transport Policy (NUTP), the CMP places people—not vehicles—at the core of transport planning. It analyses traffic patterns, forecasts future demand, and proposes a multimodal transport network with dedicated corridors for buses, BRT, metro, cycling tracks, pedestrian infrastructure, and last-mile connectivity (MoUD 2016).

CMPs are mandatory for cities seeking funding under central schemes like AMRUT and Metro Rail projects. They are expected to include aspects such as parking policy, Transit-Oriented Development (TOD), Intelligent Transport Systems (ITS), and environmental sustainability through emissions reduction and modal shift (MoHUA 2015; MoHUA 2023).

The CMP process involves extensive data collection, stakeholder consultation, and scenario building to ensure that transport systems align with broader urban development objectives. Integration with the Master Plan and Development Plan is critical to ensure coherence in spatial and transport planning (MoHUA 2015).

Despite their increasing adoption, implementation of CMP recommendations remains a challenge due to fragmented governance, lack of dedicated urban transport authorities, and limited technical capacity in smaller cities. Addressing these issues is vital for achieving inclusive and sustainable urban mobility (NIUA 2021; MoHUA 2022).

3.1.8 City Sanitation Plan (CSP)

A City Sanitation Plan (CSP) is a strategic document that outlines the goals, strategies, and action plans for achieving universal sanitation coverage, environmental sustainability, and public health in urban areas. Initiated under the National Urban Sanitation Policy (MoUD 2008), and further advanced by the Swachh Bharat Mission (SBM-Urban), CSPs focus on holistic sanitation management, including safe containment, transportation, treatment, and disposal of human waste, along with solid waste and greywater management (MoHUA 2014).

CSPs are prepared by Urban Local Bodies (ULBs) or state-level agencies through participatory approaches and detailed baseline assessments. They include ward-level mapping of existing sanitation infrastructure, service gaps, hygiene behaviour, vulnerable populations, and institutional capacity. The goal is to develop an implementable roadmap that ensures citywide inclusive sanitation (MoHUA 2015).

These plans are typically structured around seven key components: access to toilets, safe septage and sewerage management, solid waste management, stormwater drainage, water supply linkages, behavioural change communication, and governance reforms. Integration with city budgets and alignment with Development Plans or Smart City Proposals is encouraged to ensure implementation convergence (MoHUA 2015; MoHUA 2016).

With increasing focus on Faecal Sludge and Septage Management (FSSM), CSPs are being updated to include decentralized treatment, private sector participation, and monitoring frameworks. However, smaller towns often face challenges due to limited financial and technical resources. Addressing these gaps through institutional support, capacity-building, and inter-agency coordination is critical for achieving sanitation outcomes (NIUA 2021; MoHUA 2022).

3.1.9 Smart City Plan

A Smart City Plan is an integrated, technology-driven strategy that outlines a city's vision, goals, and interventions under the Smart Cities Mission (SCM), launched by the Government of India in 2015. Unlike traditional urban plans, Smart City Plans emphasize area-based development, digital governance, sustainable infrastructure, and citizen-centric services to enhance urban quality of life (MoHUA 2015, 2023).

Each selected city under the mission prepares a Smart City Proposal (SCP), which includes a vision statement, pan-city initiatives, and an area-based development strategy—typically focusing on retrofitting, redevelopment, or greenfield development in a specific zone. These proposals are selected through competitive rounds and implemented by Special Purpose Vehicles (SPVs) formed at the city level (MoUD, 2016).

Smart City Plans integrate multiple urban systems: intelligent transport, real-time utility monitoring, ICT-based service delivery, climate-resilient infrastructure, and spatial analytics for better planning. The mission encourages convergence with other schemes such as AMRUT, PMAY, and Swachh Bharat Mission, while also incorporating global frameworks like the Sustainable Development Goals (SDGs) and New Urban Agenda (UN 2016).

In practice, Smart City Plans serve as dynamic tools to reimagine urban development with a focus on sustainability, inclusivity, efficiency, and digital transformation. The use of GIS, IoT, and real-time data systems underpins these plans, making them more adaptive and responsive to citizen needs (MoHUA 2022; NIUA 2021).

Despite their innovation, challenges persist—particularly in project financing, digital divide, legacy infrastructure integration, and ensuring inclusivity in tech-led solutions. Moving forward, institutionalising the learnings of Smart City Plans into mainstream planning frameworks remains critical (MoHUA 2016–17).

Together, the various types of urban development plans in India—from long-term statutory instruments like the Master Plan and Development Plan to focused, sectoral strategies such as CMPs, CSPs, and Smart City Plans—form a comprehensive and interlinked planning ecosystem. Each plan serves a unique purpose, scale, and timeframe, yet their coherence and convergence are essential for sustainable urban transformation. With increasing emphasis on digitalization, resilience, inclusivity, and participatory governance, urban planning in India is gradually evolving from a rigid land-use-centric model to a more integrated, flexible, and people-oriented approach. Strengthening institutional capacities, enabling data-driven decision-making, and ensuring cross-sectoral alignment will be key to translating these plans into actionable and equitable urban outcomes.

3.2 Strategies, Tools, and Urban Development Policies

Urban development in India is no longer confined to the preparation of spatial plans alone; it increasingly relies on a wide range of strategic tools, planning instruments, and policy innovations that enable dynamic and responsive urban governance. These strategies provide the technical, financial, and participatory mechanisms necessary for implementing urban plans, addressing service delivery gaps, fostering resilience, and ensuring inclusive growth.

With the emergence of complex urban challenges—ranging from climate vulnerability and mobility stress to informal settlements and digital divide—urban governance demands flexible, multi-scalar approaches. Strategic urban planning tools such as Local Area Plans, Transit-Oriented Development frameworks, and Heritage Management Plans provide targeted interventions within the larger city planning framework. Simultaneously, digital tools like GIS, MIS, and e-Governance platforms are revolutionising the way cities collect data, engage with citizens, and deliver services (MoHUA 2015; MoHUA 2022).

Equally important are participatory methods and policy frameworks that empower communities, improve accountability, and enhance the effectiveness of urban interventions. From the constitutional decentralization brought in by the 74th Amendment to innovations under the Smart Cities Mission and ClimateSmart Cities frameworks, India's urban policy landscape is undergoing significant transformation, embedding sustainability, equity, and technology into the core of city management.

The following subsections examine some of the key strategic and operational tools being adopted in India's urban planning ecosystem.

3.2.1 Strategic Urban Planning Tools

Strategic urban planning tools are focused, project-driven instruments that complement statutory land use plans by addressing specific thematic, spatial, or sectoral issues within urban areas. Unlike long-term Master Plans, which often remain static, these tools are dynamic and can be tailored to respond to emerging urban challenges, local needs, and implementation priorities (MoHUA 2015).

Common examples include Local Area Plans (LAPs), which focus on detailed spatial development and infrastructure improvements within a defined neighbourhood or ward; Transit-Oriented Development (TOD) strategies that integrate land use with high-capacity public transport corridors; and Heritage Management Plans designed to protect and revitalize culturally significant areas (MoUD 2016; NIUA 2021).

Tools such as City Resilience Strategies, promoted under climate frameworks like CSCAF and the National Mission on Sustainable Habitat (NMSH), support cities in identifying climate risks and planning adaptive infrastructure. Similarly, Land Pooling Policies, already operational in states like Delhi and Andhra Pradesh, provide an alternative to conventional land acquisition for urban expansion and redevelopment (MoHUA 2015).

The introduction of City Investment Plans, City Development Plans (CDPs) under JnNURM, and Area-Based Development (ABD) proposals under the Smart Cities Mission further illustrate how strategic tools enable cities to prioritize infrastructure, leverage financial resources, and monitor performance outcomes (MoHUA 2015; MoHUA 2023).

By embedding flexibility and responsiveness into urban governance, these tools allow urban local bodies to bridge the gap between vision and execution. However, their effectiveness relies heavily on inter-agency coordination, stakeholder engagement, and capacity-building support—particularly in Tier 2 and Tier 3 cities where technical expertise is limited (UN-Habitat III, 2016; MoUD 2016).

3.2.2 Participatory Planning and Technology in Urban Management

Participatory planning is central to inclusive, accountable, and responsive urban governance. Recognising the limitations of top-down planning models, India's urban policy frameworks increasingly promote the involvement of citizens, civil society, and local institutions in the planning, design, and monitoring of urban development projects. The 74th Constitutional Amendment Act laid the foundation for such participatory processes by mandating the devolution of planning powers to Urban Local Bodies (ULBs) and ensuring the formation of ward committees and district planning committees (MoHUA 2015).

In practice, participatory planning has been institutionalized through tools such as public consultations during Master Plan preparation, community engagement during Local Area Planning, and feedback loops under Smart City Proposals. The Smart Cities Mission, for instance, made citizen engagement a prerequisite during proposal formulation, encouraging cities to crowdsource ideas, conduct surveys, and use online platforms to gauge local priorities (MoHUA 2015).

The role of technology in urban management has grown rapidly alongside participatory models. Digital tools such as online grievance redressal systems, city dashboards, real-time service tracking, and e-governance platforms are now integral to city functioning. These systems help enhance transparency, improve service delivery, and strengthen the accountability of municipal institutions (MoHUA 2023).

Moreover, platforms like the India Urban Observatory, Ease of Living Index, and Municipal Performance Index leverage digital tools to measure and compare city performance, enabling data-driven decision-making. At the local level, GIS mapping, spatial analytics, and mobile applications have transformed how cities collect information, engage with citizens, and plan urban services (MoHUA 2022; NIUA 2021).

While these innovations mark significant progress, challenges persist in the form of digital illiteracy, uneven internet access, and limited institutional capacity in smaller towns. To overcome these, future urban strategies must combine participatory governance with inclusive digital access and continuous institutional learning.

3.2.3 GIS, MIS, and E-Governance Tools

Geographic Information Systems (GIS), Management Information Systems (MIS), and e-Governance platforms have become essential tools in modern urban planning and management. These technologies enable cities to collect, store, analyse, and visualize spatial and non-spatial data, leading to more informed and efficient decision-making across sectors such as land use, infrastructure, mobility, environment, and public services (MoHUA 2015).

GIS is particularly valuable in preparing base maps, zoning proposals, infrastructure layouts, and environmental assessments. It supports dynamic updates to development plans, improves accuracy in property taxation, and facilitates climate risk mapping and vulnerability assessments under initiatives like the Climate Smart Cities Assessment Framework (MoHUA 2022). Several cities, including Bhopal, Pune, and Surat, have successfully adopted GIS-based systems for integrated urban management.

MIS platforms enable real-time monitoring and performance tracking of municipal services. They are widely used in sectors such as water supply, waste management, sanitation, and urban housing to manage inventories, workflows, and citizen feedback. These systems are also essential for reporting under national programs such as AMRUT, SBM, and PMAY-U (MoHUA 2023; MoUD 2016).

E-Governance tools bridge the gap between governments and citizens by offering digital services such as birth and death registration, building plan approvals, property tax payments, and grievance redressal through unified online portals. Under the Smart Cities Mission and Digital India framework, ULBs have been encouraged to digitize records, implement mobile-based apps, and create integrated command and control centres for urban operations (MoHUA 2015; NIUA 2021).

Despite their potential, the effective use of these tools is constrained by lack of skilled personnel, inadequate IT infrastructure, and fragmented data systems in many smaller municipalities. Strengthening digital capacity, ensuring data interoperability, and protecting citizen data privacy are critical steps towards realising the full benefits of technology-driven urban governance.

The evolving landscape of urban governance in India reflects a decisive shift toward integrated, participatory, and technology-enabled planning. Strategic urban tools provide the flexibility to respond to localized needs, while participatory approaches deepen democratic engagement and ownership of urban transformation. At the same time, GIS, MIS, and e-Governance systems enhance precision, transparency, and efficiency in decision-making and service delivery. However, the effectiveness of these tools depends not just on their technical robustness but also on institutional capacity, cross-sectoral coordination, and equitable digital access. As India's cities continue to grow in complexity, these strategies and tools will play a pivotal role in operationalising urban plans and translating policy goals into meaningful outcomes.

3.3 Some Key Urban Policies

India's urban transformation is significantly shaped by a set of national policies and centrally sponsored missions that provide financial support, institutional guidance, and thematic focus for urban development. These policies are designed to address critical aspects such as housing, mobility, water supply, sanitation, environment, and urban governance—many of which are essential for implementing city-level plans and improving quality of life. While each policy or mission targets specific sectors, their convergence under a broader urban framework ensures coordinated action and measurable outcomes. Together, they reflect a shift from project-centric to outcome-oriented urban governance, with increasing emphasis on inclusivity, resilience, digitalization, and decentralized planning. The following subsections briefly highlight some of the most influential urban policies currently shaping India's cities.

3.3.1 Smart Cities Mission (SCM)

Launched in 2015, the Smart Cities Mission (SCM) aims to promote cities that provide core infrastructure, clean and sustainable environments, and a decent quality of life through smart solutions and citizen-centric planning. It introduced Area-Based Development (ABD) and Pan-City initiatives, implemented through Special Purpose Vehicles (SPVs) at the city level (Smart Cities Guidelines, 2015). With a strong emphasis on digital governance, ICT integration, and public participation, the mission has redefined urban project delivery and data-led management in India's cities.

3.3.2 Atal Mission for Rejuvenation and Urban Transformation (AMRUT)

AMRUT, launched in 2015, focuses on improving infrastructure in 500 cities, particularly in areas such as water supply, sewerage, drainage, urban transport, and green spaces. It introduced Service Level Improvement Plans (SLIPs) and promoted reforms in municipal finance, e-governance, and urban planning capacity (MoHUA 2023). AMRUT 2.0 continues this momentum with a focus on universal water access and convergence with climate goals.

3.3.3 Pradhan Mantri Awas Yojana – Urban (PMAY-U)

PMAY-U, launched in 2015, aims to ensure "Housing for All" in urban areas by 2022 through verticals like In-situ Slum Redevelopment, Affordable Housing in Partnership, Credit-Linked Subsidy Scheme, and Beneficiary-Led Construction. It emphasizes secure tenure, women ownership, and convergence with basic services (MoHUA 2023; MoHUA 2016–17).

3.3.4 National Urban Transport Policy (NUTP)

First introduced in 2006 and revised in 2014, NUTP emphasizes moving people rather than vehicles. It promotes public transport, non-motorized transport (NMT), Transit-Oriented Development (TOD), and multi-modal integration as core principles for sustainable urban mobility (MoUD 2014). It also advocates institutional reforms and dedicated urban transport authorities in cities.

3.3.5 National Policy on Urban Street Vendors (NPUSV)

This policy, notified in 2009 and reinforced by the Street Vendors Act (2014), recognizes street vendors as integral to the urban economy. It provides for vending zones, vendor committees, and issuance of identity cards, aiming to protect livelihoods while ensuring public space management (MoHUPA 2009; GoI 2014).

3.3.6 Swachh Bharat Mission – Urban (SBM-U)

SBM-U, launched in 2014, aims to eliminate open defecation and improve solid waste management through behavioural change, infrastructure provisioning, and citizen participation. It introduced tools like ODF+, ODF++ certification, decentralized waste processing, and faecal sludge management (FSM), becoming one of India's largest urban sanitation drives (MoHUA 2014; MoHUA 2023).

3.3.7 Urban Land Ceiling and Regulation Act (ULCRA)

Enacted in 1976 and repealed in most states since the early 2000s, ULCRA aimed to control land speculation and ensure equitable land distribution. While intended to enable affordable housing and planned growth, it was criticized for stalling development and fuelling informality, prompting its gradual phase-out (Govt. of India, 1976; MoHUA 2015).

3.3.8 Environmental and Sustainability Policies

India's urban environmental policy landscape includes frameworks like the Environment Protection Act (1986), Coastal Regulation Zone (CRZ) Notification, and Eco-Sensitive Zone guidelines, all of which influence urban land use and infrastructure decisions. Cities are increasingly integrating climate action, biodiversity, and ecosystem restoration into planning through tools like CSCAF and SDG localization (GoI 1986; MoEF 2011).

3.3.9 National Mission on Sustainable Habitat (NMSH) *(optional)*

Part of India's National Action Plan on Climate Change, NMSH focuses on sustainable urban planning, energy-efficient buildings, and resilient public transport systems. Though still under implementation, its vision aligns closely with evolving city-level climate strategies and planning reforms (MoUD 2010; MoEF, 2010).

3.3.10 National Urban Policy Framework (NUPF)

Developed in 2018 by the Ministry of Housing and Urban Affairs, the National Urban Policy Framework (NUPF) serves as a strategic vision document guiding India's urban transformation. It is built around 10 functional areas and grounded in 16 principles such as inclusiveness, subsidiarity, transparency, and resilience. While not a statutory policy, it offers a unified, integrative framework for states, ULBs, and institutions to align urban development efforts, promote cross-sectoral coordination, and move towards people-centric and sustainable urbanization (MoHUA 2018).

India's urban policy architecture has evolved significantly over the past two decades, moving from fragmented sectoral schemes to integrated, mission-driven, and performance-oriented programs. These policies—whether focused on housing, mobility, sanitation, or governance—have provided essential direction and funding support for cities to scale up infrastructure and services. However, the challenge now lies in ensuring convergence, contextualisation, and capacity at the local level. Policies like the NUPF offer a critical bridge between vision and action, reinforcing the need for strategic coherence, institutional innovation, and long-term sustainability in India's urban future.

3.4 Impact of Urban Development Policies on Metro and Mega Cities

India's metropolitan and mega cities—such as Delhi, Mumbai, Bengaluru, and Kolkata—are at the forefront of the country's urban transition. These cities experience intense demographic pressure, economic dynamism, environmental stress, and infrastructural complexity. Consequently, they have become primary sites for policy experimentation and large-scale urban investment. National missions like AMRUT, Smart Cities, PMAY-U, and SBM have prioritized metropolitan regions for funding and reform, while frameworks like the NUPF and CSCAF have encouraged strategic, climate-resilient, and people-centric approaches. However, despite these advancements, cities continue to face persistent challenges in policy implementation, coordination, and equitable service delivery. The following subsections examine the challenges, success stories, and institutional gaps in implementing urban development policies in metro and mega cities.

3.4.1 Challenges in Implementation

Despite the wide reach and ambitious scope of national urban development policies, metro and mega cities in India face several implementation challenges. One of the most persistent issues is institutional fragmentation, where multiple agencies—such as municipal corporations, development authorities, utility boards, and parastatals—operate in silos without effective coordination. This often leads to overlaps in jurisdiction, conflicting mandates, and delays in project execution.

Financing urban infrastructure remains another major barrier. While central schemes provide funding, metro cities frequently face gaps in resource mobilization, land acquisition costs, and operation and maintenance expenditures. Urban local bodies often struggle with limited revenue generation capacity, dependency on grants, and delays in fund disbursement, especially in projects involving private participation or multilateral support.

Capacity constraints within municipal institutions further affect implementation. Technical expertise in urban planning, procurement, and data analysis is often lacking, particularly in managing large-scale, technology-integrated projects like those under the Smart Cities Mission. In addition, rigid bureaucratic structures and outdated planning regulations hinder innovation and responsiveness to changing urban dynamics.

Policy integration is also a significant challenge. While missions such as AMRUT, PMAY, and SBM aim for convergence, cities often implement them in isolation, leading to inefficiencies and missed opportunities for holistic urban transformation. Moreover, participatory planning remains limited in practice, with citizen engagement often confined to tokenistic consultations rather than meaningful involvement in decision-making.

Environmental concerns are increasingly emerging in metro cities, where rapid urbanization, informal expansion, and vehicular congestion contribute to air and water pollution, loss of green spaces, and increased vulnerability to climate risks. Existing policies offer frameworks for sustainable development, but enforcement remains weak due to institutional inertia and political pressures.

Together, these challenges highlight the need for strengthening local governance, reforming institutional structures, and building sustained urban capacity to fully realize the potential of national urban policies in India's largest and most complex cities.

3.4.2 Successful Examples and Best Practices

Despite numerous challenges, several metro and mega cities in India have demonstrated notable successes in implementing urban development policies through innovation, institutional coordination, and community engagement. These examples offer valuable lessons in translating policy frameworks into on-ground outcomes.

Ahmedabad's Bus Rapid Transit System (BRTS), known as Janmarg, is widely regarded as a best practice in sustainable urban transport. Developed with support from the National Urban Transport Policy, the system integrates dedicated corridors, smart ticketing, and multimodal connectivity. Its success lies in proactive planning, phased implementation, and institutional commitment, making it a model replicated in other cities.

Pune has made significant progress in participatory planning and e-governance under the Smart Cities Mission. The city established an Integrated Command and Control Centre (ICCC), GIS-based property tax systems, and citizen feedback mechanisms. These digital initiatives improved transparency, service delivery, and responsiveness, aligning with the mission's core objectives.

Indore stands out for its achievements in sanitation and solid waste management. Under the Swachh Bharat Mission, the city adopted door-to-door collection, source segregation, decentralized composting, and a well-structured grievance redressal system. Indore's consistent top ranking in Swachh Survekshan reflects its administrative efficiency and citizen participation.

Bhubaneswar's Smart City Proposal is often cited for its inclusive approach and urban design innovations. The city emphasized child-friendly infrastructure, non-motorized transport, heritage-sensitive planning, and resilience strategies, supported by extensive stakeholder consultations. The focus on cultural identity alongside digital infrastructure makes Bhubaneswar a standout example of integrated urban transformation.

Chennai's implementation of AMRUT has seen major reforms in urban water supply and sewerage services, including the expansion of piped networks and improvements in service quality. These projects were planned with Service Level Improvement Plans (SLIPs), ensuring accountability and performance monitoring.

These examples demonstrate that successful policy implementation depends not only on funding or frameworks but also on leadership, inter-agency collaboration, contextual design, and a strong connection between planning and execution. Scaling such practices across other cities will require adaptive governance, peer learning, and continuous institutional support.

3.4.3 Gaps and Overlaps in Urban Policy Execution

While India's urban policy landscape has grown richer and more comprehensive over the years, gaps and overlaps in execution remain a recurring concern, especially in complex metropolitan environments. These issues often stem from the coexistence of multiple centrally sponsored schemes, sectoral policies, and planning institutions operating without clear coordination or alignment.

A major overlap occurs between land use and infrastructure planning. While spatial development is guided by Master Plans and Development Plans, sectoral missions like AMRUT, SBM, or Smart Cities often operate independently of these statutory plans. As a result, infrastructure investments may not fully align with land use patterns or future growth areas, leading to inefficiencies and underutilisation of assets.

There are also institutional gaps between urban local bodies and parastatal agencies. For instance, water supply and housing boards often operate at the state level, while city governments are responsible for urban governance and planning. This fragmentation results in duplicated efforts, conflicting project timelines, and challenges in citizen accountability.

Policy mandates also tend to overlap. Smart Cities and AMRUT, for example, both include components related to mobility, green spaces, and water infrastructure, but they follow different planning and reporting frameworks. This can create confusion at the local level and stretch already limited technical capacity.

Another gap lies in the mismatch between urban policy aspirations and local implementation capabilities. While national policies increasingly promote resilience, inclusivity, and climate action, many cities lack the institutional readiness, financial autonomy, and trained personnel to adopt these principles effectively. Smaller metropolitan areas, in particular, struggle to access funding, retain skilled professionals, and implement integrated urban solutions.

Addressing these gaps requires reforming institutional structures to promote convergence, empowering local governments with planning authority and fiscal autonomy, and developing unified frameworks that align city planning, service delivery, and policy goals. Strengthening horizontal and vertical integration remains crucial to improving the coherence and impact of urban policies in India's metro and mega cities.

India's metro and mega cities are central to the country's urban growth story, yet they also bear the brunt of its most complex challenges. Urban development policies have provided a much-needed framework for reform and investment, and many cities have demonstrated that well-executed strategies can yield measurable improvements in mobility, sanitation, housing, and governance. However, the full potential of these policies is often constrained by fragmented institutions, overlapping mandates, and capacity limitations. Bridging these gaps will require a systemic shift toward integrated governance, empowered local bodies, and long-term strategic thinking. Only then can India's metropolitan regions truly become inclusive, resilient, and sustainable engines of national development.

CHAPTER

4

Metropolitanization

4.1 Introduction

The 21st century has been marked by an unprecedented transformation in the scale, form, and dynamics of human settlements. Among the most prominent manifestations of this transformation is the phenomenon of metropolitanization. As urbanization accelerates globally, cities have expanded beyond their traditional municipal boundaries, giving rise to complex and integrated metropolitan regions that function as engines of economic growth, centres of innovation, and loci of significant social and environmental challenges.

Metropolitanization is not merely a quantitative expansion of urban space but represents a qualitative shift in the way cities interact with their hinterlands and with each other. The emergence of polycentric urban regions, with intricate networks of transport, infrastructure, housing, and services, has redefined the spatial organisation of human settlements. Globally, metropolitan areas account for the majority of a nation's gross domestic product (GDP), often serve as political and cultural capitals, and act as gateways for global economic integration (UN-Habitat 2020; World Bank 2015).

In the Indian context, the metropolitan question is both urgent and evolving. With over 30 per cent of its population residing in urban areas and over 53 metropolitan areas identified in the Census of India 2011, the country is undergoing a rapid transformation that demands new frameworks for urban governance, infrastructure planning, and social inclusion. The recent push towards smart urbanization, coupled with efforts to reform planning capacity and decentralize governance, has brought metropolitan regions to the forefront of India's development discourse (Census of India 2011; MoHUA 2023). Yet, this transformation is not without its complexities. Metropolitan areas often experience the most acute forms of socio-spatial inequality, ecological degradation, and institutional fragmentation. These regions face mounting pressure to deliver sustainable development outcomes while navigating between multiple jurisdictions, economic imperatives, and cultural identities. Moreover, as India moves towards becoming the third-largest economy in the world, the governance and planning of metropolitan areas are becoming increasingly central to achieving its broader development goals (NIUA 2021; MoHUA 2023; UN-Habitat 2020).

This chapter seeks to unpack the concept of metropolitanization by tracing its historical roots, examining global and Indian trends, identifying key characteristics and governance issues, and outlining the need for metropolitan planning. Drawing on empirical studies, policy frameworks, and planning experiences, the chapter provides a comprehensive exploration of metropolitanization as both a process and a planning challenge. It also sets the stage for more detailed case studies in subsequent chapters, where real-world examples will illustrate the diverse trajectories and responses of metropolitan regions.

4.1.1 Historical Evolution of Metropolitanization

The origins of metropolitanization can be traced to the early emergence of human settlements and trade-based urban centres in antiquity. Cities such as Mohenjo-daro, Babylon, and Alexandria were not only hubs of administration and culture but also reflected complex spatial and economic relationships with their hinterlands. However, it was the industrial revolution in the 18th and 19th centuries that catalysed the first wave of large-scale urban expansion, giving rise to the modern city. The introduction of mechanized production, rail transport, and mass migration led to the densification and spatial spread of urban areas, particularly in Europe and North America.

The post-World War II period witnessed a second wave of metropolitan growth driven by rapid industrialization, state-led development, and population booms in the global South. Cities such as São Paulo, Mumbai, Cairo, and Lagos expanded beyond their core municipalities, engulfing surrounding towns, villages, and rural landscapes. The phenomenon was marked by both horizontal sprawl and vertical intensification, facilitated by the rise of automobile infrastructure, housing estates, and administrative reclassification of peri-urban zones (Wang et al. 2024).

In India, the process of metropolitanization gained momentum during the post-independence decades. The adoption of five-year plans emphasized industrial growth and public sector development, leading to the spatial concentration of employment in urban centres. The influx of rural migrants into cities like Delhi, Kolkata, and Chennai initiated an unplanned, organic expansion of urban territories, eventually giving rise to metropolitan regions. During the 1990s, with the liberalization of the Indian economy, the growth of the services sector and global capital investments further transformed urban dynamics, especially in metropolitan centres such as Bengaluru, Hyderabad, and Pune (Kebza 2024).

The Census of India began recognising *metropolitan areas* as urban agglomerations with a population of over one million. The 2001 and 2011 censuses marked significant changes in the number and spread of metropolitan regions, highlighting the extent of urban sprawl and the functional integration of satellite towns and peri-urban regions into core cities (Census of India 2011). By 2011, India had officially identified 53 metropolitan areas, indicating a paradigm shift in the scale and scope of urbanization.

Parallel to this quantitative expansion, the qualitative dimensions of metropolitanization have also evolved. The boundaries between urban and rural areas have blurred, creating transitional landscapes often termed the urban-rural continuum. Moreover, the governance of metropolitan regions has grown increasingly complex, involving multiple tiers of administration, overlapping jurisdictions, and sectoral authorities with fragmented mandates (NITI Aayog 2021; Artioli and Galès 2025).

The contemporary phase of metropolitanization is characterized by digital connectivity, mobility corridors, and polycentric spatial forms. With the proliferation of smart technologies, regional planning instruments, and international collaboration on climate goals, metropolitan regions are now positioned as key actors in addressing global sustainability challenges. However, the historical trajectory reveals that metropolitanization is not a linear or uniform process; it is shaped by political economy, technological transitions, and socio-cultural factors unique to each context.

4.2 Metropolitanization

Metropolitanization refers to the dynamic process through which urban growth extends beyond the formal boundaries of a city to incorporate surrounding towns, peri-urban zones, and rural hinterlands into a functionally integrated urban region. Unlike mere population growth or spatial expansion, metropolitanization entails a complex restructuring of social, economic, and political systems at a regional scale. It transforms isolated urban centres into networks of interdependent settlements, often governed by multiple administrative entities but functioning as cohesive economic, labour, and infrastructural systems.

Globally, metropolitanization has emerged as a dominant urban form due to several converging factors. These include the liberalization of markets, global investment flows, decentralization policies, improvements in mobility and communication infrastructure, and the shift from manufacturing-based economies to services and knowledge sectors (Wang et al. 2024). Metropolitan regions typically offer agglomeration advantages—such as proximity to markets, talent pools, logistics networks, and institutional services—that foster innovation and drive national economic growth.

In the Indian context, metropolitanization has intensified over the past three decades, primarily driven by economic liberalization, the rise of the IT and service sectors, rapid migration from rural areas, and infrastructure-led urban expansion. Cities such as Delhi, Mumbai, Bengaluru, and Hyderabad have absorbed surrounding municipalities and census towns, often forming contiguous urban corridors with complex land-use patterns and varying levels of governance. These corridors represent the spatial manifestation of India's economic reorganization and reflect emerging forms of regional urbanism (NITI Aayog 2021).

The process of metropolitanization is not limited to megacities. It also manifests in the transformation of tier-2 and tier-3 cities into regional hubs that develop strong economic and functional linkages with larger metropolitan centres. As these cities grow, they attract investments, talent, and services, gradually integrating into larger urban ecosystems. Examples include the Pune-Mumbai-Nashik triangle, the Delhi-Meerut-Ghaziabad corridor, and the emerging Bhubaneswar-Cuttack region.

One of the core implications of metropolitanization is the growing mismatch between spatial growth and institutional capacities. While urban areas expand seamlessly across administrative borders, governance structures often remain fragmented, leading to issues in planning, infrastructure provisioning, and service delivery. Furthermore, metropolitanization frequently intensifies socio-economic inequalities by displacing low-income communities, straining natural resources, and exposing vulnerabilities in public health, housing, and mobility systems (Artioli and Galès 2025; UN-Habitat 2016).

Despite these challenges, metropolitanization presents significant opportunities for inclusive development if appropriately planned and managed. The convergence of population, capital, and innovation in metropolitan regions can be leveraged to enhance competitiveness, improve living standards, and foster climate-resilient urbanism. Realising these outcomes, however, requires a paradigm shift in governance—from jurisdictional fragmentation to regional coordination; from infrastructure-centric approaches to people-centric planning; and from sectoral policies to integrated metropolitan frameworks.

As the subsequent sections will explore, understanding the features, trajectories, and institutional structures of metropolitanization is critical to addressing the challenges of 21st-century urbanization—particularly in rapidly transforming contexts such as India.

4.2.1 Key Characteristics

Metropolitan areas are distinguished from other urban forms by their scale, structure, and complexity. These characteristics are not only physical or demographic but also institutional, economic, and social in nature. The process of metropolitanization results in urban systems that are fundamentally different from traditional city forms due to the following key attributes:

1. **Polycentric Spatial Structure:** One of the defining features of metropolitan regions is the emergence of multiple urban nodes within a single, functionally connected region. Unlike monocentric cities, where economic and administrative functions are concentrated in a single core, metropolitan regions often consist of a central city surrounded by several secondary centres, satellite towns, and suburban nodes. These sub-centres may serve distinct roles—industrial, residential, commercial, or educational—and are interconnected by transportation and infrastructure networks (Wang et al. 2024).
2. **Peri-Urban and Fringe Expansion:** Metropolitanization leads to the rapid transformation of rural and semi-rural areas into urban zones. This expansion blurs the traditional boundaries between rural and urban, giving rise to peri-urban landscapes characterized by mixed land uses, informal settlements, industrial activity, and transitional governance. These fringe areas often face a lack of infrastructure and regulatory ambiguity, making them vulnerable to unplanned growth and environmental degradation (NITI Aayog 2021).
3. **Functional Integration:** Metropolitan areas function as cohesive systems despite administrative fragmentation. Daily commuting patterns, shared markets, interdependent labour pools, and unified logistics systems create strong economic and social linkages across municipal boundaries. Functional integration also implies the need for shared infrastructure—such as transport corridors, water supply, and waste management systems—that span across jurisdictions (Artioli and Galès 2025).
4. **Administrative and Jurisdictional Complexity:** A typical metropolitan region comprises multiple municipalities, development authorities, panchayats, and specialized agencies. This multi-level governance results in overlapping mandates, coordination challenges, and inconsistencies in planning and service delivery. The absence of unified metropolitan governance often hampers long-term infrastructure development, housing policy, and environmental management (UN-Habitat 2020).
5. **Economic Centrality and Agglomeration:** Metropolitan areas tend to concentrate a disproportionate share of national GDP, investment, and employment. They attract corporate headquarters, universities, research institutions, and financial services, contributing to economies of scale and innovation. The clustering of firms and services within metro regions leads to agglomeration benefits, but also increases the risk of congestion, land speculation, and socio-spatial inequality (UN-Habitat 2016).

6. **Social and Demographic Diversity:** Due to migration and mobility, metropolitan regions are highly heterogeneous. They are home to a diverse mix of income groups, cultures, languages, and occupations. This diversity contributes to social vibrancy but also creates challenges related to integration, social cohesion, housing affordability, and equitable access to urban amenities (Kebza 2024).
7. **Infrastructure Intensity and Environmental Pressures:** The demand for transport, energy, water, and waste systems in metropolitan areas is significantly higher than in smaller urban areas. This often results in infrastructure overload, service deficits, and environmental stress. Air and water pollution, traffic congestion, and the urban heat island effect are particularly acute in densely populated metropolitan regions (Land 2022).
8. **Strategic Role in National and Global Networks:** Metropolitan areas act as nodes in national and international networks of trade, finance, culture, and governance. They serve as command centres for economic activity and are often the focal points for foreign investment, global connectivity, and international diplomacy. Their influence extends beyond their geographical limits, shaping regional and national development trajectories.

These characteristics collectively make metropolitan regions both powerful drivers of development and complex arenas of planning and governance. Understanding these features is essential to designing policies and strategies that align with their scale, diversity, and interdependencies.

4.3 Metropolises in the World

The global landscape of urbanization has evolved significantly over the past century, with metropolitan regions emerging as dominant urban forms across continents. These urban configurations have transcended conventional city boundaries to become extensive, complex regions that integrate economic, social, and spatial systems. The emergence of global metropolises reflects a transformation not only in size but also in function, governance, and connectivity. As the engines of national and regional economies, metropolises now house the majority of the global urban population and play critical roles in shaping international flows of capital, labour, culture, and knowledge.

Understanding the evolution and diversity of metropolises worldwide is essential for grasping the larger phenomenon of metropolitanization. While definitions may vary across contexts, several core attributes define what constitutes a metropolis in comparative global urbanism.

4.3.1 Definition of Metropolis

The term "metropolis" originates from the Greek word *mētēr* (mother) and *polis* (city), historically referring to a "mother city" or a central city with influence over surrounding settlements. In modern usage, a metropolis is generally defined as a large, densely populated urban area that serves as a central node in regional, national, or global systems. However, the specific criteria for designating a metropolis vary depending on demographic thresholds, functional characteristics, and governance frameworks.

Internationally, organisations such as the United Nations, OECD, and the World Bank adopt varying classifications. The United Nations defines metropolitan areas as contiguous urban agglomerations with more than one million inhabitants, functioning as unified economic and social entities (UN-Habitat 2020). The OECD, meanwhile, uses the concept of "functional urban areas" (FUAs), which are determined by commuting patterns and economic integration rather than administrative boundaries.

In many contexts, a metropolis is distinguished not only by its size but also by its institutional complexity, economic centrality, and infrastructural intensity. It often acts as the administrative capital, a financial hub, and a centre of higher education, healthcare, culture, and technology. Global metropolises such as New York, Tokyo, London, and Shanghai exemplify these characteristics—hosting global headquarters, serving as decision-making centres, and forming part of interconnected urban networks.

In the Indian context, the term "metropolis" is commonly associated with urban agglomerations that cross the one million population mark as per Census definitions. These include both megacities—such as Delhi, Mumbai, and Kolkata—and a growing number of tier-2 and tier-3 cities experiencing rapid metropolitanization. The Census of India (2011) defines a "metropolitan city" as one with a population of over one million, encompassing not just the core city but also adjacent municipalities and urban outgrowths that together form an integrated agglomeration.

Beyond population, however, several functional criteria are used to identify a metropolis:

- A high level of employment in secondary and tertiary sectors.
- Regional dominance in terms of economic output, connectivity, and service provision.
- Daily commuting zones that extend far beyond the administrative limits of the core city.
- Diverse and dense land use patterns, typically including central business districts, industrial corridors, educational clusters, and informal settlements.

The lack of a globally standardized definition of a metropolis reflects the diversity in how urban systems develop and function. Yet, the consensus remains that a metropolis is more than just a large city—it is a complex, evolving system that performs a strategic role in shaping broader socio-economic and spatial transformations.

4.3.2 Global Trends in Metropolises

Over the last few decades, metropolises have become the epicentres of global demographic, economic, and technological transformations. The proliferation of metropolitan regions reflects the broader shift in urbanization patterns from compact, mono-nodal cities to sprawling, multi-nodal urban regions. These trends are shaped by forces such as globalization, digitalization, climate change, and migration, resulting in metropolises that are larger, more connected, and more complex than ever before.

One of the most prominent global trends is the rapid rise in the number of megacities and large metropolitan areas. According to the United Nations (UN-Habitat 2020), the number of urban agglomerations with populations exceeding one million increased from 83 in 1950 to over 550 in 2018, and this number continues to grow. Notably, the majority of this growth has occurred in developing regions, particularly in Asia and Africa, where cities are experiencing exponential expansion without corresponding improvements in infrastructure or governance.

Another trend is the emergence of polycentric metropolitan regions. In countries such as the United States, China, Germany, and Brazil, metropolitan growth has led to the formation of urban corridors and regional city clusters. Examples include the BosWash corridor in the northeastern United States, the Pearl River Delta in China, and the Rhine-Ruhr region in Germany. These regions often function as interconnected systems of cities, with specialized economic functions distributed across multiple urban nodes and supported by high-speed transport and digital infrastructure.

A third trend is the increasing functional integration between metropolitan regions and their surrounding rural or semi-urban areas. This is particularly evident in developing countries, where peri-urban expansion and rural-urban migration have blurred the boundaries between urban and rural land uses. These metropolitan hinterlands often serve as reservoirs of labour, food, and ecological services while also facing risks such as land-use conflict, informal housing growth, and environmental degradation (Wang et al. 2024).

Technological transformation has also reshaped global metropolises. The adoption of digital infrastructure, data analytics, and artificial intelligence is increasingly central to urban management in cities such as Singapore, Seoul,

Amsterdam, and Dubai. These smart cities aim to improve mobility, energy efficiency, and governance through digitally integrated systems. However, such developments are often accompanied by rising concerns over digital divides, data privacy, and technological exclusion, especially in less affluent metropolitan contexts (Artioli and Galès 2025).

Environmental sustainability and resilience have emerged as critical priorities in the global metropolitan discourse. As climate change intensifies, metropolitan regions face increasing threats from floods, heatwaves, air pollution, and resource scarcity. Cities such as New York, Copenhagen, and Tokyo have initiated resilience plans and green infrastructure investments to mitigate these impacts. At the same time, cities in the global South often struggle to balance growth with sustainability due to capacity constraints and governance fragmentation (UN-Habitat 2016).

Finally, global metropolises are becoming key actors in international policy forums and governance networks. Through platforms such as C40 Cities, UCLG (United Cities and Local Governments), and ICLEI (Local Governments for Sustainability), metropolitan leaders are influencing global agendas on climate action, urban equity, and sustainable development. This increasing global engagement reflects the recognition that metropolitan regions are not just administrative units but strategic spaces for tackling transboundary challenges.

These trends illustrate that while metropolises differ in form and function across the world, they share common patterns of growth, integration, and stress. Understanding these patterns is crucial for framing responsive planning and governance approaches—especially for countries like India, where metropolitanization is both rapid and structurally unique.

4.3.3 Distribution of Metropolises

The spatial distribution of metropolises across the globe reveals deep patterns of demographic concentration, economic centrality, and geopolitical influence. While metropolises can be found on every continent, their size, density, and functional specialization often reflect broader regional and national development trajectories. The distribution of metropolises is closely tied to historic trade routes, patterns of colonization, industrialization, and more recently, the integration of economies into global networks (Elliott 1997; Wang et al. 2024).

According to United Nations data, the world's metropolitan areas are predominantly concentrated in Asia, followed by Africa, Latin America, and Europe. In 2018, nearly half of the world's megacities—defined as urban agglomerations with over 10 million people—were located in Asia (UN-Habitat 2020). Cities like Tokyo, Delhi, Shanghai, Mumbai, Beijing, and Manila rank among the most populous metropolitan regions globally, reflecting both natural population growth and rural-to-urban migration (UN-Habitat 2016).

Africa is experiencing a rapid shift in its urban landscape, with metropolises such as Lagos, Cairo, Kinshasa, and Nairobi expanding rapidly. These cities serve as national economic hubs but are also facing significant stress in terms of infrastructure, governance, and environmental degradation (UN-Habitat 2020). The African continent is projected to host several new megacities by 2050 due to sustained population growth and urban expansion (Artioli and Le Galès 2025).

In Latin America, metropolitan regions such as São Paulo, Mexico City, Buenos Aires, and Bogotá have long served as economic and political capitals, exhibiting high levels of urban primacy—where a single city dominates the urban hierarchy (UN-Habitat 2020; Wang et al. 2024).

European metropolitan areas tend to be more compact, planned, and functionally integrated within regional networks. Cities like Paris, London, Berlin, and Madrid have long-standing metropolitan planning frameworks that support transit-oriented development, heritage preservation, and environmental sustainability (Artioli and Le Galès, 2023).

In North America, the United States and Canada have several sprawling metropolitan regions characterized by low-density suburbs, high car dependency, and expansive transport networks. The New York Metropolitan Area, Los Angeles, and Chicago are among the largest (UN-Habitat 2020), while in Canada, Toronto and Vancouver lead in terms of growth and international connectivity (Wang et al. 2024). These metropolitan regions are notable for their advanced governance structures, emphasis on regional planning, and use of data and technology in urban management (Marwaha, Gupta, and Bhatia 2024).

Australia's metropolises—such as Sydney, Melbourne, and Brisbane—are also significant in terms of spatial planning and sustainability leadership. While fewer in number due to the country's overall population size, Australian metropolitan areas have high per capita urbanization rates and are considered models for liveable city design (UN-Habitat 2020).

Importantly, the rise of secondary metropolises or "emerging metropolises" is being observed across developing countries. These are cities that are not yet global megacities but are experiencing rapid growth and regional influence. Examples include Pune and Surat in India, Medellín in Colombia, and Bandung in Indonesia (UN-Habitat 2016; NITI Aayog 2021). These cities often lack the institutional capacity of established metropolises, making them both highly dynamic and increasingly vulnerable to unregulated growth.

The global distribution of metropolises highlights an uneven yet intensifying pattern of urban concentration. While each metropolitan region develops within a unique socio-political context, they share common challenges of managing scale, complexity, and sustainability. This distribution sets the context for understanding how India's metropolitan areas are positioned within the global urban hierarchy and why they require differentiated, region-sensitive planning frameworks.

4.4 Metropolitan Areas/Regions in India

India's experience of metropolitanization is deeply shaped by its post-colonial development trajectory, rapid economic liberalization, and persistent rural-to-urban migration. Unlike many other countries where metropolitan growth has been guided by early institutional frameworks and consolidated urban governance models, Indian metropolitan regions have evolved more organically—often in response to economic opportunity, political centralization, and demographic pressure. These regions have expanded far beyond their core municipalities to incorporate peri-urban areas, industrial corridors, and emerging satellite towns, creating spatial configurations that are dense, diverse, and highly dynamic.

As of the Census of India 2011, there are 53 officially recognized metropolitan areas—defined as urban agglomerations with populations exceeding one million. These regions are not just statistical units but represent distinct socio-spatial formations that demand coordinated planning, infrastructure provisioning, and governance reforms. The following subsections examine the trends, governance transformations, and classifications associated with metropolitan regions in India.

4.4.1 Trends

The metropolitan landscape in India has undergone substantial transformation over the past few decades, marked by both demographic expansion and spatial reconfiguration. Between the 2001 and 2011 censuses, the number of metropolitan cities in India increased from 35 to 53, reflecting the increasing concentration of population and economic activities in urban regions (Census of India 2011). This trend signifies not only the growth of traditional metropolitan centres like Delhi, Mumbai, and Kolkata but also the emergence of newer urban agglomerations such as Surat, Lucknow, Patna, and Indore as key metropolitan nodes.

Much of this growth is attributed to rural-to-urban migration, high natural population growth, and the reclassification of rural areas into statutory towns. Additionally, the development of infrastructure such as highways, industrial corridors, and metro rail systems has led to the physical integration of adjoining municipalities and villages into larger metropolitan frameworks. This has resulted in the creation of urban corridors—such as the Delhi-Gurugram-Noida-Ghaziabad belt or the Mumbai-Pune-Nashik triangle—that function as extended metropolitan regions with interlinked economies and shared infrastructure (NITI Aayog 2021).

India's metropolitan regions are also becoming increasingly polycentric. Unlike the historical core-periphery model where the central city dominates, many metro regions now exhibit multiple urban centres with specialized economic roles. For example, the Delhi Metropolitan Region includes nodes like Noida (IT and manufacturing), Gurugram (corporate services), and Faridabad (industrial base), each contributing to the region's composite identity.

Another important trend is the vertical intensification of city cores alongside horizontal expansion into peri-urban areas. While central business districts witness high-rise development and commercial densification, the urban fringes see informal housing, slums, and industrial clusters. This dual growth pattern contributes to socio-spatial inequalities and raises complex challenges related to infrastructure, housing, and environmental sustainability (UN-Habitat 2016).

Furthermore, many Indian metropolitan regions are becoming central to national development strategies. Initiatives such as the Smart Cities Mission, AMRUT, and DMIC (Delhi-Mumbai Industrial Corridor) have specifically targeted metropolitan regions for infrastructure upgrades, investment promotion, and smart urban management. However, these initiatives often operate parallel to existing municipal structures, raising concerns about institutional coordination and accountability (Marwaha, Gupta, and Bhatia 2024).

In summary, the trends shaping metropolitan areas in India point to their growing centrality in the country's socio-economic future. However, they also expose the systemic limitations of planning and governance mechanisms that are still largely designed for isolated urban municipalities rather than integrated metropolitan systems.

4.4.2 The Changing Role of Metropolitan Governance (Post-2014 Reforms)

Governance in India's metropolitan regions has historically been characterized by institutional fragmentation, overlapping jurisdictions, and limited capacity at the local level. However, the period following 2014 has witnessed a gradual yet significant shift in the approach toward metropolitan governance, driven by national-level urban reforms, digitalization efforts, and increasing recognition of the need for integrated metropolitan planning.

One of the foundational steps toward rethinking urban governance was the rollout of the Smart Cities Mission (SCM) in 2015. This initiative introduced a new model of decentralized, data-driven urban management by establishing Special Purpose Vehicles (SPVs) for project implementation. While these SPVs often operate parallel to Urban Local Bodies (ULBs), they represent a shift towards professionalized urban governance and inter-agency collaboration. Many of the cities chosen under SCM were part of larger metropolitan agglomerations, thus indirectly promoting metropolitan-level infrastructure and IT integration (MoHUA 2017).

Simultaneously, the Atal Mission for Rejuvenation and Urban Transformation (AMRUT) expanded the scope of city governance by encouraging convergence between urban services like water supply, sewerage, and mobility. While AMRUT did not explicitly target metropolitan governance structures, it provided a financing mechanism for shared infrastructure across municipalities that form part of a metro region. This has enabled coordinated projects between core cities and their adjoining municipalities, particularly in water, transport, and green space development (UN-Habitat 2016).

Another important policy push came through the 14th and 15th Finance Commissions, which emphasized performance-based grants to local governments and encouraged intergovernmental coordination. These grants provided incentives for ULBs to improve transparency, digitalization, and service delivery—functions that are crucial for metropolitan-scale governance.

From a constitutional standpoint, the 74th Constitutional Amendment Act (1992) had envisioned the establishment of Metropolitan Planning Committees (MPCs) to prepare spatial plans at the metropolitan level. However, in practice, MPCs have remained either dormant or ineffective in most states due to lack of clarity in their functions, political interference, and poor integration with State Town Planning Departments. Post-2014, there have been renewed efforts in some metropolitan regions—particularly in Mumbai, Pune, and Bengaluru—to reactivate these committees or explore alternatives such as Regional Development Authorities and Urban Observatories (NITI Aayog 2021).

The NITI Aayog's 2021 report on Urban Planning Capacity in India also highlighted the need for creating metropolitan-level institutions that can coordinate between various agencies including development authorities, ULBs, regional transport bodies, and environmental regulators. The report calls for a new cadre of urban planners, the establishment of an All-India Urban Planning Service, and capacity-building efforts specifically focused on metropolitan governance (NITI Aayog 2021).

Additionally, digital governance tools such as Integrated Command and Control Centres (ICCCs), City Dashboards, and GIS-based infrastructure mapping are increasingly being adopted in metropolitan areas. These platforms allow for cross-jurisdictional data sharing, real-time monitoring, and predictive planning—thereby enabling more responsive and coordinated metropolitan management (Marwaha, Gupta, and Bhatia 2024).

In essence, while metropolitan governance in India remains a work in progress, the post-2014 period has ushered in a governance model that is more performance-oriented, technology-driven, and metropolitan in scope, albeit still limited by statutory ambiguities and institutional resistance. The current trajectory suggests a shift from city-centric to regionally integrated governance systems, where coordination, capacity, and citizen participation will be central to the effectiveness of India's metropolitan future.

4.4.3 List of Metropolitan Areas in India

The Census of India 2011 formally recognizes 53 metropolitan urban agglomerations, each with a population of over one million. These regions comprise a central statutory town (or city) and its adjoining towns or urban outgrowths that form a continuous urban spread and are functionally linked through economic, social, or infrastructural ties.

These metropolitan areas are not merely administrative units; they reflect the evolving realities of urban expansion, regional integration, and economic concentration in India. The list includes both longstanding megacities like Mumbai and Delhi, as well as rapidly growing secondary metros such as Surat, Bhopal, and Jaipur. While some are governed through established development authorities or planning boards, many continue to face challenges of coordination across municipal corporations, councils, and panchayat jurisdictions.

This classification by the Census provides a uniform national framework for identifying urban agglomerations that function as metropolitan regions. However, it is important to note that this list is demographic, not necessarily aligned with statutory or functional metropolitan planning regions as defined by various state-level agencies. Consequently, many of these regions still lack formalized governance structures to manage them as unified spatial or planning units.

The next section delves deeper into how these areas have evolved in terms of growth trends, planning needs, and systemic challenges.

4.5 Growth Trends and Processes

The growth of metropolitan areas in India has been both rapid and spatially uneven, reflecting the complex interplay of demographic pressures, economic transitions, policy interventions, and infrastructure investments. Unlike the compact and planned development of smaller cities, metropolitan growth is typically characterized by both vertical intensification in city cores and horizontal expansion into peri-urban and rural areas. This duality produces intricate spatial patterns, makes service delivery more challenging, and increases institutional demands on already stressed governance systems.

Over the past two decades, metropolitan growth has been heavily influenced by liberalization, globalization, and large-scale investments in the real estate and infrastructure sectors. Economic corridors, ring roads, industrial zones, IT

Table 4.1 List of 53 metropolitan areas, as per Census of India 2011.

RANK	*CITY/URBAN AGGLOMERATION*	*POPULATION (2011)*	*STATUTORY BODY*	*SPECIALTY*	*INCLUDES*
1	Greater Mumbai UA (Maharashtra)	18,414,288	Municipal Corporation of Greater Mumbai, MMRDA	*Financial capital of India, Bollywood hub*	Mumbai city, suburbs, Thane, Navi Mumbai
2	Delhi UA (Delhi) / NCR	16,314,838	Municipal Corporation of Delhi (MCD), NDMC, DDA, NCRPB	*National capital, political centre, diverse culture*	Delhi and parts of Haryana, Uttar Pradesh, and Rajasthan
3	Kolkata UA (West Bengal)	14,112,536	Kolkata Municipal Corporation (KMC)	*Major port city, cultural capital of India*	Kolkata, Howrah, Bidhannagar, South 24 Parganas
4	Chennai UA (Tamil Nadu)	8,696,010	Greater Chennai Corporation	*Automotive industry, IT hub*	Chennai, Tambaram, Avadi, Ambattur
5	Bengaluru UA (Karnataka)	8,520,435	Bruhat Bengaluru Mahanagara Palike (BBMP)	*IT hub, "Silicon Valley of India"*	Bengaluru, Whitefield, Yelahanka
6	Hyderabad UA (Telangana)	7,749,334	Greater Hyderabad Municipal Corporation (GHMC), HMDA	*IT, pharmaceutical industries*	Hyderabad, Secunderabad, Gachibowli
7	Ahmedabad UA (Gujarat)	6,357,693	Ahmedabad Municipal Corporation (AMC)	*Textile industry, historic monuments*	Ahmedabad, Gandhinagar, Maninagar
8	Pune UA (Maharashtra)	5,049,968	Pune Municipal Corporation (PMC)	*Education, IT, and cultural heritage*	Pune, Pimpri-Chinchwad, Chakan
9	Surat UA (Gujarat)	4,591,246	Surat Municipal Corporation (SMC)	*Diamond and textile industries*	Surat, Hazira, Udhna
10	Jaipur UA (Rajasthan)	3,046,163	Jaipur Municipal Corporation	*Tourism, cultural heritage*	Jaipur, Amer, Sanganer

Contd.

Table 4.1 *Cond.*

RANK	*CITY/URBAN AGGLOMERATION*	*POPULATION (2011)*	*STATUTORY BODY*	*SPECIALTY*	*INCLUDES*
11	Kanpur UA (Uttar Pradesh)	2,920,067	Kanpur Municipal Corporation	*Leather industries, education hub*	Kanpur city and suburbs
12	Lucknow UA (Uttar Pradesh)	2,901,474	Lucknow Municipal Corporation	*Cultural heritage, administrative capital*	Lucknow city and outskirts
13	Nagpur UA (Maharashtra)	2,497,777	Nagpur Municipal Corporation	*Orange production, logistics hub*	Nagpur city and suburbs
14	Patna UA (Bihar)	2,348,801	Patna Municipal Corporation	*Educational hub, historical importance*	Patna city and adjoining areas
15	Indore UA (Madhya Pradesh)	2,167,447	Indore Municipal Corporation	*Cleanest city, industrial hub*	Indore city and nearby areas
16	Vadodara UA (Gujarat)	1,822,221	Vadodara Municipal Corporation	*Petrochemicals, cultural hub*	Vadodara city and suburbs
17	Bhopal UA (Madhya Pradesh)	1,798,218	Bhopal Municipal Corporation	*Administrative capital, lakes*	Bhopal city and nearby regions
18	Coimbatore UA (Tamil Nadu)	1,752,101	Coimbatore Municipal Corporation	*Textile and manufacturing industries*	Coimbatore city and suburbs
19	Ludhiana UA (Punjab)	1,618,879	Ludhiana Municipal Corporation	*Hosiery, bicycles, and industrial hub*	Ludhiana city and adjoining areas
20	Agra UA (Uttar Pradesh)	1,585,704	Agra Municipal Corporation	*Tourism, Taj Mahal*	Agra city and surroundings
21	Nashik UA (Maharashtra)	1,486,053	Nashik Municipal Corporation	*Religious tourism, wine industry*	Nashik city and nearby vineyards

Contd.

Table 4.1 *Cond.*

RANK	*CITY/URBAN AGGLOMERATION*	*POPULATION (2011)*	*STATUTORY BODY*	*SPECIALTY*	*INCLUDES*
22	Faridabad UA (Haryana)	1,414,050	Faridabad Municipal Corporation	*Industrial centre*	Faridabad city and adjoining areas
23	Meerut UA (Uttar Pradesh)	1,424,908	Meerut Municipal Corporation	*Sports goods, historical significance*	Meerut city and suburbs
24	Rajkot UA (Gujarat)	1,390,640	Rajkot Municipal Corporation	*Engineering and jewellery industries*	Rajkot city and industrial zones
25	Kalyan-Dombivli UA (Maharashtra)	1,247,327	Kalyan-Dombivli Municipal Corporation	*Residential and industrial*	Kalyan, Dombivli, surrounding areas
26	Vasai-Virar UA (Maharashtra)	1,222,390	Vasai-Virar Municipal Corporation	*Real estate, coastal significance*	Vasai, Virar, Nalasopara
27	Varanasi UA (Uttar Pradesh)	1,201,815	Varanasi Municipal Corporation	*Religious tourism, cultural heritage*	Varanasi city and surrounding areas
28	Srinagar UA (Jammu & Kashmir)	1,180,570	Srinagar Municipal Corporation	*Tourism, handicrafts*	Srinagar city and surrounding villages
29	Aurangabad UA (Maharashtra)	1,171,330	Aurangabad Municipal Corporation	*Historical tourism, industrial base*	Aurangabad city and suburbs
30	Dhanbad UA (Jharkhand)	1,162,472	Dhanbad Municipal Corporation	*Coal mining, industrial hub*	Dhanbad city and adjoining areas
31	Amritsar UA (Punjab)	1,183,705	Amritsar Municipal Corporation	*Golden Temple, religious tourism*	Amritsar city and nearby villages
32	Navi Mumbai UA (Maharashtra)	1,119,477	Navi Mumbai Municipal Corporation	*Planned city, IT hub*	Navi Mumbai and adjoining industrial areas

Contd.

Table 4.1 *Cond.*

RANK	*CITY/URBAN AGGLOMERATION*	*POPULATION (2011)*	*STATUTORY BODY*	*SPECIALTY*	*INCLUDES*
33	Allahabad UA (Uttar Pradesh)	1,117,094	Prayagraj Municipal Corporation	*Religious tourism, cultural heritage*	Allahabad city and surrounding areas
34	Howrah UA (West Bengal)	1,077,075	Howrah Municipal Corporation	*Industrial hub, transport gateway*	Howrah city and adjoining regions
35	Gwalior UA (Madhya Pradesh)	1,054,420	Gwalior Municipal Corporation	*Tourism, historical forts*	Gwalior city and surrounding areas
36	Jabalpur UA (Madhya Pradesh)	1,044,105	Jabalpur Municipal Corporation	*Defence industries, tourism*	Jabalpur city and nearby regions
37	Vijayawada UA (Andhra Pradesh)	1,034,358	Vijayawada Municipal Corporation	*Industrial hub, cultural centre*	Vijayawada city and surrounding suburbs
38	Madurai UA (Tamil Nadu)	1,017,865	Madurai Municipal Corporation	*Religious tourism, cultural heritage*	Madurai city and surrounding areas
39	Jamshedpur UA (Jharkhand)	1,033,096	Tata Steel and others	*Steel production, industrial significance*	Jamshedpur city and adjoining areas
40	Raipur UA (Chhattisgarh)	1,010,087	Raipur Municipal Corporation	*Industrial hub, administrative capital*	Raipur city and outskirts
41	Kota UA (Rajasthan)	1,001,694	Kota Municipal Corporation	*Education hub (coaching), industrial base*	Kota city and adjoining regions
42	Guwahati UA (Assam)	963,429	Guwahati Municipal Corporation	*Gateway to Northeast India, tourism*	Guwahati city and adjoining areas
43	Chandigarh UA (Chandigarh)	960,787	Chandigarh Municipal Corporation	*Planned city, administrative capital*	Chandigarh and surrounding areas

Contd.

Table 4.1 *Cond.*

RANK	CITY/URBAN AGGLOMERATION	POPULATION (2011)	STATUTORY BODY	SPECIALTY	INCLUDES
44	Solapur UA (Maharashtra)	951,558	Solapur Municipal Corporation	*Textile industries*	Solapur city and suburbs
45	Hubli-Dharwad UA (Karnataka)	943,857	Hubli-Dharwad Municipal Corporation	*Cotton trade, industrial hub*	Hubli, Dharwad, and adjoining regions
46	Bareilly UA (Uttar Pradesh)	898,167	Bareilly Municipal Corporation	*Furniture, cane industries*	Bareilly city and outskirts
47	Moradabad UA (Uttar Pradesh)	889,810	Moradabad Municipal Corporation	*Brassware production*	Moradabad city and surrounding areas
48	Mysore UA (Karnataka)	887,446	Mysuru Municipal Corporation	*Tourism, cultural heritage*	Mysuru city and nearby regions
49	Tiruchirappalli UA (Tamil Nadu)	846,915	Tiruchirappalli Municipal Corporation	*Educational hub, cultural significance*	Tiruchirappalli city and outskirts
50	Tiruppur UA (Tamil Nadu)	844,769	Tiruppur Municipal Corporation	*Textile industry*	Tiruppur city and surrounding areas
51	Salem UA (Tamil Nadu)	831,038	Salem Municipal Corporation	*Steel production, mango cultivation*	Salem city and suburbs
52	Aligarh UA (Uttar Pradesh)	828,215	Aligarh Municipal Corporation	*Lock industry, educational centre*	Aligarh city and outskirts
53	Thiruvananthapuram UA (Kerala)	744,983	Thiruvananthapuram Municipal Corporation	*Tourism, administrative capital*	Thiruvananthapuram city and nearby areas

Note: *The full dataset includes intermediate metropolitan areas like Patna, Bhopal, Ludhiana, Coimbatore, Lucknow, Varanasi, and others, each meeting the one million population threshold.*

Source: Census of India (2011). *Provisional Population Totals – Urban Agglomerations and Cities.* Office of the Registrar General & Census Commissioner, Government of India.

parks, metro systems, and expressways have restructured the spatial organization of metropolitan regions by encouraging decentralization and the emergence of multiple urban centres within a single region. For instance, the Delhi National Capital Region (NCR) and the Mumbai Metropolitan Region (MMR) have experienced extensive urbanization well beyond their municipal boundaries—into Gurugram, Noida, Faridabad, and Navi Mumbai respectively—creating polycentric metropolitan regions (NITI Aayog 2021; UN-Habitat 2016).

These growth dynamics are not always planned. In many cases, the expansion of metropolitan boundaries occurs through informal means such as the proliferation of unregulated colonies, rural-urban conversions, and land speculation. Peri-urban areas often emerge faster than the capacity of municipal institutions to manage them, resulting in patchy service provision, environmental degradation, and unclear land ownership (Artioli and Le Galès 2025). Moreover, the classification of many census towns within metropolitan regions reflects this organic and often unregulated expansion, as these areas functionally behave as urban spaces but lack statutory recognition and infrastructure provisioning.

A significant feature of this growth is the increasing spatial mismatch between employment centres and housing zones. The rapid increase in real estate prices in city cores has pushed large sections of the population to the urban fringes, while jobs remain concentrated in central business districts or newly created economic zones. This mismatch leads to extensive daily commuting, traffic congestion, and a higher carbon footprint—all common to India's growing metropolitan regions (Kebza 2024).

Growth has also been highly sector-driven, with metropolitan economies increasingly dependent on services, finance, real estate, information technology, and logistics. However, this sectoral concentration often results in spatial inequality, where investment clusters around affluent corridors while low-income populations are displaced or relocated to under-serviced peripheries. This trend exacerbates socio-economic disparities and complicates inclusive planning at the metropolitan scale (UN-Habitat 2016).

Despite these challenges, the growth of metropolitan areas has been vital to India's economic trajectory. These regions account for a significant share of the country's GDP, employment, innovation output, and tax revenues. They are also central to national infrastructure projects such as industrial corridors, dedicated freight routes, and smart mobility systems. However, without robust and inclusive planning mechanisms, the growth of metropolitan areas can become unsustainable, exclusionary, and environmentally damaging.

The following subsections further analyse the characteristics of this growth and the challenges it presents for sustainable metropolitan development.

4.5.1 Characteristics of Growth

Metropolitan growth in India is distinguished by its scale, speed, and spatial complexity. Unlike planned urban expansion, metropolitan growth often unfolds in response to a mix of market forces, infrastructural interventions, and demographic pressures. This results in a patchwork of urban forms—ranging from vertical towers in central business districts to sprawling low-income settlements on the periphery. Several defining characteristics have emerged in recent decades.

One key characteristic is the expansion of built-up areas into adjoining municipalities, gram panchayats, and census towns. This outward spread, often termed urban sprawl, is typically low-density and land-intensive. It results from the scarcity of affordable land within core cities and is accelerated by new highway networks, ring roads, and large-scale housing projects. These new developments often lack adequate infrastructure such as sewerage systems, public transport, and healthcare facilities, which puts pressure on both municipal finances and regional ecosystems (NITI Aayog 2021).

Another significant feature is the transformation of economic geography. Metropolitan growth is increasingly polycentric, with multiple nodes of commercial, industrial, and residential activity distributed across the region. This can be seen in regions like the National Capital Region, where Gurugram, Noida, and Faridabad have emerged as economic hubs, or in the Mumbai Metropolitan Region, where Navi Mumbai, Thane, and Kalyan perform distinct urban functions. Such polycentricity brings opportunities for decentralization but also creates challenges in terms of infrastructure synchronization and inter-agency coordination (UN-Habitat 2016).

The demographic structure of metropolitan areas is marked by high migration inflows. These include both skilled professionals attracted by the formal economy and large numbers of informal workers employed in construction, services, logistics, and domestic labour. This dual labour market contributes to the emergence of informal housing, slum clusters, and rental arrangements that operate outside the formal regulatory framework. Consequently, social segregation intensifies as high-end gated communities and slum pockets often coexist within the same spatial zones (Artioli and Le Galès 2025).

Additionally, growth is highly influenced by speculative land markets. The anticipation of urban expansion and infrastructural projects often leads to large-scale land acquisition and price inflation. This speculative behaviour reshapes local land-use patterns, displaces traditional agrarian livelihoods, and increases the vulnerability of marginalized groups who lack secure tenure or legal recognition. In many cities, public land is encroached or auctioned without comprehensive land-use planning, adding to governance complexity (Kebza 2024).

Technological integration is another emerging aspect. With the rollout of metro rail networks, smart traffic systems, and digital governance platforms, metropolitan growth is increasingly intertwined with data and automation. While these interventions can improve service delivery and planning accuracy, their uneven implementation often creates islands of efficiency amidst broader systemic gaps (Marwaha, Gupta, and Bhatia 2024).

Finally, growth is marked by a persistent mismatch between infrastructure provision and population needs. Roads, housing, public transport, and waste management systems often lag behind the pace of expansion, resulting in service bottlenecks and deteriorating environmental quality. The focus on elite-centric infrastructure such as expressways, flyovers, and commercial parks also diverts attention from the everyday needs of low-income populations.

These characteristics illustrate that metropolitan growth is not a uniform or neutral process. It is shaped by economic priorities, governance choices, and socio-political inequalities that determine who benefits from growth and who is excluded. Recognizing these patterns is crucial for planning cities that are not only economically vibrant but also inclusive and sustainable.

4.5.2 Growth Challenges

While metropolitan regions are key drivers of economic growth and innovation, their rapid and often unplanned expansion has generated a complex set of challenges. These challenges are multidimensional—spanning environmental degradation, governance breakdown, infrastructure shortfalls, and socio-spatial inequities. Without targeted interventions, these issues can undermine the sustainability and liveability of India's metropolitan future.

Spatial Mismatch and Urban Sprawl

The horizontal expansion of metropolitan areas frequently leads to inefficient land use. Peri-urban zones develop without integrated planning, resulting in fragmented neighbourhoods disconnected from mass transit, health services, or economic centres. This not only increases travel time and fuel dependency but also reduces the efficiency of service delivery.

- In cities like Bengaluru and Hyderabad, the sprawl has extended into villages beyond the municipal boundary, where urban services remain absent or underdeveloped.
- Real estate-led development often prioritizes speculative investment over inclusive housing, further distorting the urban form.

Infrastructure Overload and Service Deficits

Rapid growth has outpaced infrastructure capacity in most metropolitan regions. Core urban infrastructure such as roads, drainage, solid waste systems, and electricity grids are under stress, especially in high-density informal settlements.

Key service delivery gaps include:

- Intermittent water supply and frequent outages
- Inadequate sewerage and stormwater drainage systems
- Growing demand for public transport but insufficient coverage
- Poor waste segregation and overloaded landfills

These deficits not only affect the quality of life but also pose public health and environmental risks.

Institutional Fragmentation

Governance in metropolitan areas often suffers from fragmentation and lack of coordination among multiple agencies. Most metros include numerous municipal bodies, parastatal agencies, and departments with overlapping responsibilities.

For instance, land-use planning may be under a development authority, while infrastructure provision falls under municipal corporations or state-level agencies.

The absence of a metropolitan-level statutory planning institution weakens accountability and creates implementation bottlenecks (NITI Aayog 2021).

Socio-Spatial Inequality and Informality

Metropolitan growth frequently exacerbates socio-economic divides. High-income, gated enclaves coexist with informal settlements, reflecting deep inequalities in housing access, amenities, and mobility.

Challenges include:

- Limited affordable housing leading to slum proliferation
- Displacement of urban poor due to infrastructure or beautification projects
- Informal employment with no social protection
- Unequal access to education, healthcare, and green spaces

These inequalities are not incidental—they are often embedded in planning and investment choices that prioritize elite interests.

Environmental Stress and Climate Risk

Environmental degradation is an increasingly urgent consequence of unregulated metropolitan growth.

Major concerns include:

- Air and water pollution due to vehicular emissions, construction activity, and industrial discharge
- Loss of urban wetlands, forests, and green buffers to real estate projects
- Increased vulnerability to urban floods, heatwaves, and poor air quality
- Inadequate solid waste and construction debris management

For example, Chennai's 2015 floods and Bengaluru's 2022 lake flooding incidents were closely linked to uncontrolled urbanization over natural drainage paths.

Land Conflicts and Displacement

Metropolitan expansion often involves large-scale land acquisition, either for public infrastructure or private real estate development. These processes are often non-transparent and exclusionary, particularly for marginalized rural or peri-urban communities.

- Displacement without proper rehabilitation leads to economic vulnerability and social unrest.
- Land-use changes in metropolitan peripheries are also driven by speculative markets, with minimal regulatory oversight.

Overdependence on a Few Economic Sectors

Metropolitan economies are frequently dependent on a narrow band of sectors—particularly real estate, finance, IT, and service industries. This economic concentration creates vulnerabilities during downturns (e.g., the COVID-19 pandemic exposed the fragility of service-based metro economies).

Moreover, the informal economy, which supports a large share of metropolitan employment, remains excluded from formal planning, infrastructure, and social protections.

These growth-related challenges demand a shift in how metropolitan development is conceived and managed. Planning must move from reactive service delivery toward anticipatory, inclusive, and regionally integrated strategies. The next sections will explore how issues of sustainability, inclusivity, and governance further intersect with these challenges.

4.6 Problems and Characteristics of Urban Sustainability

The sustainability of metropolitan regions is increasingly under threat due to rapid urban expansion, resource-intensive lifestyles, and ecological imbalances. As engines of growth, these regions consume disproportionately high amounts of energy, land, and materials. However, this growth has come at the cost of environmental degradation, rising climate risks, and socio-spatial disparities. Ensuring sustainability in metropolitan contexts requires more than just green technologies—it demands systemic reforms in land use, governance, mobility, infrastructure, and public participation.

Urban sustainability, in the context of metropolitanization, refers to the ability of large, complex urban systems to grow in a manner that is ecologically balanced, socially inclusive, economically resilient, and institutionally adaptive.

4.6.1 Key Sustainability Challenges

1. Ecological Degradation and Resource Strain

Metropolitan areas are hotspots for air, water, and soil pollution due to high concentrations of vehicles, industries, and construction activity. Expansion into natural ecosystems—such as wetlands, forests, and agricultural land—has severely impacted regional ecologies.

Key stressors include:

- Air pollution caused by traffic congestion, diesel generators, and construction dust
- Deterioration of rivers and lakes due to untreated sewage and solid waste dumping
- Depletion of groundwater and overextraction of natural resources
- Loss of biodiversity due to land conversion and habitat fragmentation

For example, Delhi and Mumbai face persistent air quality crises, while cities like Hyderabad and Bengaluru have lost over 50% of their surface water bodies in recent decades (Land 2022).

2. Climate Vulnerability

With climate change intensifying, metropolitan regions are highly exposed to extreme weather events. Densely built-up areas with low green cover and inadequate drainage are particularly vulnerable to urban floods, heatwaves, and water scarcity.

- Climate-related risks in metros include:
- Urban heat islands resulting from dense concrete structures and low vegetation
- Intense rainfall leading to flash floods in areas with poor drainage
- Rising sea levels threatening coastal metros like Chennai, Mumbai, and Kolkata
- Increased vector-borne diseases due to poor sanitation and stagnant water

Most metropolitan areas lack dedicated climate adaptation strategies and remain reactive rather than proactive in their approach (Artioli and Le Galès 2025).

3. *Energy and Mobility Challenges*

Metros consume more energy per capita than smaller cities due to transportation demands, high-rise construction, and industrial activity. A growing dependency on private vehicles has increased fossil fuel use and emissions, while public transport systems remain underfunded and fragmented.

Issues include:

- Overburdened and polluting public bus systems
- Underutilization of metro infrastructure due to poor last-mile connectivity
- Low adoption of non-motorized transport like walking and cycling
- Poor integration of transport planning with land-use zoning

Efforts toward electric mobility, renewable energy, and low-carbon infrastructure are in early stages and require long-term institutional support.

4. *Inadequate Waste and Water Management*

Solid waste management continues to be one of the most poorly managed sectors in metropolitan governance. Open dumping, lack of segregation, and insufficient treatment capacity are widespread.

Sustainability bottlenecks include:

- Mixed collection of biodegradable and hazardous waste
- Illegal dumping in peri-urban zones and riverbeds
- Water supply losses due to outdated pipelines and illegal connections
- Untreated wastewater discharge into water bodies

Some cities have introduced decentralized waste processing and reuse systems, but these are still isolated pilots.

5. *Institutional Silos and Weak Sustainability Integration*

Many sustainability issues are rooted in institutional fragmentation. Different agencies handle land, water, energy, housing, and transport, often without coordination. Sustainability goals are often sidelined in favour of short-term economic priorities or infrastructure-driven development.

Barriers to integrated sustainability include:

- Absence of unified metropolitan environmental governance authorities
- Weak implementation of Environmental Impact Assessments (EIAs)
- Poor citizen participation in environmental decision-making
- Lack of integration of sustainability into Master Plans and Regional Plans

In conclusion, while metropolitan areas offer enormous potential to lead the transition toward sustainable urban futures, they currently reflect some of the deepest contradictions in modern urbanism—high productivity alongside deep precarity, global connectivity alongside ecological collapse. Addressing these issues will require cross-sectoral planning, ecological restoration, and a shift in values toward long-term environmental and social wellbeing.

4.7 Issues Related to Quality of Life, Inclusivity, and Equity

Metropolitan regions are often perceived as zones of opportunity, economic mobility, and modern living. However, beneath the veneer of prosperity lies a reality marked by deep social inequalities, spatial segregation, and inadequate access to basic services. The accelerated pace of metropolitan growth, combined with speculative urban development, has produced patterns of exclusion that significantly undermine the quality of life for large sections of the population—especially the poor, informal workers, migrants, and other vulnerable groups.

Inclusivity and equity are not just normative ideals but critical components of sustainable urban systems. Without equitable access to housing, mobility, education, health, and public spaces, metropolitan areas risk reinforcing existing disparities and generating new forms of social fragmentation.

4.7.1 Challenges to Quality of Life

The quality of life in metropolitan areas is shaped by multiple interrelated factors—housing conditions, access to services, affordability, public safety, environmental quality, and a sense of belonging. While affluent neighbourhoods enjoy world-class amenities, marginalized populations are often forced to live in overcrowded, underserviced settlements.

Key issues affecting quality of life in Indian metros include:

- **Housing stress**: Skyrocketing real estate prices have made home ownership unaffordable for the majority. This pushes low- and middle-income families to the peripheries or into informal housing.
- **Overcrowding and congestion**: High population densities, unregulated construction, and poor transport infrastructure result in time-consuming commutes, stress, and air pollution.
- **Health and sanitation**: Informal settlements often lack access to clean drinking water, drainage, waste disposal, and primary healthcare. This contributes to the spread of water-borne and respiratory illnesses.
- **Public safety and gendered vulnerabilities**: Lack of adequate lighting, safe public transport, and responsive policing disproportionately

affects women, children, and senior citizens, especially in low-income neighbourhoods.

- **Disparities in service delivery**: While central business districts and elite residential colonies enjoy reliable utilities and green spaces, many fringe areas face intermittent power, poor roads, and non-functional amenities.

The 2020 Ease of Living Index by the Ministry of Housing and Urban Affairs further highlighted intra-city disparities in citizen perception of liveability, governance, safety, and economic opportunity across metropolitan regions (NIUA 2020).

4.7.2 Informal Economy and Livelihood Challenges

Informality is a defining characteristic of India's metropolitan regions. A large share of the urban population relies on informal employment for survival—ranging from domestic work, construction, vending, driving, and waste collection to small-scale manufacturing. Despite contributing significantly to the urban economy, these workers are often excluded from planning frameworks, economic protections, and basic services.

Challenges faced by the informal workforce include:

- **Precarity of income and work**: Most informal workers have no formal contracts, minimum wage protection, or social security coverage.
- **Evictions and harassment**: Street vendors and hawkers often face eviction drives in the name of beautification or traffic management without being offered alternative spaces or legal recourse.
- **Exclusion from housing**: Without formal employment or documentation, many workers are unable to access rental housing or credit, pushing them into informal settlements.
- **Lack of recognition in planning**: Urban development plans and infrastructure projects often fail to account for the role and needs of informal workers—such as access to vending zones, shelters, restrooms, or transit hubs.
- **Digital and financial exclusion**: Increasing digitalization in governance and service delivery is often inaccessible to informal workers, especially migrant labourers with low literacy or smartphone access.

The COVID-19 lockdown highlighted the structural neglect of informal workers, with millions left stranded in cities without food, income, or transport (UN-Habitat 2016; Marwaha, Gupta, and Bhatia 2024).

Despite their marginalization, informal workers are indispensable to metropolitan functioning. They provide low-cost goods and services, support supply chains, and keep the city operational—especially in crises. Urban policy must shift from criminalization and neglect to enabling and integration-based approaches.

4.8 TOD and Participatory Planning

In response to increasing congestion, environmental degradation, and urban sprawl, Transit-Oriented Development (TOD) has emerged as a critical planning strategy for India's metropolitan regions. TOD seeks to restructure cities around efficient, inclusive, and sustainable public transport systems. By integrating land use and mobility planning, it encourages compact, mixed-use development within walkable distances from transit nodes. However, for TOD to contribute meaningfully to social equity, it must be embedded within participatory planning frameworks that reflect the needs of all urban residents—particularly those often left out of formal planning processes (LRTP 2021; UN-Habitat 2016b).

4.8.1 TOD Goals

The Ministry of Housing and Urban Affairs defines TOD as a type of urban development that maximizes residential, business, and leisure space within walking distance of public transport. Its formalization in Indian urban policy was reinforced through the Metro Rail Policy (2017) and Smart Cities Mission guidelines. The goals of TOD include improving connectivity, reducing private vehicle dependency, and optimising land utilization along transit corridors.

The main objectives of TOD include:

- Densifying areas along metro and BRT corridors through revised Floor Space Index (FSI) norms
- Encouraging compact, vertical, and mixed-use development to reduce travel time and urban sprawl
- Prioritising walkability, cycling infrastructure, and seamless last-mile connectivity
- Discouraging car use through limited parking, high road-use charges, and improved public transport options
- Enhancing real estate value capture mechanisms for cross-subsidising affordable housing and green infrastructure

Cities such as Delhi, Ahmedabad, Pune, and Kochi have introduced TOD-based frameworks either as part of metro expansion or Development Plan revisions (LRTP, 2021; Marwaha et al., 2024). However, the success of these policies has been mixed. Many TOD projects remain dominated by high-end real estate interests, while the poor and informal sectors are displaced or excluded due to rising land values and restrictive zoning.

Moreover, the institutional fragmentation of metropolitan governance—where land use, transport, and housing are managed by separate entities—often weakens the integrated approach that TOD demands (NITI Aayog 2021). Financing gaps, regulatory resistance, and limited community engagement further dilute the equitable potential of TOD.

4.8.2 Participatory Planning

While TOD addresses spatial and infrastructural integration, participatory planning addresses the political and social dimensions of metropolitan development. It ensures that planning processes are not exclusively expert-led or technocratic but include the lived experiences, aspirations, and struggles of diverse urban communities.

Participatory planning in the Indian context has gained visibility through movements for housing rights, slum upgrading, street vending, and inclusive budgeting. However, formal integration into statutory planning remains weak and inconsistent.

Core elements of participatory planning include:

- **Community consultations and ward sabhas** for shaping local improvement projects
- **Participatory budgeting**, where citizens decide how portions of municipal budgets are spent—pioneered in cities like Pune and Bengaluru
- **Citizen feedback loops and grievance redressal platforms** integrated into Smart City dashboards and mobile applications
- **Co-design processes** in neighbourhood upgrading, street redesign, or park revitalization, often through civil society–government partnerships

Despite its potential, participatory planning often remains limited to elite residents' welfare associations or donor-funded pilot projects. Vulnerable groups—including slum dwellers, migrants, and informal workers—rarely have sustained access to institutional platforms or technical knowledge needed to engage in statutory planning processes (UN-Habitat 2016b; Artioli and Le Galès 2025).

To scale up participatory planning, metropolitan governance must:

- Institutionalize inclusive forums at neighbourhood and ward levels
- Mandate public consultations in all major planning exercises
- Ensure gender and caste diversity in participatory bodies
- Build digital and legal literacy among citizens to navigate planning systems

Inclusive planning is not only a democratic imperative but also essential for ensuring that metropolitan infrastructure, housing, and services reflect the actual needs and realities of urban residents—not just those of formal or powerful stakeholders.

4.9 Inner City Issues and Urban Renewal

Inner-city areas in Indian metropolises represent a paradox of high historical value and deep infrastructural decay. These zones—often the oldest parts of the city—serve as the cultural, administrative, and economic foundations of metropolitan regions. They host major markets, government institutions, historic neighbourhoods, and dense mixed-use developments. Yet, they are also some of the most neglected urban environments, suffering from congestion, deteriorating infrastructure, overpopulation, and environmental stress.

Urban renewal in inner cities has become a critical planning priority—not only for preserving heritage and improving quality of life but also for unlocking the economic and spatial potential of centrally located urban land. However, renewal efforts in India have often been fragmented, top-down, or exclusionary, with limited participation from long-term residents and vulnerable communities.

4.9.1 Key Issues in Inner City Areas

1. **Infrastructure Obsolescence**: Many inner-city areas still rely on colonial-era or pre-independence infrastructure. Water pipelines, drainage systems, roads, and electricity networks are outdated and unable to meet contemporary demands. Frequent power cuts, waterlogging, poor sanitation, and traffic bottlenecks are common issues.
2. **Congestion and Overuse**: Central business districts such as Chandni Chowk (Delhi), Kalbadevi (Mumbai), and George Town (Chennai) are burdened by intense commercial activity, vehicular traffic, and pedestrian movement, often far exceeding their designed capacity. Street vendors, informal parking, and encroachments further exacerbate congestion.
3. **Poor Housing Conditions**: Residential areas in inner-city zones often comprise old, poorly maintained buildings with high tenancy densities. These include *chawls*, *katras*, and informal rentals that lack proper ventilation, safety standards, and structural stability. Fire hazards and building collapses are frequent risks.
4. **Heritage Neglect and Encroachment**: Many historic buildings, temples, mosques, markets, and public squares are at risk due to unregulated construction, commercialization, and lack of conservation. In several

cases, heritage sites are encroached upon or used as storage areas and informal workplaces, degrading their architectural and cultural value.

5. **Livelihood Disruption and Gentrification**: Renewal projects often aim to beautify or redevelop inner cities but end up displacing small vendors, artisans, and low-income tenants. Markets are 'modernized' without considering existing livelihoods, while evictions are carried out without resettlement. Gentrification displaces the very communities that sustain the economic vibrancy of inner cities.
6. **Absence of Public Space and Amenities**: Inner-city areas have very few open spaces, parks, or public amenities. Overcrowded streets, inadequate sanitation, and encroached public lands diminish quality of life and limit recreational or social interaction opportunities.

4.9.2 Urban Renewal Initiatives in India

Several urban renewal programmes have attempted to address these issues, with varying degrees of success:

- **Jawaharlal Nehru National Urban Renewal Mission (JnNURM)** promoted infrastructure upgrades in inner-city wards, including housing, roads, and sanitation.
- **HRIDAY (Heritage City Development and Augmentation Yojana)** focused on revitalizing historic cores in cities like Varanasi, Amritsar, and Ajmer through heritage-sensitive urban design and public realm improvements.
- **Smart Cities Mission** has funded area-based development in central districts, integrating IT solutions with infrastructure renewal. However, criticisms remain regarding gentrification and top-down project implementation.

4.9.3 The Way Forward

Effective inner-city renewal must balance redevelopment with conservation, and modernization with inclusivity. Key strategies include:

- **Heritage-led regeneration** with adaptive reuse, facade restoration, and streetscape enhancement
- **In-situ upgradation** of housing rather than demolition and relocation
- **Multi-stakeholder partnerships** involving local businesses, residents, and civic groups
- **Flexible zoning regulations** to allow mixed-use and cultural preservation
- **Transit and walkability improvements** to reduce congestion without displacing livelihoods

The future of metropolitan sustainability is tied not just to new infrastructure on the periphery but also to the revival of its inner core. Inner-city renewal is not merely a physical project—it is a socio-cultural and economic mission that must centre people as much as it does infrastructure.

4.10 Urban Development Schemes in Metropolitan Contexts

Over the past two decades, the Government of India has launched several flagship urban development schemes aimed at improving infrastructure, liveability, and service delivery in cities. While most of these schemes are officially city-centric, in practice, they have had profound implications for India's metropolitan regions. These schemes have influenced how metros are planned, governed, and financed, often introducing new models of service delivery, project implementation, and institutional frameworks.

Metropolitan regions, by virtue of their scale and economic importance, have been primary recipients of funding and policy attention under these missions. However, implementation has varied across metros, and many of these schemes have faced criticism for being technocratic, exclusionary, or poorly integrated with existing governance systems.

Below is an overview of key urban development programmes and their relevance to metropolitan planning.

1. Smart Cities Mission (SCM)

Launched in 2015, the Smart Cities Mission aimed to promote "cities that provide core infrastructure, clean and sustainable environment, and application of 'smart' solutions." A total of 100 cities were selected under the mission, including major metro municipalities like Pune, Ahmedabad, Chennai, and Bhubaneswar.

Key features:

- Creation of Special Purpose Vehicles (SPVs) for decentralized implementation
- Area-Based Development (ABD) strategies to upgrade specific neighbourhoods
- Integration of ICT (Information and Communication Technologies) for governance, safety, mobility, and waste management
- Funding model: 50:50 contribution from Centre and State, with convergence encouraged from private and PPP sources

Impacts and challenges

In metropolitan regions, Smart Cities funding has upgraded select central zones but left many peripheral areas unaffected

Critics note the exclusion of slums and informal areas in ABD projects, leading to fragmented development and spatial inequality (Habitat III India Report, 2016)

2. Atal Mission for Rejuvenation and Urban Transformation (AMRUT)
AMRUT was introduced alongside SCM in 2015 as a continuation of earlier infrastructure schemes like UIDSSMT under JNNURM. It focuses on universal service delivery in core urban areas with population over one hundred thousand.

Focus sectors:

- Water supply
- Sewerage
- Urban transport
- Stormwater drainage
- Green spaces

Relevance to metropolitan planning:

- Though focused on municipal areas, AMRUT projects contribute to improving base infrastructure in metro regions
- Encourages State Annual Action Plans (SAAPs) that can be scaled to include multiple ULBs within metropolitan clusters (NITI Aayog 2021).

3. HRIDAY (Heritage City Development and Augmentation Yojana)
Launched in 2015, HRIDAY focused on cities with rich cultural heritage, aiming to preserve urban heritage through city-level interventions.

Key interventions:

- Streetscape redesign in heritage precincts
- Conservation of monuments, water bodies, and temples
- Upgradation of public spaces and infrastructure in old city cores

Metropolitan impact:

- Though HRIDAY targeted smaller heritage cities like Varanasi and Amritsar, its methodology and lessons are highly applicable to inner-city renewal in larger metros
- It demonstrated the potential of heritage-led regeneration when combined with community participation (MoHUA 2015)

4. Jawaharlal Nehru National Urban Renewal Mission (JNNURM)
Operational from 2005 to 2014, JNNURM was India's first major urban reform-linked investment programme. It aimed to fast-track infrastructure development in 65 cities, most of which were part of larger metropolitan agglomerations.

Components:

- Urban Infrastructure and Governance (UIG)
- Basic Services to the Urban Poor (BSUP)

Achievements:

- Funded over 1,000 projects in sectors like transport, water, sewerage, and housing
- Introduced urban reforms such as e-governance, double-entry accounting, and property tax automation

Criticism:

- Slow project completion and limited community participation
- Poor integration with regional or metropolitan-level planning

These urban development schemes have significantly influenced the form and function of India's metropolitan areas. They have introduced new financial models (like PPPs and SPVs), emphasized results-based planning, and exposed the capacity gaps within urban local bodies. However, their impact on long-term metropolitan sustainability is limited by their city-centric scope, lack of coordination among agencies, and insufficient alignment with spatial planning frameworks.

For future metropolitan development, *national missions must* evolve to:

- Foster **region-level planning** across municipal boundaries
- Address **inclusivity and equity** beyond beautification or infrastructure-centric goals
- Prioritize **integration of informal settlements** and community-led processes
- Embed **resilience and climate adaptation** within programme guidelines

4.11 Issues and Challenges in Metropolitan Areas

India's metropolitan regions are dynamic engines of growth but also complex ecosystems facing layered and persistent challenges. As these regions expand—both demographically and spatially—they encounter institutional, environmental, infrastructural, and socio-economic issues that demand governance frameworks far more sophisticated than those designed for single-municipality cities.

This section explores the key systemic challenges that hinder sustainable and equitable metropolitan development.

4.11.1 Fragmented Governance

Perhaps the most fundamental challenge is the fragmentation of governance across multiple administrative bodies. Metropolitan regions often include dozens of municipal corporations, municipalities, census towns, development authorities, and special-purpose agencies, each with overlapping responsibilities but limited coordination.

Key issues include:

- Absence of unified metropolitan-level planning authorities in most states
- Weak or inactive Metropolitan Planning Committees (MPCs), despite the 74th Constitutional Amendment
- Conflicting priorities between state governments, parastatals (e.g., metro rail corporations), and local bodies
- Fragmented accountability for essential services such as transport, solid waste, and water supply

For example, in the Delhi NCR, over 10 local bodies and agencies operate without a singular spatial vision or implementation framework, leading to disjointed development (NITI Aayog 2021; UN-Habitat 2016b).

4.11.2 Infrastructure Overload

The scale and density of India's metropolitan regions put enormous pressure on physical infrastructure. Rapid growth often outpaces investment, resulting in declining service quality and overstretched systems.

Critical challenges include:

- Congested roads and inadequate public transport networks
- Frequent power shortages and aging electricity grids
- Water scarcity due to overextraction and inefficient distribution
- Overflowing landfills and insufficient waste processing facilities
- Poor stormwater management leading to annual urban floods

These issues disproportionately affect low-income residents and fringe areas, reinforcing spatial inequality and public health risks.

4.11.3 Environmental Degradation

Metropolitan expansion has often occurred at the expense of ecological integrity. Natural ecosystems—wetlands, forests, lakes, and riverbanks—have been encroached upon or degraded, undermining urban resilience.

Environmental challenges include:

- High air pollution levels due to vehicular emissions, construction dust, and industry
- Loss of open spaces and green buffers due to unregulated development
- Groundwater depletion and pollution of surface water bodies
- Increased heat island effect from high-rise, high-density urban forms

Cities such as Delhi, Chennai, and Bengaluru are routinely cited among the most polluted and ecologically strained metros, with climate impacts becoming more frequent and intense (Land 2022).

4.11.4 Housing Shortages and Slums

Metropolitan regions face acute housing shortages, particularly for the economically weaker sections. The formal housing market caters mostly to middle- and high-income groups, while the urban poor are left to depend on informal solutions.

Challenges include:

- A massive shortfall in affordable housing units
- Proliferation of slums and informal settlements lacking tenure security
- Weak implementation of in-situ slum rehabilitation policies
- Displacement without rehabilitation in the name of development or beautification

The 2012 Technical Group on Urban Housing Shortage estimated over 18.78 million units of deficit in urban India, a significant share of which is concentrated in metro cities.

4.12 The Need for Metropolitan Planning

As India's metropolitan regions evolve into sprawling, complex urban systems, the limitations of traditional city-centric planning have become increasingly evident. Existing planning tools—such as municipal master plans or individual sectoral schemes—are inadequate for managing the multi-jurisdictional, functionally integrated nature of metropolitan areas. Without coordinated spatial and institutional strategies, metros risk deepening inequality, infrastructure stress, and ecological vulnerability.

Metropolitan planning is thus not just a technical process—it is a governance imperative. It involves a shift from fragmented, inward-looking plans toward integrated, multi-scalar strategies that can manage the scale, diversity, and dynamics of metropolitan growth.

Why Metropolitan Planning is Urgent

1. **Functional Integration Across Jurisdictions**: Metropolitan areas operate as unified labour markets, transport networks, housing regions, and environmental systems, despite being divided among multiple administrative bodies. Planning for only one municipality in isolation leads to service duplication, infrastructure gaps, and land-use conflicts.
2. **Infrastructure and Service Coordination**: Essential services like roads, water, sewerage, transport, and waste management are regional in nature. Coordinated planning ensures interoperability of systems, optimizes resource allocation, and improves overall efficiency.

3. **Disaster and Climate Resilience**: Urban floods, heatwaves, and air pollution do not respect administrative boundaries. Regional-scale resilience planning—such as integrated watershed management or mobility strategies—is essential for mitigating metropolitan climate risks (NITI Aayog 2021).
4. **Sustainable Land Use and Mobility**: Without metropolitan planning, peri-urban growth becomes informal and disconnected from transit infrastructure, leading to unproductive sprawl. Metropolitan planning allows densification, mixed-use development, and transit integration to be synchronized across the region.
5. **Inclusive Development**: Metropolitan planning helps identify and support the needs of low-income and marginalized communities across the entire region—not just in politically visible urban cores. It enables equitable housing, employment zones, and social infrastructure.
6. **Institutional Efficiency**: Currently, multiple agencies plan and operate independently, leading to misaligned priorities and resource wastage. A unified metropolitan plan can offer a common spatial framework, define institutional responsibilities, and guide investment.
7. **National Development Linkages**: India's metros are central to national priorities—industrial corridors, economic zones, and digital infrastructure all converge here. Metropolitan planning ensures these mega-projects are integrated into local development needs rather than imposed top-down.

In short, metropolitan planning bridges the gap between micro-level service provision and macro-level economic and environmental objectives. It offers a platform to reimagine Indian cities not as siloed municipal territories, but as living regions—dynamic, diverse, and deeply interconnected.

The next section explores what constitutes a metropolitan plan and what features make it effective and responsive to contemporary urban challenges.

4.13 Key Features of a Metropolitan Plan

A metropolitan plan is far more than an expanded city master plan. It is a strategic, multi-jurisdictional spatial framework that aims to coordinate growth, infrastructure, and service delivery across the entire metropolitan region. Unlike traditional master plans that often stop at administrative boundaries, metropolitan plans integrate diverse areas—central cities, satellite towns, peri-urban zones, and rural linkages—into one cohesive vision.

The key features of a robust metropolitan plan include:

1. Regional Scope with Sub-Regional Sensitivity
A metropolitan plan addresses the needs of the entire urban agglomeration but also recognizes the diversity within it. It integrates:

- Central business districts and commercial cores
- Peri-urban villages and urbanizing panchayats
- Industrial corridors, special economic zones, and logistics hubs
- Natural ecosystems like wetlands, rivers, and green belts

This balance between macro-vision and micro-planning ensures both regional coherence and local relevance (NITI Aayog 2021).

2. Integrated Land Use and Transport Planning
Land use is not planned in isolation but is coordinated with mobility patterns and transport investments. Key goals include:

- Mixed-use zoning near transit nodes (TOD principles)
- Preservation of ecological buffers and hazard-prone areas
- Promotion of walkable, compact development over sprawl
- Alignment of housing zones with employment centres to reduce commute burdens

This reduces congestion, pollution, and public spending while improving accessibility and efficiency.

3. Multilevel Governance and Interagency Coordination
Metropolitan plans are not the sole domain of municipal corporations—they involve collaboration between:

- Development authorities
- State urban development departments
- Public utilities and transport boards
- Urban local bodies (ULBs)
- Civil society and private sector partners

Plans must clearly assign roles, promote horizontal integration, and include mechanisms for cross-jurisdictional collaboration (UN-Habitat 2016b).

4. Data-Driven and Evidence-Based
Contemporary metropolitan planning is grounded in robust data. This includes:

- Satellite and GIS-based land-use mapping
- Travel behaviour and transport demand models
- Real-time service performance metrics
- Environmental and demographic datasets
- Public perception and grievance mapping

Plans that are not based on real-time, disaggregated data often misrepresent ground realities and result in mismatched infrastructure provision (Marwaha, Gupta, and Bhatia 2024).

5. Inclusion of Informality and Vulnerability Analysis
Most Indian metros contain significant informal economies and housing clusters. A metropolitan plan must:

- Map slums, informal vending zones, and housing deficits
- Assess social vulnerability to eviction, flooding, or displacement
- Create space for informal livelihoods and community participation
- Avoid eviction-based redevelopment in favour of in-situ upgrading

Without this, plans risk becoming instruments of exclusion rather than equity.

6. Financial and Investment Frameworks
A good metropolitan plan is not just a land-use document—it is an investment roadmap. It links:

- Infrastructure priorities with fiscal strategies
- Land value capture and public-private partnerships
- Affordable housing finance and transit project viability
- Budget forecasting for lifecycle costs of public services

The LRTP 2045 Report for Mumbai, for example, links regional transport plans with proposed financing mechanisms and phasing strategies (LRTP 2021).

7. Monitoring, Review, and Flexibility
Metropolitan plans should be dynamic documents with:

- Key performance indicators (KPIs) and outcome metrics
- 5–10-year midterm reviews and course correction protocols
- Institutionalized mechanisms for grievance redressal and citizen feedback
- Flexibility to accommodate emerging technologies, crises, and innovations

With these features in place, metropolitan plans can guide long-term, inclusive, and environmentally responsible urban transformation. However, executing such plans requires not just institutional coordination but also the use of advanced tools and digital platforms—a theme explored in detail in the next section. This ensures that plans remain relevant, inclusive, and responsive to change.

4.14 Role of Technology in Metropolitan Planning

Technology is playing an increasingly pivotal role in shaping the way metropolitan regions are planned, governed, and serviced. As Indian metros grow in scale and complexity, digital platforms, geospatial systems, and artificial intelligence (AI) tools offer unprecedented opportunities for data-driven governance, predictive planning, and participatory engagement.

Yet, technology is not a substitute for vision, equity, or institutional reform. It must be embedded within inclusive and transparent frameworks that serve both efficiency and justice. This section explores how digital innovations are transforming metropolitan planning, while also identifying the risks and limitations that must be addressed.

4.14.1 Data-Driven Planning

Modern metropolitan planning relies on large volumes of data—spatial, demographic, environmental, economic, and behavioural. Traditional master plans, often based on outdated or incomplete data, are being replaced or supplemented by real-time, multi-source data ecosystems.

Applications of data in metropolitan planning include:

- GIS-based land use monitoring and encroachment mapping
- Population density and household vulnerability heatmaps
- Mobility analysis using smart card, GPS, and traffic sensor data
- Environmental modelling of air, water, and noise pollution
- Tracking service delivery performance in water, waste, and electricity sectors

For instance, the Mumbai Metropolitan Region Development Authority (MMRDA) uses GIS tools to monitor land development, identify informal housing clusters, and assess proximity to infrastructure corridors (MMRDA 2024).

Data analytics improves responsiveness, transparency, and targeting—especially when integrated with public feedback platforms and grievance systems.

4.14.2 Artificial Intelligence in Urban Management

AI is increasingly being deployed to automate, optimize, and forecast urban services and infrastructure needs in metropolitan regions. Its ability to handle vast datasets and learn from complex patterns enables more accurate decision-making and early warning systems.

Key uses of AI include:

- Real-time traffic control and route optimization using adaptive signals
- Predictive maintenance for water pipelines, transformers, and sewers
- Land use classification from satellite imagery using machine learning

- AI-driven flood risk modelling based on rainfall and terrain data
- Chatbots and NLP tools in e-governance portals for public service delivery

Cities like Surat and Pune have implemented AI-backed traffic systems and smart water distribution networks, while Delhi NCR's Command and Control Centres are deploying analytics to track pollution levels and emergency response (Marwaha, Gupta, and Bhatia 2024).

However, AI adoption also requires skilled professionals, quality datasets, and accountability measures to ensure it supports public interest rather than reinforcing exclusion.

4.14.3 Smart Governance Platforms and Dashboards

Smart governance platforms serve as digital command centres that integrate data from multiple agencies and departments. These include:

- **Integrated Command and Control Centres (ICCCs)**: Operational in over 70 Indian cities under the Smart Cities Mission, ICCCs collect and visualize data on transport, safety, energy use, solid waste, and emergencies.
- **City Dashboards**: Provide real-time information on service status, pollution, water levels, and citizen feedback.
- **e-Governance and Citizen Portals**: Platforms for applications, payments, grievance redressal, and participatory planning tools.

For example, the Bhopal ICCC includes air quality monitors, smart lighting, and crime tracking modules, while Pune's public dashboard shares live bus movement and service complaints.

These tools help improve inter-departmental coordination, transparency, and citizen engagement—key priorities in metropolitan governance.

4.14.4 Risks and Ethical Considerations

While technology holds immense promise, its deployment must be critically assessed to avoid unintended consequences:

- **Digital Divide**: Access to smartphones, data, and digital literacy is unequal, particularly among informal workers, women, and older adults. Over-reliance on tech can exclude large populations from planning processes.
- **Data Privacy and Surveillance**: With increasing data collection comes the risk of surveillance, data misuse, and lack of consent in low-regulation environments.

- **Algorithmic Bias**: AI systems trained on biased or incomplete datasets can perpetuate historical inequalities—e.g., denying services to informal settlements due to their invisibility in official maps.
- **Technocratic Urbanism**: Technology can be used to justify top-down, elite-centric projects that prioritize aesthetics or control over community needs.

Addressing these concerns requires clear data protection frameworks, inclusive design, regulatory oversight, and a human-centric approach to technology use in cities (Artioli and Le Galès 2025; UN-Habitat 2016b).

In conclusion, technology must be seen as a facilitator—not a driver—of sustainable metropolitan development. When aligned with inclusive planning, ethical governance, and community participation, digital tools can significantly enhance the effectiveness, responsiveness, and resilience of India's metropolitan regions.

4.15 Examples of Metropolitan Plans

Several Indian metropolitan regions have taken steps—albeit at varying levels of maturity—towards preparing integrated plans that go beyond traditional municipal boundaries. These plans reflect diverse institutional arrangements, planning approaches, and levels of implementation.

The **Mumbai Metropolitan Region** presents one of India's longest-standing attempts at regional planning. Managed by the Mumbai Metropolitan Region Development Authority (MMRDA), the regional plan seeks to integrate land use, transport, and environmental conservation. Yet, despite a comprehensive framework, implementation has been hampered by fragmented governance and weak enforcement in ecologically sensitive zones.

In the **National Capital Region**, planning is overseen by the NCR Planning Board (NCRPB), which attempts to balance growth across Delhi, Haryana, Uttar Pradesh, and Rajasthan. The plan's emphasis on transport corridors and decongestion of Delhi is notable, though administrative friction among states continues to affect consistency in implementation.

The **Pune Metropolitan Region**—through PMRDA—has more recently adopted GIS-based tools and flexible development controls for managing urban expansion beyond the municipal corporation limits. However, like many newer regional bodies, it faces challenges in integrating peri-urban governance and managing resistance from local stakeholders.

Meanwhile, **Delhi's Draft Master Plan 2041** introduces themes of environmental resilience, TOD, and inclusive redevelopment. However, its alignment with the larger regional framework remains limited, and concerns over the exclusion of informal workers persist.

Internationally, the Paris Île-de-France Plan serves as an example of strong regional coordination, focusing on balanced housing distribution, transport integration, and heritage preservation. However, it too grapples with socio-spatial inequities between inner and outer metropolitan zones.

These examples highlight both progress and pitfalls in metropolitan planning. While institutional models vary, the recurring lessons point toward the need for strong coordination, inclusive frameworks, and continuous adaptation—all of which will be examined in greater detail through focused case studies in the chapters ahead.

4.16 Stages of Metropolitan Planning

Metropolitan planning is a cyclical, multi-stage process that blends spatial vision, governance coordination, public participation, and monitoring. It is not a one-time technical document but an evolving framework shaped by regional needs, institutional capacity, and citizen engagement. While each region may adopt slightly different sequences or tools, a broad six-stage process is commonly followed in practice and recommended in national reports (NITI Aayog 2021; UN-Habitat 2016b).

1. Visioning and Goal Setting
The planning process begins with a shared vision for the metropolitan region. This vision defines the broad aspirations of the region—whether it's compact, transit-oriented growth, environmental sustainability, inclusive housing, or innovation hubs. This stage typically involves multi-stakeholder consultations, scenario building, and review of local development priorities. It forms the normative basis for all spatial and investment decisions that follow (UN-Habitat 2016b).

2. Data Collection and Analysis
This stage involves building a comprehensive evidence base using demographic data, land use maps, infrastructure inventories, ecological assets, and transport patterns. Tools such as GIS mapping, satellite imagery, and census data are combined with field surveys and institutional datasets. Advanced models may simulate population growth, mobility patterns, or land demand scenarios to guide planning decisions (Marwaha, Gupta, and Bhatia 2024; MMRDA 2024).

3. Drafting the Plan
Based on the vision and evidence, planners prepare a draft metropolitan spatial plan. This includes proposed land use categories, regional transport frameworks, affordable housing zones, economic corridors, ecological protections, and phasing strategies. Plans often include development control regulations (DCRs) and zoning norms aligned with regional goals. At this stage, institutional roles,

implementation models, and financing frameworks are also mapped out (LRTP 2021; NITI Aayog 2021).

4. **Public Participation**
This stage ensures **democratic legitimacy**. The draft plan is released for public feedback through consultations, focus groups, hearings, exhibitions, and digital platforms. Participation helps surface local needs—especially from communities typically excluded from formal planning such as informal workers, tenants, and peri-urban residents. In cities like Pune and Delhi, citizen inputs have shaped TOD, street design, and heritage conservation strategies (UN-Habitat 2016b).

5. **Implementation**
Post-approval, the plan moves to the execution stage. Metropolitan authorities coordinate with local bodies, utilities, and parastatals to translate spatial proposals into projects—such as transit lines, green infrastructure, or new housing clusters. This phase includes institutional setup, resource allocation, inter-departmental integration, and sometimes legal reform to align with the plan (Marwaha, Gupta, and Bhatia 2024).

6. **Monitoring and Review**
A successful plan incorporates ongoing performance tracking. Indicators such as modal share, housing coverage, water stress, or green space per capita are monitored using digital dashboards and citizen feedback tools. Plans include built-in review cycles (typically every 5–10 years) to reassess goals, respond to crises (like pandemics or floods), and revise spatial strategies. Tools like Integrated Command and Control Centres (ICCCs) and urban observatories support data-driven monitoring (NITI Aayog 2021; Marwaha, Gupta, and Bhatia 2024).

By institutionalizing these stages and embedding flexibility into the process, metropolitan planning can move from paper to practice. It is through this structured yet adaptive approach that India's metropolitan regions can achieve inclusive, resilient, and future-ready urban development.

4.17 Metropolitan Statistical Tools and Indicators

Metropolitan planning is only as effective as its ability to measure, monitor, and respond to on-the-ground realities. As India's metros continue to evolve, there is a growing emphasis on data-backed evaluation systems that assess urban performance across sustainability, infrastructure, governance, resilience, and quality of life. These statistical tools and indicators form the backbone of evidence-based planning and policy recalibration.

4.17.1 Urban Sustainability and Liveability Indices

The National Institute of Urban Affairs (NIUA), in collaboration with the Ministry of Housing and Urban Affairs (MoHUA), has introduced comprehensive indices to assess urban performance. The Ease of Living Index (EoLI) and the Municipal Performance Index (MPI) are two major tools for comparative benchmarking.

The Ease of Living Index evaluates cities across four main pillars—Quality of Life, Economic Ability, Sustainability, and Governance—with sub-indicators like housing affordability, public transport access, air quality, and citizen satisfaction. The 2020 EoLI covered over 100 cities and provided metropolitan municipalities like Bengaluru, Pune, and Surat with data-driven feedback loops to improve urban services (NIUA 2020).

These indices are not just ranking mechanisms—they are increasingly influencing fiscal transfers, scheme evaluations, and regional prioritization within Smart Cities and AMRUT missions.

4.17.2 Resilience, Infrastructure, and Environmental Metrics

Beyond liveability, metropolitan regions require specialized metrics for resilience and infrastructure health. These include:

- **Service-level benchmarks** for water, sanitation, solid waste, and transport (MoHUA, SLB Framework)
- **Disaster risk and vulnerability indices** developed under the National Disaster Management Authority (NDMA)
- **Urban Green Cover and Blue Infrastructure Index** for assessing ecological assets
- **Urban Heat Risk and Flood Exposure mapping**, especially for cities like Chennai and Mumbai

Many metros have begun using **real-time SCADA systems**, smart sensors, and utility-level dashboards to measure uptime, energy use, waste flow, and leakages in core infrastructure systems.

4.17.3 Role of Dashboards and Integrated Monitoring Tools

With increasing adoption of **digital governance**, real-time dashboards and integrated data platforms have become essential statistical tools. Key examples include:

- **Smart Cities Mission Dashboards**, accessible via MoHUA, showing live service performance
- **Integrated Command and Control Centres (ICCCs)** that consolidate city-wide data feeds

- **Open data platforms** like DataSmart Cities and OpenCity.in that allow civil society to visualize and interpret metropolitan data

These tools help planners monitor key performance indicators (KPIs), identify stress points, and course-correct policies mid-cycle. They also enable citizen accountability, as residents can now track urban performance in real time.

4.17.4 Toward a Unified Metropolitan Indicator Framework

Despite these innovations, India still lacks a comprehensive metropolitan-level indicator framework that goes beyond municipal boundaries. Current tools focus on city-level governance units, while metros function as multi-jurisdictional entities. A robust metropolitan indicator system should integrate:

- Regional mobility performance
- Cross-jurisdiction infrastructure integration
- Affordable housing access across the region
- Environmental risk monitoring beyond ULB limits
- Social equity, informality, and migrant inclusion metrics

The move toward such integrated systems is already visible in pilot platforms like the NCRPB Geoportal and the proposed Urban Observatories under the NITI Aayog reform recommendations (NITI Aayog 2021; MMRDA 2024).

4.18 Conclusion

Metropolitanization in India represents one of the most transformative shifts in the country's urban trajectory. It reflects not just demographic concentration or economic centrality but a deeper reorganization of how space, society, and governance interact in rapidly expanding urban regions. These metropolitan areas are no longer singular cities—they are multi-nodal, multi-jurisdictional ecosystems shaped by dynamic flows of people, infrastructure, capital, and governance frameworks.

This chapter has examined metropolitanization through a comprehensive lens, beginning with its global and national definitions, historical emergence, and evolving characteristics. It traced the governance transitions that have shaped post-2014 metropolitan reforms in India and explored the challenges associated with rapid growth, sustainability, and socio-spatial equity. Through the lens of key urban development schemes and tools like TOD, participatory planning, and smart governance, it unpacked both the promise and the pitfalls of current metropolitan planning efforts.

By detailing the stages of metropolitan planning and the critical features that make such plans effective—such as regional integration, data use, and inclusive frameworks—the chapter has outlined what it takes to operationalize metropolitan governance meaningfully. The role of technology and statistical tools in measuring progress and identifying systemic gaps has further highlighted the importance of evidence-based planning.

Ultimately, India's metropolitan areas are sites of both immense opportunity and profound contradiction. They drive national economic growth but are equally sites of exclusion, environmental degradation, and infrastructural stress. Effective metropolitan planning must therefore be more than a technical exercise—it must be a process rooted in democratic participation, institutional reform, spatial justice, and ecological responsibility.

As the upcoming chapters turns toward detailed case studies, it becomes clear that the real test of metropolitan planning lies not in documents and visions but in implementation on the ground—across corridors, constituencies, and communities that together define the future of urban India.

CHAPTER

5

National Urban Policy Framework

5.1 Introduction

India is undergoing an unprecedented urban transition, with its urban population projected to reach over 600 million by 2036. This demographic shift presents both vast opportunities for economic growth and significant challenges in terms of planning, infrastructure, service delivery, environmental management, and social equity. Yet, despite the growing importance of cities, urban development in India has long been characterized by fragmented governance, sectoral planning, and misaligned institutional mandates (NIUA 2021; NITI Aayog 2021). The need for a coherent and integrative urban policy framework that can unify national priorities, guide sub-national actions, and promote sustainability led to the formulation of the National Urban Policy Framework (NUPF) in 2018 by the Ministry of Housing and Urban Affairs (MoHUA).

The NUPF was designed as a strategic, non-statutory document that responds to the complex realities of India's cities. It draws upon constitutional mandates such as the 74th Amendment, the principles of cooperative federalism, and India's commitments to international frameworks including the 2030 Agenda for Sustainable Development and the New Urban Agenda. Positioned as a bridge between vision and implementation, the NUPF aims to align fragmented urban initiatives—such as Smart Cities Mission, AMRUT, and PMAY-U—under a common strategic direction (MoHUA 2018; UN-Habitat and OECD 2024).

The framework departs from earlier technocratic and top-down models of planning by advocating for people-centric, resilient, and regionally balanced urbanization. Its structure is anchored around 16 guiding principles and 10 functional areas that offer a holistic lens for viewing urban transformation. As noted in the Global State of National Urban Policy report, national urban policies like the NUPF are crucial for fostering vertical and horizontal coordination, improving urban resilience, and ensuring that cities become drivers of inclusive and sustainable growth (UN-Habitat and OECD 2024).

This chapter presents a detailed analysis of the National Urban Policy Framework, beginning with its vision and principles, and progressing through its functional areas, recommended interventions, and expected outcomes. It also reflects on its current influence, monitoring systems, and the challenges that remain in translating policy into action.

5.2 Vision and Strategic Intent

The National Urban Policy Framework envisions a future where Indian cities are inclusive, safe, resilient, and sustainable—aligned with both the global sustainable development agenda and the constitutional commitment to decentralized urban governance. At its core, the NUPF seeks to create an enabling environment where all levels of government, along with civil society and the private sector, can collectively respond to urban challenges and realise the full potential of urbanization as a driver of national development (MoHUA 2018).

The framework emphasizes that cities are not isolated entities but dynamic systems embedded within wider regional and national contexts. Therefore, urban transformation requires coordinated, multi-scalar strategies that integrate land use, infrastructure, environment, economy, and governance. This strategic intent reflects a shift from traditional plan-based development to a more adaptive, integrated, and principle-led approach that empowers cities while ensuring national coherence.

The NUPF aligns closely with India's global commitments, including the Sustainable Development Goals, particularly Goal 11 on sustainable cities and communities, as well as the New Urban Agenda adopted at Habitat III. It encourages cities to adopt a systems-thinking approach, address regional disparities, promote social equity, and ensure environmental sustainability (UN-Habitat and OECD, 2024).

The framework also highlights the need to transition from sectoral interventions to integrated solutions. It advocates convergence between centrally sponsored schemes such as AMRUT, Smart Cities, PMAY-U, and SBM, so that resources are used efficiently, outcomes are measurable, and benefits are equitably distributed. Through its vision, the NUPF serves as a unifying policy architecture that connects urban aspirations with actionable strategies at every level of governance (NIUA 2021; NITI Aayog 2021).

5.3 Core Principles

The National Urban Policy Framework is built around sixteen guiding principles that offer a normative foundation for shaping India's urban future. These principles, often referred to as the "sutras" of the framework, are not just philosophical statements but are intended to influence planning processes, policy choices, and institutional behaviour across levels of government. Together, they embody the values of decentralization, inclusivity, efficiency, and sustainability, while encouraging cities to become enablers of opportunity and innovation (MoHUA 2018).

The sixteen core principles of the NUPF are as follows:

- **Subsidiarity**: Empower the lowest competent level of governance to take decisions and deliver services.
- **Integration**: Encourage the convergence of policies, programs, and departments across sectors and levels of government.
- **Inclusiveness**: Ensure that all urban residents, including marginalized and vulnerable groups, are included in planning and development.
- **Equity**: Promote fair access to resources, opportunities, and services for all segments of society.
- **Sustainability**: Balance economic growth with environmental protection and social well-being for future generations.
- **Circularity**: Optimize resource use through waste reduction, reuse, and regeneration in the urban economy.
- **Efficiency**: Enhance the use of financial, human, and natural resources through innovative and smart approaches.
- **Resilience**: Build the capacity of cities to withstand and recover from economic, environmental, and social shocks.
- **Safety**: Design urban spaces and systems that prioritise safety and security, especially for women, children, and the elderly.
- **Transparency**: Promote openness and accountability in governance and urban service delivery.
- **Participation**: Facilitate meaningful involvement of citizens in planning, budgeting, and implementation processes.
- **Regionalization**: Recognize the interdependence between urban and rural areas and promote balanced regional development.
- **Affordability**: Ensure that housing, transport, and basic services remain financially accessible to all urban residents.
- **Innovation**: Encourage new ideas, technologies, and institutional practices to solve complex urban challenges.
- **Heritage**: Preserve and integrate natural, cultural, and built heritage in urban development strategies.
- **Financial Self-Sufficiency**: Enable cities to raise and manage their own revenues and investments sustainably.

These principles offer a common ethical and operational language for urban policy and planning in India, fostering alignment between national aspirations and local actions. They also set the tone for the ten functional areas that follow, ensuring that interventions are grounded in inclusive, people-centric, and future-ready approaches (UN-Habitat and OECD 2024; NIUA 2021).

5.4 Key Functional Areas

The National Urban Policy Framework identifies ten key functional areas that form the operational core of India's urban transformation agenda. These areas represent the domains where strategic interventions are most needed to make cities inclusive, sustainable, resilient, and productive. Together, they help bridge the gap between the high-level vision of the NUPF and the practical realities of urban governance and planning (MoHUA 2018).

Each functional area is interconnected and designed to reflect the comprehensive nature of urban ecosystems. A brief overview of the ten areas is provided below:

1. **Urban Planning and Design**: Promotes integrated, inclusive, and future-ready spatial planning at all levels. Emphasizes the use of GIS, heritage-sensitive planning, public spaces, and low-carbon infrastructure.
2. **Housing and Inclusivity**: Encourages affordable, adequate, and safe housing for all, with a focus on slum rehabilitation, rental housing, tenure security, and gender-inclusive designs.
3. **Economic Development**: Aims to position cities as engines of economic growth through support for innovation, MSMEs, local entrepreneurship, and informal sector integration.
4. **Mobility and Transport**: Advocates for multi-modal, accessible, and low-emission mobility solutions. Supports public transport, non-motorized transport, last-mile connectivity, and Transit-Oriented Development (TOD).
5. **Environment and Sustainability**: Integrates climate resilience, disaster risk reduction, and natural resource management into urban development. Promotes circular economy practices and ecological restoration.
6. **Water, Waste and Sanitation**: Focuses on universal access to clean water and sanitation, solid waste management, faecal sludge treatment, and decentralized infrastructure for service delivery.
7. **Energy and Green Technology**: Encourages the use of renewable energy, energy-efficient buildings, and green technologies to reduce urban carbon footprints and build energy-secure cities.
8. **Social Infrastructure**: Stresses the importance of equitable access to health, education, recreation, and care services, particularly for marginalized communities.
9. **Governance**: Promotes accountable, decentralized, and participatory governance models that empower Urban Local Bodies and improve inter-agency coordination.

10. **Urban Finance**: Supports fiscal autonomy and financial sustainability through municipal revenue reforms, value capture, public-private partnerships, and innovative financing tools.

These functional areas are not isolated silos, but rather overlapping spheres that must be addressed through integrated urban strategies. Cities are encouraged to customize their interventions based on local needs while aligning with the broader principles and strategic intent of the NUPF (UN-Habitat and OECD 2024; NIUA 2021).

5.5 Interventions and Actions

The National Urban Policy Framework is not merely a vision document—it is intended as a guide for targeted interventions that can translate principles into practice. It encourages multi-level action at the national, state, and local levels, tailored to specific urban contexts while maintaining alignment with shared strategic goals. These interventions span policy reform, institutional strengthening, capacity building, spatial planning, infrastructure development, and citizen participation (MoHUA 2018).

Key interventions and actions proposed under the NUPF include:

At the National Level:

- Formulate model laws and planning templates to guide state-level urban reforms.
- Align central schemes and missions (e.g., AMRUT, PMAY, SBM, SCM) with NUPF's core principles.
- Promote research, innovation, and knowledge-sharing platforms through national institutes and networks.
- Establish a national urban observatory for monitoring outcomes and benchmarking progress.

At the State Level:

- Enact enabling legislation to empower Urban Local Bodies (ULBs) and regional planning authorities.
- Support metropolitan and district-level planning frameworks that promote regional coordination.
- Strengthen town and country planning departments through staffing, training, and digital systems.
- Facilitate urban–rural integration through shared service delivery models and coordinated investments.

At the Local Level:

- Prepare integrated plans that combine land use, infrastructure, resilience, and inclusivity goals.
- Implement participatory budgeting and planning processes at ward and neighbourhood levels.
- Leverage geospatial technologies, MIS, and e-governance platforms for decision-making and transparency.
- Promote green infrastructure, affordable housing, and mobility improvements aligned with functional area targets.

Cross-Cutting Actions:

- Build institutional capacity through dedicated training programs and municipal cadre reforms.
- Create mechanisms for inter-agency and inter-governmental coordination.
- Mobilize private investment through blended finance, PPPs, and innovative funding models.
- Localize SDGs and climate targets through municipal plans, performance metrics, and incentives.

These actions are designed to catalyse systemic reform by embedding flexibility, responsiveness, and accountability into urban development. The framework places emphasis on enabling environments rather than prescriptive mandates, allowing cities and states to innovate within a shared strategic structure (NITI Aayog, 2021; NIUA, 2021; UN-Habitat and OECD 2024).

5.6 Expected Outcomes

The National Urban Policy Framework envisions a transformation in how Indian cities are planned, governed, financed, and experienced. If implemented effectively, the NUPF is expected to produce a range of systemic, social, environmental, and economic outcomes that align with national development priorities and global sustainability goals. These outcomes are not limited to infrastructure or service delivery, but extend to institutional reforms, urban resilience, and quality of life improvements (MoHUA 2018; UN-Habitat and OECD 2024).

Key expected outcomes of the NUPF include:

- Improved spatial planning that is integrated, inclusive, and future-ready.
- Balanced regional development through coordinated metropolitan and city-region strategies.
- Strengthened institutional capacities at state and city levels, supported by professionalized urban cadres.

- Greater fiscal autonomy and financial sustainability of Urban Local Bodies.
- More equitable access to housing, infrastructure, and services for all, especially marginalized groups.
- Enhanced environmental sustainability through adoption of circular economy, climate-resilient infrastructure, and low-carbon solutions.
- Increased citizen engagement and participatory governance in planning and decision-making processes.
- Convergence and efficiency in implementation of national missions through shared strategic alignment.
- Integration of digital technologies, GIS, and performance monitoring tools in urban management.
- Measurable progress toward Sustainable Development Goals (particularly SDG 11) and India's climate commitments.

These outcomes are designed to evolve over time and are meant to be adaptable across geographies and scales. The NUPF thus serves not just as a framework for cities, but as a guiding force for India's overall urban future—anchored in sustainability, inclusivity, and decentralization (NITI Aayog, 2021; NIUA, 2021).

5.7 Monitoring and Evaluation

A national urban policy framework can only be effective if its implementation is supported by a robust monitoring and evaluation (M&E) system. The NUPF acknowledges this need by promoting a results-based approach that allows for adaptive learning, course correction, and evidence-driven governance. Monitoring and evaluation mechanisms ensure accountability, assess the impact of urban interventions, and enable feedback loops between national, state, and local actors (MoHUA 2018; UN-Habitat and OECD 2024).

Rather than prescribing a single set of metrics, the NUPF advocates for flexible and context-sensitive monitoring strategies. It encourages the development of urban observatories, performance dashboards, and outcome-based evaluation systems at various levels of government. These tools are intended to support data-informed decision-making and track progress across the functional areas and principles outlined in the framework.

The monitoring and evaluation approach under the NUPF can be grouped into three broad focus areas: ongoing updates, emerging impacts, and the challenges associated with implementation. Each is discussed below in the following subsections.

5.7.1 Updates

Since its release in 2018, the National Urban Policy Framework has served primarily as a strategic vision document rather than a formalized policy instrument with periodic updates. While there has not been an official revision or second version of the NUPF, many of its principles have been echoed in subsequent urban initiatives, planning guidelines, and national reports, suggesting a gradual internalization of its strategic intent within India's urban policy discourse (NIUA 2021; UN-Habitat and OECD 2024).

Some updates and policy shifts aligned with the NUPF include:

- Integration of NUPF principles into capacity-building initiatives such as those led by the National Urban Learning Platform (NULP) and the National Institute of Urban Affairs.
- Emphasis on outcome-based planning and convergence across missions like AMRUT 2.0, Smart Cities 2.0 roadmap, and PMAY-U extension.
- Use of digital performance monitoring tools such as the Ease of Living Index, Municipal Performance Index, and ClimateSmart Cities Assessment Framework to support evidence-based governance.
- References to NUPF in urban planning reform discussions at NITI Aayog and Ministry-led working groups, particularly regarding state-level policy harmonization and decentralized planning.

However, despite these thematic alignments, the NUPF has not yet evolved into a statutory or regularly updated policy instrument. There is currently no national mandate requiring states or cities to formally adopt or report progress against its framework. This absence of formal institutionalization limits the potential for structured updates, and risks the NUPF remaining aspirational rather than operational in nature (NITI Aayog 2021).

Moving forward, formalising NUPF as a living document—with provisions for regular review, adaptation, and state-level localization—could significantly strengthen its influence on India's urban development trajectory.

5.7.2 Impact of NUPF

While the National Urban Policy Framework has yet to be institutionalized as a statutory mandate, its strategic influence is visible across multiple facets of India's urban governance ecosystem. The NUPF has acted as a conceptual anchor, shaping policy dialogues, influencing the design of urban missions, and promoting integrated thinking among planners and policymakers.

Some of the key areas where the NUPF has had discernible impact include:

- **Policy Convergence**: Missions such as AMRUT 2.0, Smart Cities, and PMAY-U have increasingly adopted outcome-oriented frameworks, participatory planning methods, and integrated service delivery models—principles central to the NUPF.

- **Capacity Building and Knowledge Platforms**: Institutions like the National Institute of Urban Affairs (NIUA) and the National Urban Learning Platform (NULP) have internalized NUPF principles into training modules, practitioner guides, and knowledge-sharing forums.
- **Urban Finance and Governance Reform**: Urban finance reforms supported by the Ministry of Finance and initiatives by NITI Aayog draw on NUPF's emphasis on fiscal decentralization, municipal revenue enhancement, and institutional strengthening.
- **Performance Monitoring Tools**: The development of benchmarking systems such as the Ease of Living Index, Municipal Performance Index, and CSCAF has reflected the NUPF's call for evidence-based monitoring and citizen-centric outcomes.
- **Discourse on Urban Planning Reform**: The NUPF has informed recent discussions on planning education, creation of urban planning cadres, and state-level urban policy formulation, including the report on urban planning capacity by NITI Aayog (2021).

Despite these soft impacts, the framework's limited formal adoption at the state and city levels has constrained its transformative potential. Most references to NUPF remain conceptual, without mechanisms for integration into statutory planning processes or financial allocation systems. However, its influence on framing urban challenges holistically and advocating for integrated approaches has been widely acknowledged (NIUA 2021; UN-Habitat and OECD 2024).

As India moves toward scaling up urban reforms, the strategic foundation provided by the NUPF can play a more direct and measurable role—if supported by institutional commitment and operational guidelines.

5.7.3 Challenges in Implementing NUPF

Despite its comprehensive vision and strategic clarity, the National Urban Policy Framework faces several challenges in implementation. These barriers are structural, institutional, financial, and political in nature, and have collectively limited the framework's adoption and operational impact across different levels of government.

Key challenges include:

- **Lack of statutory status**: The NUPF remains a non-binding strategic document without legal enforcement mechanisms. This limits its influence on state-level legislation, planning mandates, and budgetary allocations, leading to uneven uptake across jurisdictions.

- **Institutional fragmentation**: Urban governance in India is distributed across multiple agencies with overlapping responsibilities. The absence of a unified urban authority or platform for coordination makes it difficult to implement NUPF's integrated and cross-sectoral vision in practice (NIUA, 2021; NITI Aayog 2021).
- **Limited localization**: Few states have developed their own urban policy frameworks aligned with NUPF. Without contextual adaptation and clear implementation roadmaps at the state and municipal levels, the framework remains disconnected from local realities.
- **Weak capacity at local levels**: Urban local bodies often lack the planning expertise, financial autonomy, and technical staff necessary to internalize and act on the principles of NUPF. Inadequate training, outdated tools, and fragmented data systems further impede capacity (NITI Aayog 2021).
- **Funding and resource gaps**: Implementation of NUPF-aligned actions requires significant investment in planning systems, data platforms, and institutional reform. However, these priorities often receive limited funding under existing schemes focused on physical infrastructure delivery.
- **Political economy constraints**: Urban reforms often face resistance from entrenched interests, especially in areas like land use regulation, revenue reform, and governance restructuring. These political challenges make it difficult to institutionalize long-term, principle-based planning frameworks like the NUPF.
- **Absence of formal monitoring systems**: While the NUPF encourages outcomes-based monitoring, there is currently no official mechanism to track how well cities or states are aligning with its principles. Without metrics, incentives, or accountability, the policy risks remaining aspirational (UN-Habitat and OECD 2024).

To overcome these challenges, the NUPF must be supported by legal recognition, dedicated institutional mechanisms, state-level policy harmonization, and sustained capacity-building efforts. Strengthening the interface between national strategy and local implementation is critical to translating its vision into tangible change.

5.8 Conclusion

The National Urban Policy Framework marks a pivotal step in reimagining India's urban future. By articulating a set of shared principles and functional areas, the NUPF offers a coherent and strategic direction for managing the opportunities and complexities of urbanization. Its emphasis on subsidiarity, inclusivity, resilience, and regional integration reflects a nuanced understanding of India's diverse urban landscape, where one-size-fits-all solutions are no longer viable.

While the framework has influenced policies, missions, and institutional thinking, its impact has remained largely conceptual due to the absence of statutory backing, monitoring mechanisms, and dedicated implementation pathways. Bridging this gap between vision and practice requires concerted efforts to localize the framework, empower city institutions, and embed NUPF principles into state-level policies, statutory plans, and financing models.

As this book progresses, it will examine how India's major metropolitan regions—such as Delhi NCR, Mumbai Metropolitan Region, Kolkata, Bengaluru, and others—align with the core tenets of the NUPF. These case studies will explore the extent to which these cities have internalized the framework's functional areas, responded to its strategic intent, and addressed its principles through localized planning, infrastructure delivery, and institutional reform. In doing so, the analysis will assess the real-world applicability of the NUPF and identify pathways for strengthening its role in shaping India's metropolitan transformation.

Ultimately, the success of the National Urban Policy Framework will depend on how well it can move from a visionary document to an enabling structure that guides cities of all sizes toward inclusive, sustainable, and future-ready urbanization.

CHAPTER

6

Case Studies of Metropolitan Areas

This chapter presents in-depth case studies of selected metropolitan areas in India, with a focus on assessing their urban development trajectories through the lens of the National Urban Policy Framework (NUPF). The case studies have been carefully chosen to represent diverse geographies, governance models, economic roles, and urbanization patterns, allowing for a comprehensive understanding of how India's metropolitan regions are evolving within a common national policy framework.

Each case study is structured around the ten key functional areas outlined in the NUPF, including urban planning, urban economy, physical and social infrastructure, housing, transport and mobility, governance, urban finance, environmental sustainability, and urban information systems. These areas are critically examined in relation to the 14 core principles of the NUPF such as sustainability, inclusivity, decentralization, and collaborative governance.

By adopting a functional approach, this chapter not only traces the developmental pathways and institutional mechanisms of individual metropolitan regions but also evaluates their effectiveness and alignment with national urban objectives. Through a synthesis of official plans, government data, academic research, and policy analysis, this chapter highlights both innovations and challenges in metropolitan planning, offering insights into how the spirit of NUPF is being translated—or contested—on the ground.

The case studies begin with Delhi Metropolitan Area, given its prominence as the national capital and the complexity of its institutional arrangements. Delhi serves as a unique entry point to understand metropolitan planning in a multi-jurisdictional, politically sensitive, and rapidly urbanizing context.

6.1 Delhi Metropolitan Area (DMA)

6.1.1 Introduction

The Delhi Metropolitan Area (DMA), comprising the National Capital Territory (NCT) of Delhi and its interconnected urban peripheries, is the most politically significant and administratively complex urban region in India. It lies at the heart of the National Capital Region (NCR), a polycentric and inter-jurisdictional mega-region that includes parts of Haryana, Uttar Pradesh, and Rajasthan. The area is governed by a unique multi-layered planning framework that links central, state, and local agencies in one of the most institutionally dense urban settings in the country.

Geographically, the DMA covers approximately 1,500 square kilometres within Delhi and extends into a broader urban influence zone defined by functional integration with satellite cities such as Gurugram, Noida, Ghaziabad, and Faridabad. The area holds critical strategic importance not only due to its political role as the national capital but also as the administrative, diplomatic, and cultural nerve centre of the country.

As per Census 2011, Delhi had a population of 16.7 million, making it the second-most populous city in India. Projections from the Master Plan for Delhi 2041 (MPD-2041) estimate the population will rise to 29.1 million by 2041 under a medium growth scenario (DDA 2021). The region has experienced rapid urban expansion, propelled by high rates of in-migration, a young demographic profile, and economic opportunities concentrated in services, governance, education, and trade. However, this expansion has been accompanied by rising spatial inequities, environmental degradation, and unplanned peripheral growth.

Delhi contributes over 7% to India's GDP, making it one of the most economically productive regions in South Asia. The city is a hub for government administration, business services, information technology, trade, and education, with a large concentration of both formal and informal economic activities. It also has one of the most vibrant start-up ecosystems in the region, bolstered by access to skilled labour and digital infrastructure (DDA 2021; ADB and NCRPB 2021).

What sets the Delhi metropolitan system apart is its institutional complexity. Governance is distributed across multiple layers: the Delhi Development Authority (DDA) is the chief planning body under the Union Government; the Government of National Capital Territory of Delhi (GNCTD) administers health, education, transport, and housing; and urban local bodies (ULBs) such as the Municipal Corporation of Delhi (MCD), New Delhi Municipal Council (NDMC), and Delhi Cantonment Board oversee service delivery and civic infrastructure. At a regional level, the National Capital Region Planning Board (NCRPB) guides long-term spatial and infrastructure planning for the wider NCR.

Historically, Delhi's urban evolution has been shaped by successive layers of planning under various regimes—from the imperial cities of the Sultanate and Mughals to colonial New Delhi, and finally, post-independence planned expansion. The first Master Plan of 1962, followed by those of 2001 and

2021, established the groundwork for land-use zoning and public sector-led development. However, these plans often fell short in accommodating the actual pace and nature of urbanization, leading to the proliferation of unauthorized colonies, slums, and urban villages. The MPD-2041 attempts to address these limitations through a more flexible, inclusive, and strategic planning approach, integrating transit-oriented development, climate resilience, and mixed-use zoning as core principles.

The following sections critically examine Delhi's development under each of the ten functional areas defined by the National Urban Policy Framework (NUPF), analysing how the region aligns with the NUPF's fourteen core principles. The case study draws from statutory planning documents, policy reports, and scholarly evaluations to present a comprehensive picture of metropolitan governance and development in the capital region.

6.1.2 Alignment with NUPF Principles: Functional Area–Wise Analysis

This section examines the urban development of the Delhi Metropolitan Area through the ten key functional areas identified in the National Urban Policy Framework (NUPF). Each functional area is analysed in terms of how it is approached in Delhi's planning and governance context, and the extent to which it aligns with the fourteen core principles of the NUPF. The assessment draws upon statutory planning documents, policy reports, and academic evaluations to understand the region's institutional capacities, planning mechanisms, and implementation gaps. This structured analysis provides insights into both the strengths and systemic limitations of Delhi's metropolitan planning framework, helping to trace its trajectory toward a more inclusive, sustainable, and well-governed urban future.

6.1.2.1 Urban Planning

Urban planning in Delhi has evolved from rigid, zone-based frameworks to a more strategic and enabling vision in MPD-2041. The plan emphasizes compact growth through transit-oriented development (TOD), land pooling, regeneration of existing built areas, and flexible land-use mixes (DDA 2021). These approaches reflect the NUPF principles of integrated planning, inclusivity, and adaptability.

However, challenges remain. The dominance of top-down planning models has led to significant informal urbanization, especially in peri-urban and unauthorized colonies (Ahrar and Staub 2020). Despite attempts at community engagement during the formulation of MPD-2041, participatory frameworks at the local or ward level remain weak, limiting true alignment with the NUPF's decentralization and participatory planning ethos.

6.1.2.2 Urban Economy

Delhi's economy is a major contributor to India's GDP, dominated by service industries, government institutions, trade, logistics, and the informal sector. MPD-2041 proposes promoting clean economies, cultural and creative hubs, and knowledge districts while formalising the informal sector through zoning flexibility and shared workspace provision (DDA 2021). It supports the development of decentralized economic clusters, particularly in the CNCR.

The plan's recognition of unorganized sectors such as street vendors and home-based workers demonstrates alignment with the NUPF's focus on equity, livelihoods, and people-centric urban development. However, spatial inequality in economic opportunities persists, especially for migrants and low-income workers residing in the urban periphery (Mohapatra 2024).

6.1.2.3 Physical Infrastructure

Delhi's planning framework promotes integration of water, sanitation, energy, and waste systems under a sustainability lens. MPD-2041 envisions decentralized wastewater treatment, increased waste segregation and recycling, and expanded access to renewable energy. These efforts align with the NUPF principles of sustainability, innovation, and end-result orientation (DDA 2021).

Despite progress, there are serious gaps in implementation, especially in informal settlements. Infrastructure provisioning in slum areas is often ad hoc and fragmented, undermining inclusive access to basic services (Ahrar and Staub 2020).

6.1.2.4 Social Infrastructure

The city has made strides in improving access to education, healthcare, and public amenities. MPD-2041 emphasizes multi-use community facilities, child- and elderly-friendly spaces, and gender-sensitive planning. In particular, it aims to address infrastructure deficits in high-density, low-income areas through amenity FAR provisions and facility mixing (DDA 2021).

These strategies reflect the NUPF's values of inclusivity and accessibility. However, inequities remain between formal colonies and informal settlements. Infrastructure upgrades are often driven by pilot projects rather than systematic coverage (Mohapatra 2024).

6.1.2.5 Housing and Affordability

Housing affordability is one of Delhi's most pressing challenges. A significant portion of the population resides in unauthorized colonies, resettlement zones, or informal slums, many lacking secure tenure and basic services. MPD-2041 promotes in-situ rehabilitation, rental housing, mixed-income development, and multiple tenure options to address these issues (DDA 2021).

The plan's focus on de-densification of slums, regularization of unauthorized colonies, and PPP models reflects the NUPF's principles of inclusivity, decentralization, and innovation in financing. Yet, operational hurdles such as delays in land acquisition, legal disputes, and weak inter-agency coordination continue to hinder delivery (ADB and NCRPB 2021).

6.1.2.6 Transportation and Mobility

Delhi boasts one of the most extensive urban metro networks globally, and ongoing projects such as the Regional Rapid Transit System (RRTS) aim to further integrate regional mobility. MPD-2041 reinforces TOD strategies, non-motorized transport infrastructure, and multimodal integration. It also supports electric vehicles and shared mobility systems (DDA 2021).

The plan reflects the NUPF's principles of sustainability, accessibility, and compact urban form. However, last-mile connectivity remains weak in many peripheral zones, and increasing private vehicle ownership continues to undermine congestion and air quality goals (Mohapatra 2024).

6.1.2.7 Urban Finance

Delhi's urban finance system is marked by fiscal fragmentation. Local bodies such as the MCDs have limited autonomy and are heavily reliant on state and central transfers. MPD-2041 introduces financing tools such as value capture mechanisms, redevelopment incentives, and land monetization strategies (DDA 2021).

These approaches align with NUPF's principle of financial sustainability. Nonetheless, the underutilization of municipal bonds, weak revenue collection, and absence of integrated financial planning across agencies continue to hamper effective urban development (ADB and NCRPB 2021).

6.1.2.8 Urban Governance

Governance in Delhi is institutionally fragmented, involving multiple overlapping bodies including the DDA, GNCTD, MCDs, NDMC, and parastatals. The lack of a unified metropolitan authority hinders integrated planning and implementation. MPD-2041 advocates for improved coordination mechanisms and digital platforms to bridge gaps (DDA 2021).

While this reflects partial alignment with the NUPF's collaborative governance and transparency principles, actual practice remains limited by political contestations and administrative overlaps (Ahrar and Staub 2020). Coordination across jurisdictions within the NCR is particularly weak, despite the intent of RP-2041.

6.1.2.9 Environmental Sustainability

Environmental stress is a major challenge in Delhi. The city faces high levels of air and water pollution, loss of ecological assets, and exposure to climate risks. MPD-2041 introduces green-blue infrastructure frameworks, biodiversity parks, restoration of the Yamuna floodplain, and nature-based solutions for climate resilience (DDA 2021).

These measures are closely aligned with NUPF's sustainability and resilience principles. However, enforcement remains weak, and many environmental initiatives lack long-term financial and institutional backing (ADB and NCRPB 2021).

6.1.2.10 Urban Information Systems

Delhi has made progress in adopting digital tools for planning, governance, and citizen engagement. MPD-2041 proposes a city-level data repository, key performance indicators for monitoring, and integrated dashboards.

These developments align with NUPF's emphasis on innovation, data-driven planning, and accountability. However, institutionalising open data protocols and ensuring interoperability across departments are ongoing challenges (Mohapatra 2024).

6.1.3 Synthesis and Analysis

The Delhi Metropolitan Area presents a complex but instructive case of metropolitan development in India, offering valuable insights into the interplay between national urban policy principles and local planning realities. Across the ten functional areas of the NUPF, Delhi's statutory planning documents—especially MPD-2041 and RP-2041—demonstrate considerable conceptual alignment with the framework's fourteen core principles, yet their operationalization remains uneven.

The principle of integrated and inclusive planning is clearly visible in the structure of MPD-2041, which integrates strategies for land use, transportation, housing, environment, and economy. Its emphasis on compact development, transit-oriented planning, and mixed-use zoning showcases a shift away from rigid land use segregation toward more flexible and holistic urbanism. However, the persistence of informal settlements and unauthorized colonies—often excluded from mainstream planning until recently—reveals gaps in the inclusivity of past approaches (Ahrar and Staub 2020).

Delhi's economic strategy aligns with the NUPF's call for demand-driven and people-centric urban economies, through promotion of informal sector inclusion, creative industries, and economic decentralization. Yet, the uneven spatial distribution of economic opportunity, especially in peripheral areas, undermines equity and balanced development (Mohapatra 2024).

The city's efforts in infrastructure, mobility, and housing highlight a clear intent to align with principles of sustainability and accessibility. Plans for decentralized infrastructure systems, electric mobility, walkability, and affordable rental housing reflect this orientation. However, issues such as traffic congestion, poor last-mile connectivity, and inadequate infrastructure in informal areas persist due to implementation lags and institutional bottlenecks (DDA 2021).

Governance remains the most significant structural weakness. While the NUPF advocates collaborative and decentralized governance, Delhi's current arrangement—split across the DDA, GNCTD, multiple ULBs, and central ministries—creates fragmented accountability. The absence of a unified metropolitan planning authority dilutes policy coherence, especially in cross-sectoral domains like housing, environment, and mobility (ADB and NCRPB 2021).

Notably, environmental sustainability has been positioned at the core of both MPD-2041 and RP-2041, with detailed frameworks for air and water quality, blue-green infrastructure, and disaster resilience. These are highly aligned with the NUPF's emphasis on ecological balance and climate adaptation. However, actual enforcement and regional cooperation—particularly for river basin restoration and air pollution—are still in early stages of institutional development.

Finally, Delhi's increasing adoption of digital tools and monitoring systems reflects growing commitment to the NUPF principle of innovation and data-driven governance. Yet, unless digital infrastructure is matched with institutional capacity-building and open data integration, its transformative potential will remain limited.

In sum, Delhi's urban transformation agenda under MPD-2041 and RP-2041 resonates strongly with the normative vision of the NUPF. However, realising this vision on the ground demands far stronger institutional alignment, political commitment, and participatory mechanisms to bridge the gap between strategic intent and lived urban experience.

6.1.4 Conclusion

The Delhi Metropolitan Area reflects both the promise and complexity of metropolitan planning in India. As the seat of national power and a rapidly growing urban agglomeration, Delhi has taken significant strides in aligning its spatial and policy frameworks with the principles outlined in the National Urban Policy Framework (NUPF). The Master Plan for Delhi 2041 and the Regional Plan for NCR 2041 indicate a clear transition toward integrated, sustainable, and inclusive development strategies.

Delhi's planning system demonstrates a strong theoretical alignment with the NUPF across most functional areas. Initiatives in compact urban form, transit-oriented development, decentralized infrastructure, mixed-income housing, and environmental sustainability mirror key NUPF principles such as adaptability, people-centricity, and green urbanism. However, the efficacy of these plans is constrained by longstanding issues of institutional fragmentation, delayed implementation, and weak inter-agency coordination.

The governance structure of Delhi, straddling multiple municipal bodies, state-level agencies, and central authorities, remains the most significant obstacle to coherent metropolitan management. Without a unified governance model or empowered metropolitan authority, implementation gaps are likely to persist despite robust planning intent.

The environmental and economic strategies proposed under MPD-2041 are ambitious and forward-looking, yet their realization depends on coordinated action beyond Delhi's borders—especially with regard to air quality, river pollution, regional mobility, and economic decentralization. This necessitates not only administrative cooperation across the NCR but also the political will to implement cross-border solutions.

Delhi's experience offers several generalisable lessons for metropolitan planning in India. First, strategic planning must be accompanied by institutional reforms to ensure delivery. Second, inclusivity must move beyond rhetoric to focus on the spatial and social integration of informal settlements and peripheral communities. Third, participatory frameworks must be institutionalized at the local level to reflect community priorities in policy outcomes.

Overall, while Delhi's metropolitan planning has evolved to reflect the core values of the NUPF, its future success depends on transforming these planning frameworks into actionable, equitable, and citizen-responsive urban governance.

6.2 Kolkata Metropolitan Area (KMA)

6.2.1 Introduction

The Kolkata Metropolitan Area (KMA) is one of the oldest, most populous, and administratively complex urban regions in India. Situated along the eastern bank of the Hooghly River in West Bengal, it represents a rich blend of historical urbanism, industrial heritage, and postcolonial transformation. KMA spans approximately 1,886.67 square kilometres and includes 3 municipal corporations, 38 municipalities, and 77 non-municipal urban centres (KMDA 2005). The region is managed by the Kolkata Metropolitan Development Authority (KMDA), which serves as the apex planning body under the aegis of the Government of West Bengal.

As per the 2011 Census, KMA had a population of 14.1 million, making it the third-largest metropolitan region in India. The Vision 2025 document projected this figure to grow to nearly 20 million by 2025, with increased pressure on core infrastructure, housing, and transport systems (KMDA 2005). Unlike newer metropolitan areas, Kolkata's evolution has been shaped by its colonial past, port-based economy, and industrial corridors stretching along the Hooghly River. The spatial development of the region has been historically influenced by the availability of rail and river-based transportation, and more recently by peri-urban expansion driven by real estate and population pressure (Banerjee 2018).

The governance of KMA is layered and fragmented. While KMDA provides planning support and project implementation oversight, municipal corporations and municipalities retain control over many service delivery functions. The Land Use and Development Control Plan (LUDCP), prepared and periodically revised under the West Bengal Town and Country Planning Act of 1979, provides zoning and development control guidelines. However, coordination between planning and executing agencies remains a challenge, particularly when implementing projects that span multiple jurisdictions or require inter-agency cooperation.

Kolkata's economic identity has shifted over time from being an industrial stronghold to a more service-oriented metropolis, with increasing investments in information technology, trade, education, and finance. However, aging infrastructure, waterlogging, congestion, and environmental degradation continue to hinder urban performance. Patterns of informal growth, especially in fringe zones such as Rajarhat, Baruipur, and Bhangar, reflect the challenges of regulating peri-urban expansion (Majumdar & Sivaramakrishnan 2020).

The following sections explore the city's development through the ten key functional areas of the **National Urban Policy Framework (NUPF)**, assessing how KMA aligns with the framework's fourteen core principles. The evaluation draws upon statutory planning documents, satellite-based growth studies, and policy reviews to present a comprehensive picture of metropolitan dynamics in eastern India's largest urban region.

6.2.2 Alignment with NUPF Principles: Functional Area–Wise Analysis

The Kolkata Metropolitan Area exhibits a complex urban morphology shaped by historical trade patterns, industrial expansion, and more recent peri-urban growth. The following analysis evaluates KMA's performance across the ten functional areas defined in the National Urban Policy Framework (NUPF), assessing their alignment with NUPF's fourteen core principles such as inclusivity, sustainability, integrated planning, and resilience.

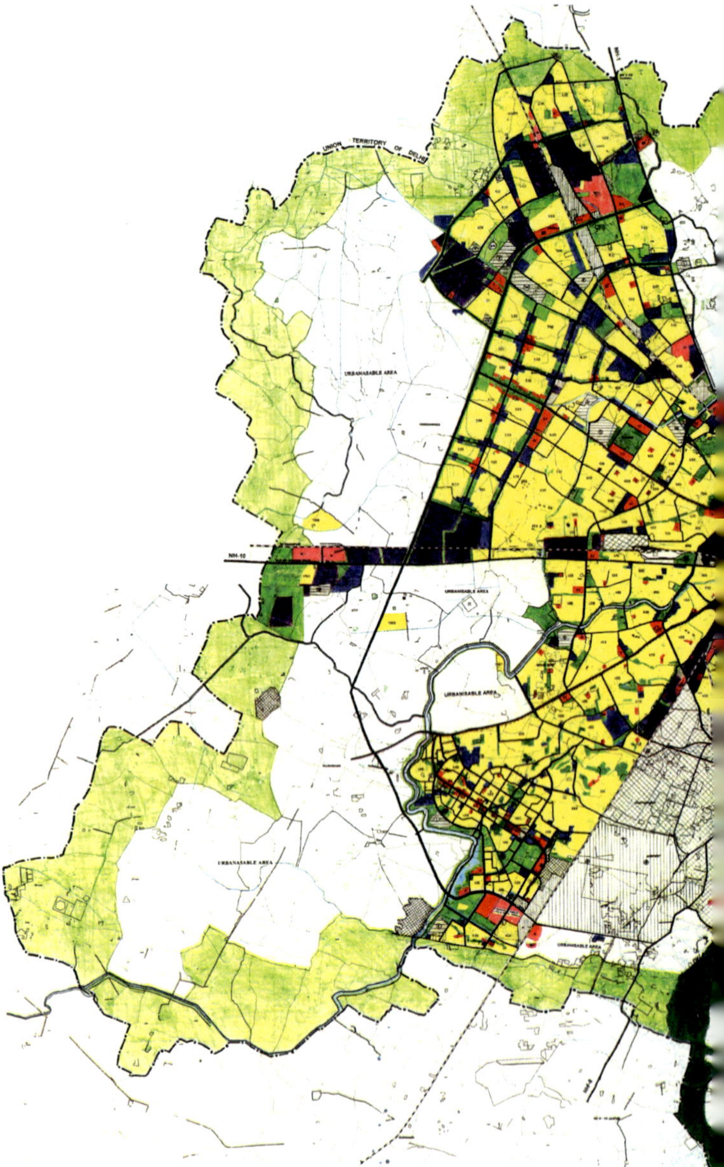

MASTER PLAN FOR

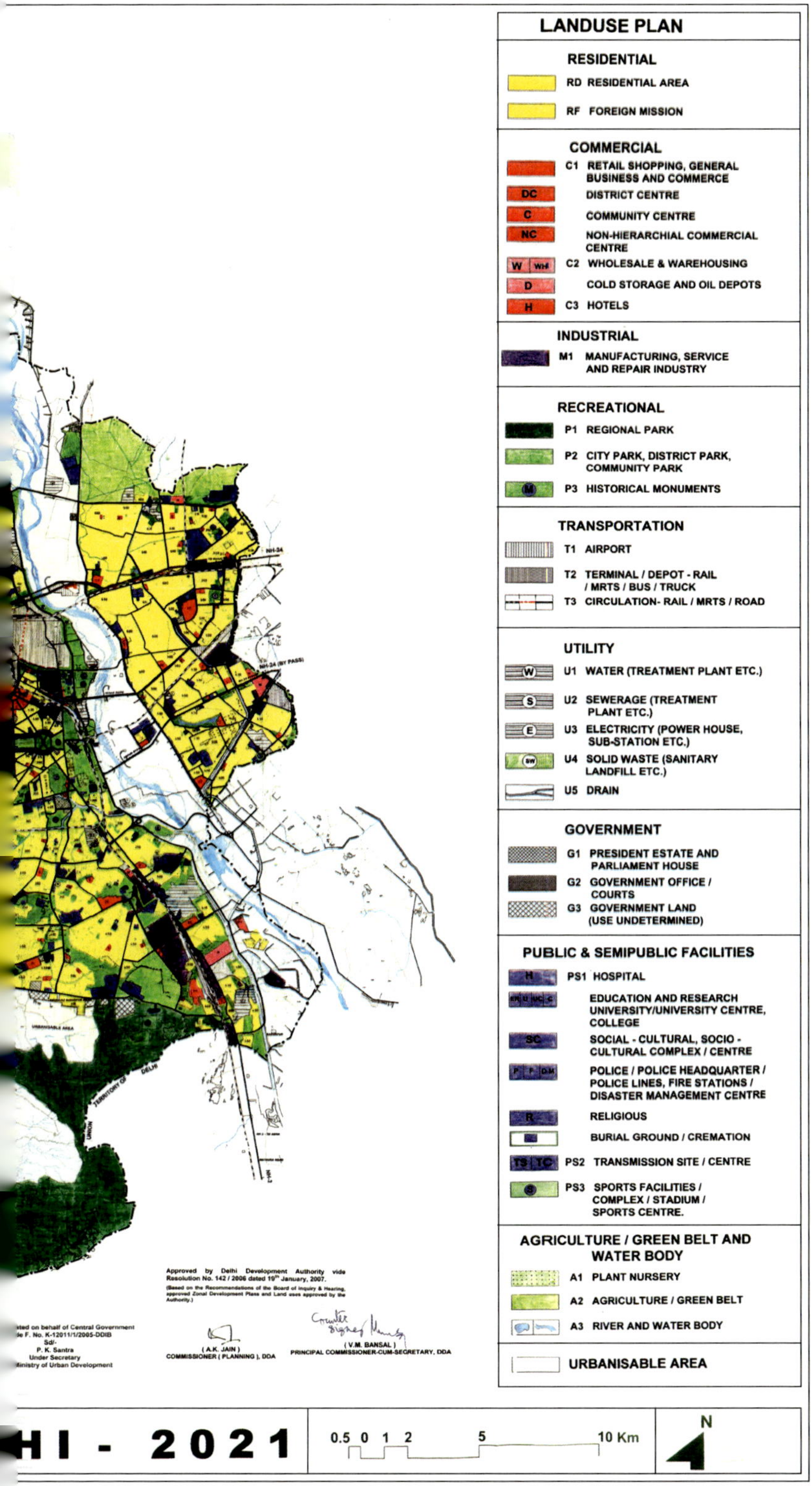
LANDUSE PLAN
RESIDENTIAL
RD RESIDENTIAL AREA
RF FOREIGN MISSION
COMMERCIAL
C1 RETAIL SHOPPING, GENERAL BUSINESS AND COMMERCE
DC DISTRICT CENTRE
C COMMUNITY CENTRE
NC NON-HIERARCHIAL COMMERCIAL CENTRE
W WH C2 WHOLESALE & WAREHOUSING
D COLD STORAGE AND OIL DEPOTS
H C3 HOTELS
INDUSTRIAL
M1 MANUFACTURING, SERVICE AND REPAIR INDUSTRY
RECREATIONAL
P1 REGIONAL PARK
P2 CITY PARK, DISTRICT PARK, COMMUNITY PARK
M P3 HISTORICAL MONUMENTS
TRANSPORTATION
T1 AIRPORT
T2 TERMINAL / DEPOT - RAIL / MRTS / BUS / TRUCK
T3 CIRCULATION- RAIL / MRTS / ROAD
UTILITY
W U1 WATER (TREATMENT PLANT ETC.)
S U2 SEWERAGE (TREATMENT PLANT ETC.)
E U3 ELECTRICITY (POWER HOUSE, SUB-STATION ETC.)
SW U4 SOLID WASTE (SANITARY LANDFILL ETC.)
U5 DRAIN
GOVERNMENT
G1 PRESIDENT ESTATE AND PARLIAMENT HOUSE
G2 GOVERNMENT OFFICE / COURTS
G3 GOVERNMENT LAND (USE UNDETERMINED)
PUBLIC & SEMIPUBLIC FACILITIES
H PS1 HOSPITAL
EDUCATION AND RESEARCH UNIVERSITY/UNIVERSITY CENTRE, COLLEGE
SC SOCIAL - CULTURAL, SOCIO - CULTURAL COMPLEX / CENTRE
POLICE / POLICE HEADQUARTER / POLICE LINES, FIRE STATIONS / DISASTER MANAGEMENT CENTRE
R RELIGIOUS
BURIAL GROUND / CREMATION
TS TC PS2 TRANSMISSION SITE / CENTRE
S PS3 SPORTS FACILITIES / COMPLEX / STADIUM / SPORTS CENTRE.
AGRICULTURE / GREEN BELT AND WATER BODY
A1 PLANT NURSERY
A2 AGRICULTURE / GREEN BELT
A3 RIVER AND WATER BODY
URBANISABLE AREA
NH-24
NH-24 (BY PASS)
UNION TERRITORY OF DELHI
NH-2
Approved by Delhi Development Authority vide Resolution No. 142 / 2006 dated 19th January, 2007.
(Based on the Recommendations of the Board of Inquiry & Hearing, approved Zonal Development Plans and Land uses approved by the Authority.)
...ted on behalf of Central Government
...de F. No. K-12011/1/2005-DDIB
Sd/-
P. K. Santra
Under Secretary
...inistry of Urban Development
(A.K. JAIN)
COMMISSIONER (PLANNING), DDA
Counter signed
(V.M. BANSAL)
PRINCIPAL COMMISSIONER-CUM-SECRETARY, DDA
...HI - 2021
0.5 0 1 2 5 10 Km
N

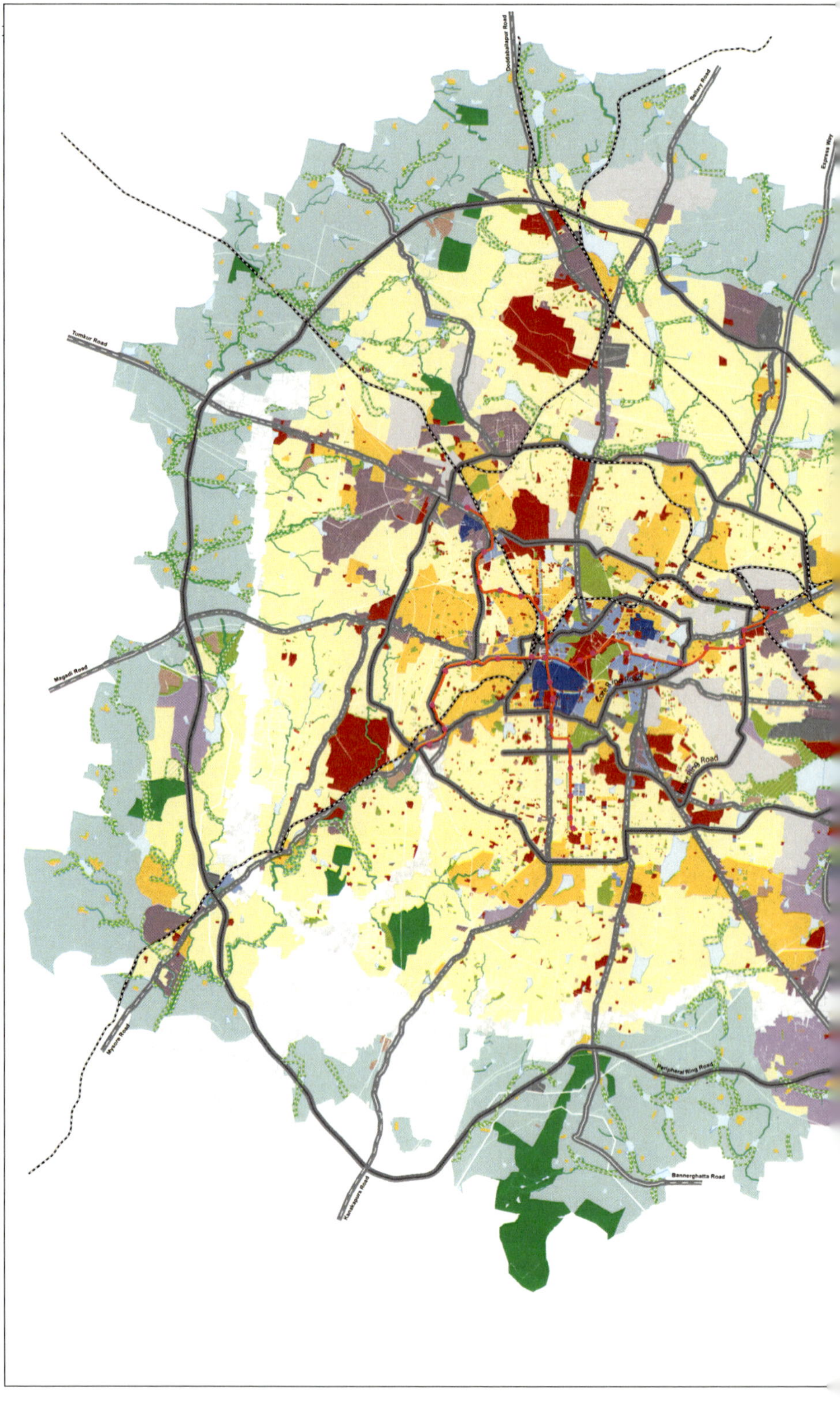

Doddaballapur Road
Bellary Road
Express Way
Tumkur Road
Magadi Road
Core Ring Road
Inner Ring Road
Mysore Road
Peripheral Ring Road
Kanakapura Road
Bannerghatta Road

BANGALORE
Revised Master Plan
2015
Proposed Land Use Map

Consolidated Map

ZONING CLASSIFICATION

MAIN ZONES

Residential
- Residential (Mixed)
- Residential (Main)

Commercial
- Commercial (Central)
- Commercial (Business)
- Mutation Corridor
- Commercial Axes

Industrial
- Industrial
- High Tech

Public and Semi-public
- Public / Semi-public

Green (Parks and Open spaces)
- State forest — *Protected land*
- Valley — *Protected land*
- Lake / tank — *Protected land*
- Parks and Green Spaces, Sport / Playgrounds, Cemeteries / Burial grounds

Traffic and Transportation
- Road / Rail / Airport Transport

Public Utilities
- Power / Water / Garbage Facility / Treatment Plant

Agricultural land

Unclassified use

Planning Perimeters
- Town Planning Scheme (TPS)
- Coordinated Planning Scheme (CPS)
- Area Improvement Perimeter
- Transport and Utilities Perimeter
- Heritage Conservation zone

CONSTRAINT AREA
- Non buildable: High Tension Line (HTL) Pipeline: Oil / Water
- Airport/Heights restrictions

OTHER INFORMATIONS

Proposed roads hierarchy
- Ring road
- Primary Urban road
- Major Urban road
- Minor Urban road
- (26) Proposed width of roads (in meters)
- Railway line
- Metro Alignment

Boundaries
- BDA LPA
- BMP Bangalore Mahanagara Palike
- LPA of BMICAPA
- village — Village
- 21 — Survey number

Hydrography
- Drain
- Sensitive Area

N

Meters
0 5,000 10,000

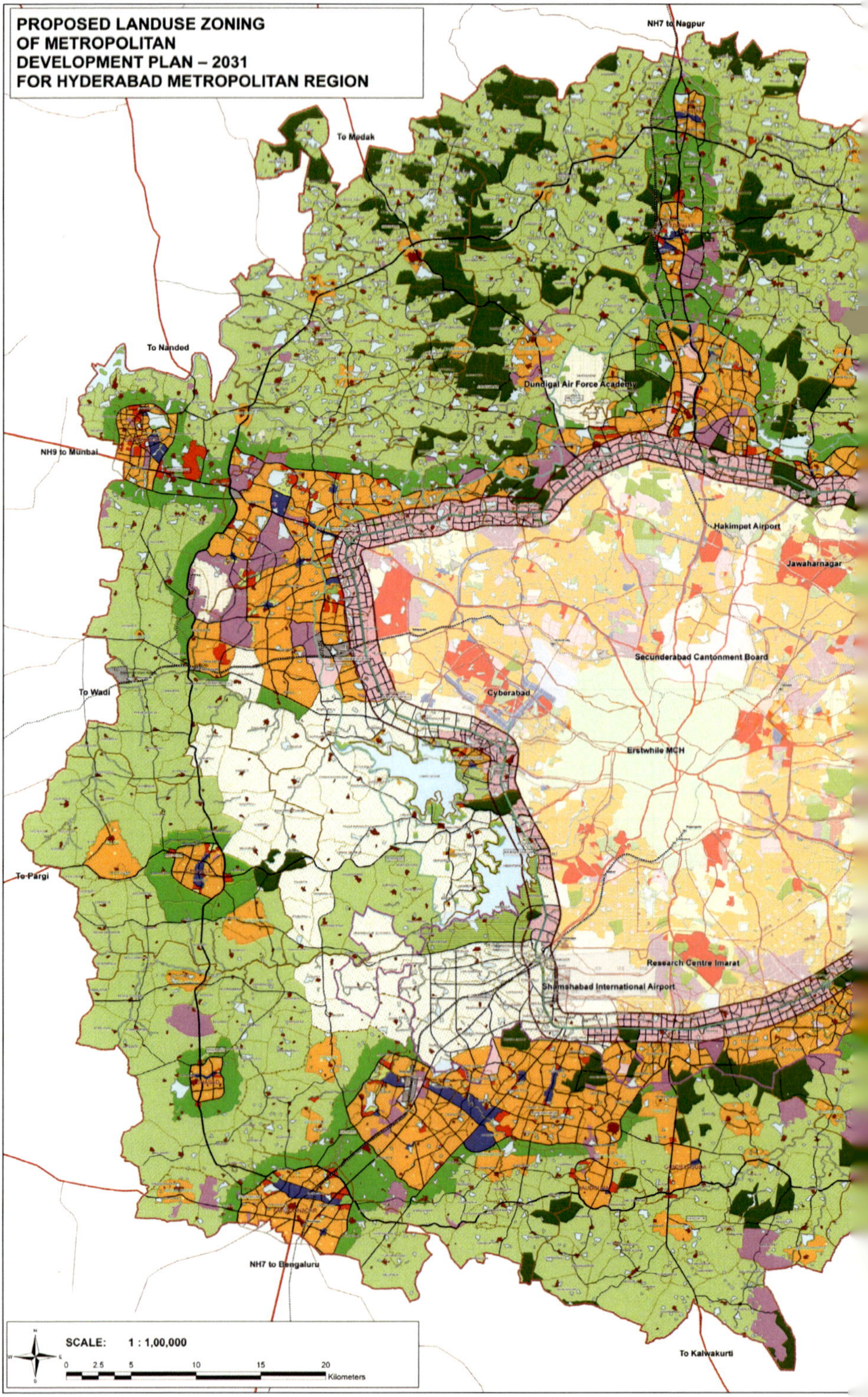
PROPOSED LANDUSE ZONING
OF METROPOLITAN
DEVELOPMENT PLAN – 2031
FOR HYDERABAD METROPOLITAN REGION
NH7 to Nagpur
To Medak
To Nanded
Dundigal Air Force Academy
NH9 to Mumbai
Hakimpet Airport
Jawaharnagar
Secunderabad Cantonment Board
To Wadi
Cyberabad
Erstwhile MCH
To Pargi
Research Centre Imarat
Shamshabad International Airport
NH7 to Bengaluru
SCALE: 1 : 1,00,000
0 2.5 5 10 15 20
Kilometers
To Kalwakurti

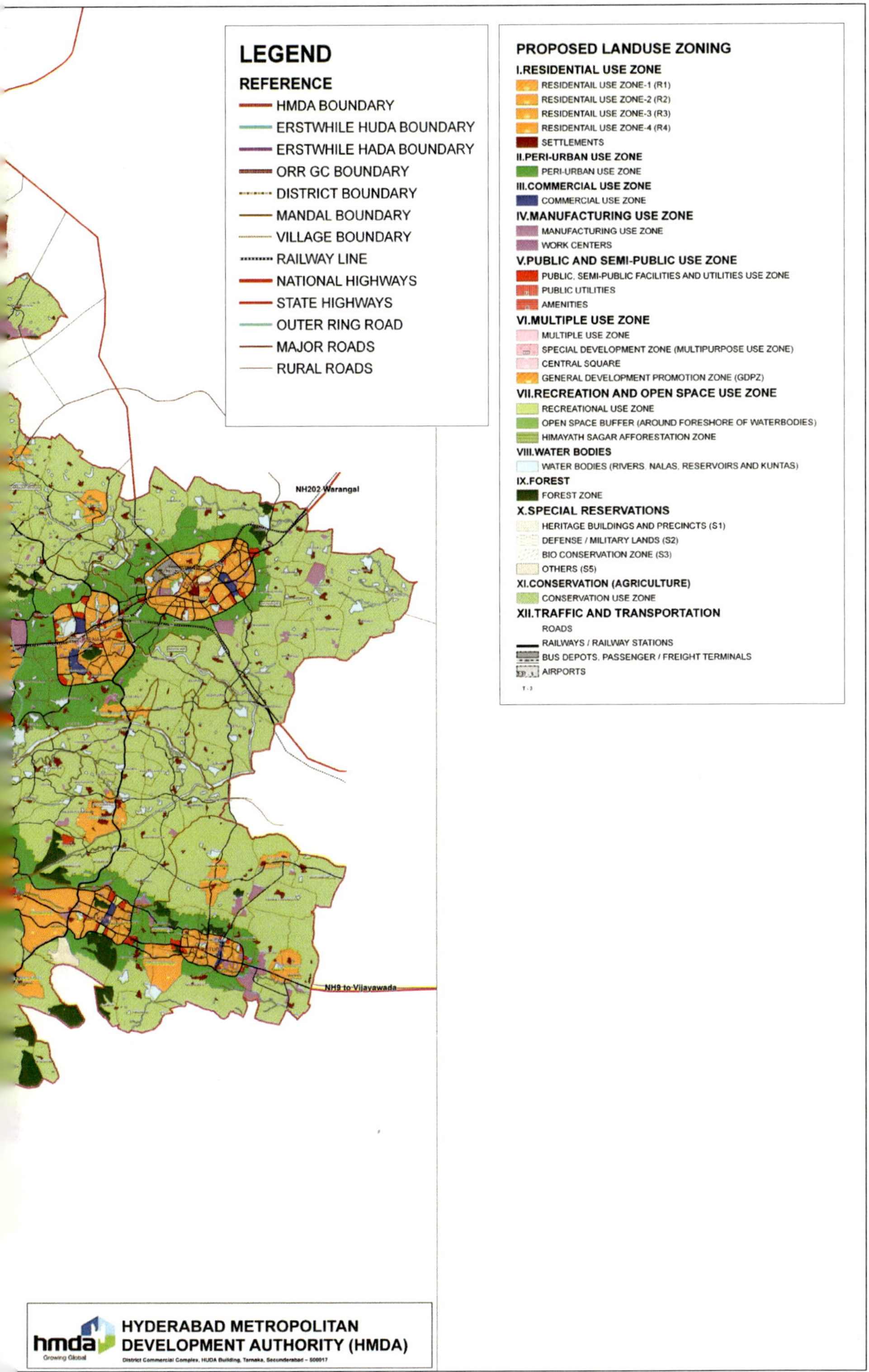
LEGEND
REFERENCE
HMDA BOUNDARY
ERSTWHILE HUDA BOUNDARY
ERSTWHILE HADA BOUNDARY
ORR GC BOUNDARY
DISTRICT BOUNDARY
MANDAL BOUNDARY
VILLAGE BOUNDARY
RAILWAY LINE
NATIONAL HIGHWAYS
STATE HIGHWAYS
OUTER RING ROAD
MAJOR ROADS
RURAL ROADS
PROPOSED LANDUSE ZONING
I.RESIDENTIAL USE ZONE
RESIDENTAIL USE ZONE-1 (R1)
RESIDENTAIL USE ZONE-2 (R2)
RESIDENTAIL USE ZONE-3 (R3)
RESIDENTAIL USE ZONE-4 (R4)
SETTLEMENTS
II.PERI-URBAN USE ZONE
PERI-URBAN USE ZONE
III.COMMERCIAL USE ZONE
COMMERCIAL USE ZONE
IV.MANUFACTURING USE ZONE
MANUFACTURING USE ZONE
WORK CENTERS
V.PUBLIC AND SEMI-PUBLIC USE ZONE
PUBLIC, SEMI-PUBLIC FACILITIES AND UTILITIES USE ZONE
PUBLIC UTILITIES
AMENITIES
VI.MULTIPLE USE ZONE
MULTIPLE USE ZONE
SPECIAL DEVELOPMENT ZONE (MULTIPURPOSE USE ZONE)
CENTRAL SQUARE
GENERAL DEVELOPMENT PROMOTION ZONE (GDPZ)
VII.RECREATION AND OPEN SPACE USE ZONE
RECREATIONAL USE ZONE
OPEN SPACE BUFFER (AROUND FORESHORE OF WATERBODIES)
HIMAYATH SAGAR AFFORESTATION ZONE
VIII.WATER BODIES
WATER BODIES (RIVERS, NALAS, RESERVOIRS AND KUNTAS)
IX.FOREST
FOREST ZONE
X.SPECIAL RESERVATIONS
HERITAGE BUILDINGS AND PRECINCTS (S1)
DEFENSE / MILITARY LANDS (S2)
BIO CONSERVATION ZONE (S3)
OTHERS (S5)
XI.CONSERVATION (AGRICULTURE)
CONSERVATION USE ZONE
XII.TRAFFIC AND TRANSPORTATION
ROADS
RAILWAYS / RAILWAY STATIONS
BUS DEPOTS, PASSENGER / FREIGHT TERMINALS
AIRPORTS
NH202 Warangal
NH9 to Vijayawada
hmda
Growing Global
HYDERABAD METROPOLITAN
DEVELOPMENT AUTHORITY (HMDA)
District Commercial Complex, HUDA Building, Tarnaka, Secunderabad – 500017

MAP OF KOLKATA METROPOLITAN AREA (KMA)

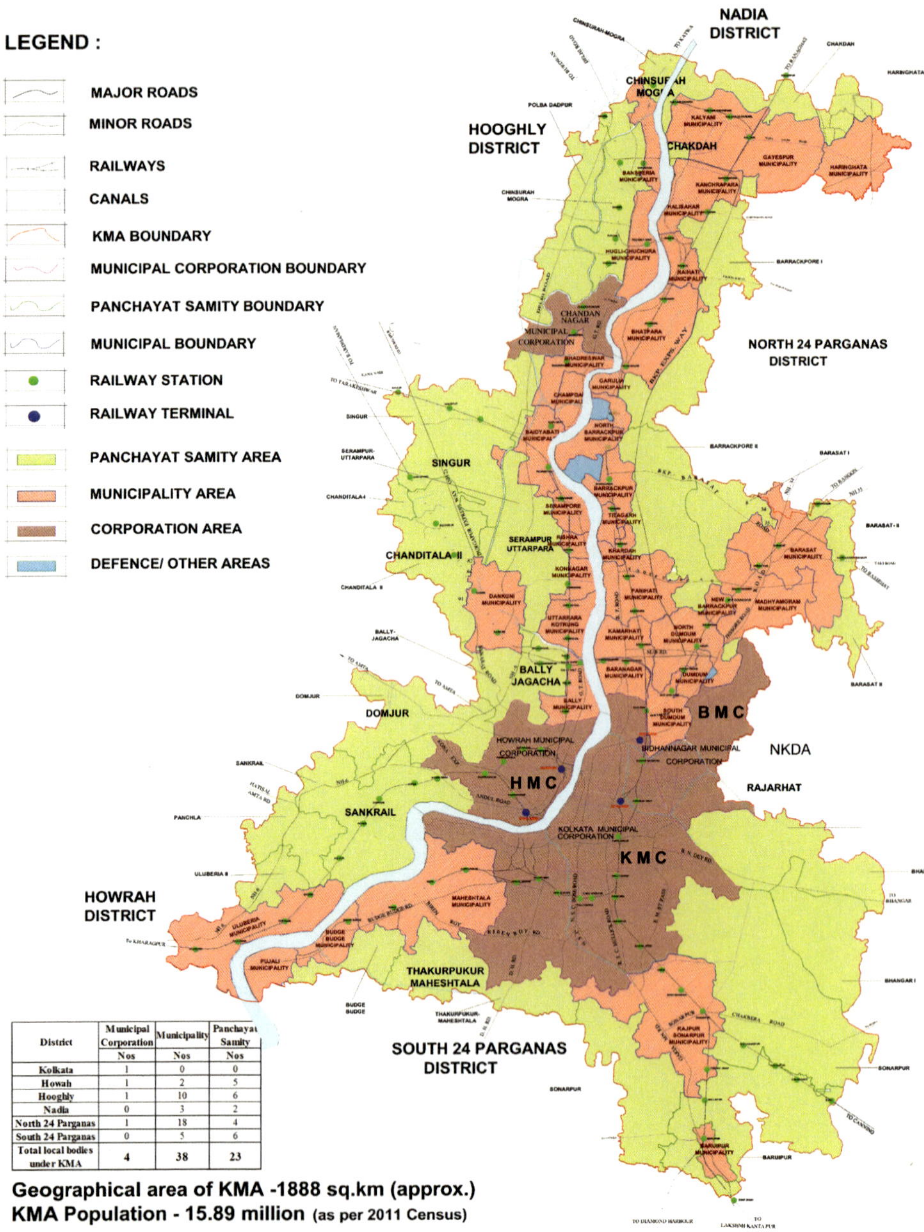

District	Municipal Corporation	Municipality	Panchayat Samity
	Nos	Nos	Nos
Kolkata	1	0	0
Howah	1	2	5
Hooghly	1	10	6
Nadia	0	3	2
North 24 Parganas	1	18	4
South 24 Parganas	0	5	6
Total local bodies under KMA	4	38	23

Geographical area of KMA -1888 sq.km (approx.)
KMA Population - 15.89 million (as per 2011 Census)

PLANNING DEPARTMENT
KOLKATA METROPOLITAN DEVELOPMENT AUTHORITY

0 1.5Km SCALE

6.2.2.1 *Urban Planning*

Urban planning in Kolkata has historically been grounded in colonial-era urban form and the subsequent industrial grid that expanded along the Hooghly River. The Perspective Plan 2025 (Vision 2025) prepared by the KMDA proposed decentralized growth, reinforcing polycentric development around sub-metropolitan centres like Barasat, Baruipur, Uluberia, and Kalyani (KMDA 2005). However, planning remains largely reactive rather than anticipatory, with informal settlements proliferating faster than serviced urban expansion.

The Land Use and Development Control Plan (LUDCP) provides statutory zoning and regulation for land use on the western bank of the Hooghly, aiming to preserve heritage, regulate densities, and improve environmental protection (KMDA 1998). While this plan reflects the NUPF principle of legal land governance and zoning clarity, it lacks dynamism in responding to changing urban patterns and emerging peri-urban realities. Furthermore, participatory planning remains limited, especially in municipal areas on the urban fringe (Banerjee 2018).

6.2.2.2 *Urban Economy*

Kolkata's economy is transitioning from its former industrial identity to a more diversified service-based model, encompassing finance, education, logistics, and information technology. The Vision 2025 document identifies economic clustering, urban logistics, and regional linkages as key drivers for future development (KMDA 2005). However, the shift has been uneven, with some municipalities like Howrah and Baranagar still heavily dependent on legacy manufacturing while newer zones like Rajarhat attract IT and commercial investment.

The informal economy plays a crucial role in Kolkata's livelihood structure, with high dependence on hawking, home-based production, and construction. Yet planning instruments do not adequately reflect the economic needs of these actors. NUPF's principles of equitability, people-centric development, and economic decentralization remain underrealized, particularly in terms of inclusive spatial integration of economic zones (Majumdar and Sivaramakrishnan 2020).

6.2.2.3 *Physical Infrastructure*

Basic infrastructure in KMA suffers from chronic deficits and uneven quality. Legacy water supply systems, outdated drainage, and low-capacity solid waste management continue to affect urban liveability, particularly in core municipalities. Though the Vision 2025 recommended integrated water and sanitation systems, progress has been fragmented and heavily dependent on state and central funding (KMDA 2005).

While newer township areas like Salt Lake and Rajarhat have better infrastructure, older parts of the city experience frequent waterlogging, waste overflow, and service discontinuities. This highlights a clear mismatch with NUPF's principles of end-result orientation and equitable service provision.

6.2.2.4 Social Infrastructure

Social infrastructure in KMA, including education, healthcare, and cultural institutions, is well-developed in the core metropolitan area but uneven in peripheral zones. Vision 2025 acknowledged these disparities and proposed a distributed model of health and education facilities, yet implementation remains patchy (KMDA 2005).

Heritage and cultural identity are central to Kolkata's urban fabric, with the LUDCP including guidelines for conservation and adaptive reuse of historic buildings (KMDA 1998). This partially reflects the NUPF principles of social inclusion and heritage-led urban regeneration. However, underfunded civic bodies and uneven demographic distribution continue to limit the reach of these services.

6.2.2.5 Housing and Affordability

Kolkata faces significant housing challenges in terms of both quantity and quality. A large share of the population resides in informal slums or unauthorized housing, especially along the railway corridors and canal banks. Vision 2025 proposed in-situ upgrading, EWS housing, and vertical redevelopment of low-income housing clusters (KMDA, 2005). Despite these strategies, there is little evidence of transformative progress in affordable housing delivery.

Informal housing dominates the urban fringe, where planning control is weakest. The city also lacks a formal rental housing framework, leaving migrant populations in precarious living conditions. This weakens alignment with NUPF principles of inclusivity, housing diversity, and integrated slum redevelopment (Banerjee 2018).

6.2.2.6 Transportation and Mobility

KMA has historically benefitted from rail and water-based transport connectivity. The Eastern Railway network and ferry services once formed the backbone of metropolitan mobility. Today, the metro network, suburban rail, and limited bus services continue to serve as key modes of transport, although capacity and coverage remain inadequate.

Vision 2025 proposed transit corridors, multi-modal hubs, and better bus rapid transit systems to promote public transport (KMDA 2005). While the city's street pattern limits large-scale interventions, the prioritization of metro expansion and TOD aligns well with the NUPF principles of compact urban form and sustainable mobility. However, non-motorized transport and last-mile connectivity remain underdeveloped (Majumdar and Sivaramakrishnan 2020).

6.2.2.7 Urban Finance

Municipal finance in KMA is a major constraint. Most municipalities face revenue deficits and rely heavily on state transfers. There is limited use of tools such as land value capture, PPPs, or monetization of public assets. Vision 2025 briefly mentions strengthening institutional capacity and fiscal reforms but lacks actionable financing strategies (KMDA 2005).

This highlights a weak alignment with the NUPF principles of commercial financing, fiscal sustainability, and financial decentralization. Without reforms in local taxation, budget management, and financial autonomy, municipalities will continue to struggle with infrastructure delivery and planning enforcement.

6.2.2.8 Urban Governance

The governance landscape in KMA involves overlapping jurisdictions across KMDA, municipal corporations, ULBs, parastatals, and state departments. KMDA functions as a planning and implementing agency but lacks enforcement power in several areas. This fragmented structure results in implementation delays, accountability gaps, and policy overlaps (KMDA 1998; Majumdar and Sivaramakrishnan 2020).

Despite the intention of integrated regional planning through Vision 2025, the lack of empowered metropolitan governance undermines the NUPF principle of collaborative and accountable governance. Inter-agency coordination remains minimal, particularly across the urban-rural continuum.

6.2.2.9 Environmental Sustainability

Kolkata faces environmental stress from air pollution, water contamination, loss of wetlands, and encroachments on floodplains. Vision 2025 highlights the importance of conserving the East Kolkata Wetlands and strengthening natural drainage systems (KMDA 2005). The LUDCP includes zoning for open spaces, water bodies, and green buffer zones (KMDA 1998).

Despite policy recognition, weak enforcement has led to widespread environmental degradation. Illegal construction, wetland infill, and insufficient sewage treatment continue to pose serious threats. This results in partial alignment with the NUPF principle of ecological resilience and urban sustainability.

6.2.2.10 Urban Information Systems

The use of GIS and spatial data is limited within municipal operations. Planning processes have yet to institutionalize robust information systems or real-time monitoring frameworks. While some municipalities have digitized land records or initiated grievance redressal portals, these are not uniformly implemented across KMA.

The absence of an integrated urban data system weakens the alignment with the NUPF's emphasis on data-driven governance and transparency. Vision 2025 called for the development of metropolitan-level information systems, but progress remains minimal (KMDA 2005).

6.2.3 Synthesis and Analysis

The Kolkata Metropolitan Area reflects the multidimensional realities of India's older metropolitan centres—marked by deep-rooted history, spatial complexity, and layered institutional arrangements. Across the ten functional areas of the NUPF, Kolkata's planning documents and policy directions display a broad conceptual awareness of national urban development goals. However, a closer assessment reveals a significant gap between planning intent and implementation effectiveness, particularly in outer municipalities and rapidly urbanising peri-urban areas.

The principle of integrated and balanced urban planning finds partial expression in the Vision 2025 document, which advocates a decentralized urban structure through hierarchical urban centres. Yet this vision has not been fully translated into spatial or governance outcomes. Much of the recent urban growth has occurred in an unregulated manner, especially in eastern and southern fringes like Rajarhat and Baruipur, leading to fragmented urbanization that undermines the compact, connected, and coordinated growth envisioned in the NUPF (KMDA 2005; Banerjee 2018).

Kolkata's economic base is transitioning, but the absence of planning tools that effectively integrate the informal sector into formal development processes limits the scope of equitable and inclusive growth. Livelihood support, especially for informal workers, remains marginal in mainstream planning documents, indicating only partial alignment with the NUPF's principles of demand-driven development and people-centricity (Majumdar and Sivaramakrishnan 2020).

Infrastructure systems across the KMA are marked by unequal coverage and dated technologies. While core urban areas benefit from older but functional water and sanitation systems, peripheral municipalities lag behind. Environmental sustainability remains a major area of concern, with the loss of wetlands and weak enforcement of conservation zones. The recognition of the East Kolkata Wetlands as a Ramsar site is symbolically important, but in practice, ecological zones face continued degradation. These trends suggest weak operational alignment with NUPF principles related to sustainability, resilience, and environmental justice.

Institutional fragmentation continues to be a fundamental barrier to the realization of cohesive planning outcomes. The KMDA, despite being the metropolitan planning authority, lacks adequate enforcement mechanisms across jurisdictions. Municipalities are under-capacitated, both financially and technically, and regional coordination between urban and rural areas remains weak. This structural disjuncture reduces the feasibility of collaborative governance and decentralized planning as advocated by the NUPF (KMDA 1998; Majumdar and Sivaramakrishnan 2020).

While Kolkata has a strong cultural identity and rich legacy in education and public health infrastructure, disparities in social and housing infrastructure across regions—especially between planned townships and informal settlements—pose continuing challenges. Vision 2025 promotes equitable distribution of services, but there is limited budgetary and administrative support to scale such provisions across the urban continuum.

Overall, the Kolkata Metropolitan Area shows partial alignment with the NUPF's core principles. While policy visioning documents capture the essence of integrated and sustainable metropolitan planning, weak institutional capacity, poor inter-agency coordination, and limited fiscal innovation remain key bottlenecks. Bridging this gap requires more than structural reforms; it calls for a shift in metropolitan governance culture—toward proactive coordination, community participation, and data-informed decision-making.

6.2.4 Conclusion

The Kolkata Metropolitan Area presents a compelling case of an older Indian metropolis grappling with the pressures of demographic growth, spatial expansion, and economic transformation, while navigating the legacies of industrialization and colonial urbanism. Although the region benefits from a well-defined statutory planning structure and a long-standing institutional body in the form of KMDA, the operationalization of metropolitan planning remains constrained by limited fiscal autonomy, institutional fragmentation, and uneven development patterns.

Documents like Vision 2025 and the Land Use and Development Control Plan (LUDCP) articulate a clear intent to decentralise growth, protect ecological assets, and promote equitable service delivery. However, these ambitions often remain aspirational due to weak implementation mechanisms, insufficient cross-jurisdictional coordination, and slow policy uptake in rapidly changing peri-urban zones.

While the metropolitan area aligns conceptually with several of the National Urban Policy Framework's core principles—such as sustainability, equity, and integrated planning—the practical decentralize of these principles is often hindered by capacity gaps at the municipal level, absence of reliable urban data systems, and low levels of community participation. In particular, the informal economy, housing insecurity, and fragile ecological zones remain areas where transformative planning interventions are urgently needed.

From a broader perspective, Kolkata's experience reinforces the need for large metropolitan regions to rethink governance models. Metropolitan planning must evolve to become more dynamic, adaptive, and participatory—particularly in cities with complex jurisdictional overlays and long-standing infrastructural deficits. The case of KMA also suggests that metropolitan policy instruments should be accompanied by robust monitoring frameworks, greater citizen engagement, and tailored fiscal tools to enable cities to realize their development visions.

Moving forward, key recommendations include the need to:

- Empower KMDA with stronger statutory authority and inter-agency coordination mandates;
- Institutionalize metropolitan-level fiscal tools such as land value capture and PPP models;
- Enhance participatory planning, particularly in fringe municipalities;
- Protect and restore ecological assets through enforceable zoning and green buffers;
- Strengthen urban data systems and integrate them into daily planning workflows.

As Kolkata continues to expand beyond its colonial grid into newer suburban and peri-urban territories, aligning its growth trajectory with the NUPF's principles will require sustained political commitment, administrative reform, and a renewed emphasis on inclusive, climate-resilient, and decentralized planning.

6.3 Bengaluru Metropolitan Area (BMA)

6.3.1 Introduction

The Bengaluru Metropolitan Area (BMA), anchored by Karnataka's capital city, is one of the fastest-growing metropolitan regions in India. Once recognised as a 'Garden City' and administrative centre, Bengaluru has transformed into India's leading technology and innovation hub, often referred to as the 'Silicon Valley of India'. With this transformation, the city has undergone rapid demographic expansion, spatial reconfiguration, and economic restructuring, making it a compelling case for metropolitan analysis through the lens of the National Urban Policy Framework (NUPF).

As of the 2011 Census, the Bangalore Urban District had a population of over 9.6 million, rising from just 380 thousand in 1901, indicating a nearly 25-fold increase in just over a century (Puttalingaiah, Irfan, and Hanjagi 2020). The region comprises a core urban agglomeration and a surrounding metropolitan spread encompassing satellite towns and peri-urban belts under the jurisdiction of the Bangalore Metropolitan Region Development Authority (BMRDA). The Revised Master Plan 2031 projects this number to cross 20 million by 2031, requiring robust infrastructure, housing, and environmental safeguards (BDA 2017).

The governance of the region is distributed between multiple institutions, including the Bruhat Bengaluru Mahanagara Palike (BBMP), Bangalore Development Authority (BDA), Bangalore Metropolitan Transport Corporation (BMTC), and BMRDA. While the BDA oversees statutory planning for the city core, the BMRDA governs the larger region extending into five districts. However, coordination among these bodies remains limited, often resulting in fragmented service delivery and overlapping mandates (Lakshmisha and Nagendra, 2025).

Bengaluru's economic transition from a government-driven administrative city to a global IT and startup capital has attracted large-scale in-migration, leading to sprawling development, gentrification, and growing strain on natural resources. The city's physical expansion into formerly rural hinterlands—particularly along Whitefield, Electronic City, and Tumakuru corridors—has created a dynamic yet uneven urban form that continues to challenge regulatory control and planning capacity.

The city's environmental assets, especially its interconnected lake systems, green zones, and ridge-valley terrain, are under severe pressure due to encroachments and unchecked construction. The failure to integrate ecological considerations into mainstream urban planning has contributed to issues such as flooding, groundwater depletion, and urban heat island effects, despite growing awareness of climate vulnerability (Sen and Nagendra 2021).

The following sections evaluate the Bengaluru Metropolitan Area across the ten functional areas outlined in the NUPF. These include urban planning, urban economy, infrastructure, mobility, housing, governance, finance, environment, social infrastructure, and urban data systems. Each area is critically examined to assess how closely BMA's policies and outcomes align with the fourteen core principles of the NUPF, such as sustainability, inclusivity, decentralization, innovation, and citizen-centric development.

6.3.2 Alignment with NUPF Principles: Functional Area–Wise Analysis

The Bengaluru Metropolitan Area (BMA) offers a unique case where globally competitive economic performance coexists with intense governance fragmentation and ecological stress. The following analysis explores the city's progress and limitations across the ten functional areas of the National Urban Policy Framework (NUPF), connecting each with the NUPF's fourteen core principles such as inclusivity, sustainability, innovation, adaptability, and decentralization.

6.3.2.1 Urban Planning

The city's planning framework is governed by the Revised Master Plan (RMP) 2031, which outlines a polycentric, TOD-based vision for a compact, liveable, and equitable Bengaluru. The plan proposes to reorganize growth along major transit corridors and arterial roads by designating multi-nodal economic and residential centres. It also advocates for a transition from conventional zone-based planning to mixed-use and dynamic land use policies that allow greater flexibility (BDA 2017).

This reflects conceptual alignment with NUPF's principles of integrated planning, flexibility, and anticipatory development. However, in practice, planning continues to be highly centralized, with minimal input from lower-tier municipalities or ward committees. Moreover, the absence of real-time urban observatories or local area plans weakens the responsiveness of planning mechanisms. Peri-urban areas beyond BBMP boundaries grow largely through layouts approved by gram panchayats, often without connection to trunk infrastructure or compliance with RMP norms (Puttalingaiah, Irfan, and Hanjagi 2020). This disconnect undermines spatial coherence and violates the NUPF principle of balanced urban-rural integration.

6.3.2.2 Urban Economy

Bengaluru's economy is characterized by a high concentration of IT, biotechnology, aerospace, and start-ups. It contributes approximately 38% of India's IT exports and ranks among the top innovation cities in Asia (Knight Frank 2020). RMP 2031 seeks to leverage this status by identifying economic corridors, formalising informal employment zones, and providing ecosystem support for micro-enterprises and skill development. It proposes clustering of knowledge industries near high-capacity transit routes, aligned with TOD and employment-housing balance models.

Despite this forward-looking vision, implementation remains uneven. The informal economy—which supports a substantial proportion of livelihoods—is poorly integrated into the spatial and infrastructure plans. Regulatory frameworks rarely accommodate hawkers, home-based workers, and service providers in land use classifications or commercial zones. This stands in contrast to NUPF's people-centric and demand-driven development principles, which encourage economic inclusion, multiple livelihood forms, and interdependency across formal and informal sectors.

6.3.2.3 Physical Infrastructure

The physical infrastructure network in Bengaluru is under significant strain. The city depends heavily on the Cauvery River, located over 100 km away, for its water supply, while peripheral areas lack piped coverage. Wastewater treatment coverage is below 50%, and solid waste management is uneven, especially in outer zones. RMP 2031 and the Urban Infrastructure Report (Knight Frank 2020) both recommend decentralized infrastructure models, improved integration of utilities, and compact urban form to reduce network costs.

The city has initiated pilot projects in waste-to-energy, decentralized sewage treatment, and rainwater harvesting. However, weak coordination between agencies such as BWSSB, BBMP, and BESCOM results in fragmented outcomes. This fragmentation contradicts the NUPF's vision of holistic, outcome-oriented infrastructure development. Moreover, capital investment remains disproportionately focused on core zones, neglecting peripheral and peri-urban communities, thereby creating service disparities.

6.3.2.4 Social Infrastructure

Bengaluru performs relatively well in tertiary education and private healthcare provisioning, but these are spatially and economically inaccessible for large sections of the population. Outer zones, including parts of Yelahanka, Kanakapura Road, and Sarjapur, face a shortage of public clinics, schools, and cultural amenities. RMP 2031 advocates for distributed infrastructure models, co-location of services, and child-friendly and elderly-friendly urban design (BDA 2017), reflecting NUPF's commitment to inclusive urban environments.

Nonetheless, underfunding and bureaucratic delays constrain infrastructure rollout, and most municipalities beyond BBMP jurisdiction lack institutional capacity to plan or maintain community-level amenities. This reinforces spatial inequality, with underserved areas continuing to depend on higher-order facilities located in central Bengaluru.

6.3.2.5 Housing and Affordability

Housing in Bengaluru is shaped by market-driven dynamics, with a growing mismatch between supply and demand. Rents and land prices in key corridors have risen sharply, pushing low-income groups to the urban periphery, often into informal settlements or gram panchayat-approved layouts lacking basic services. Slums continue to proliferate, especially along lake beds, railway corridors, and peripheral industrial zones.

RMP 2031 proposes in-situ rehabilitation, rental housing schemes, and vertical redevelopment through public-private partnerships. However, these mechanisms remain underutilized. Absence of a dedicated urban rental housing authority, limited land banks for social housing, and weak legal protections for tenants impede progress. This misalignment with NUPF's principle of affordable, tenure-diverse, and inclusive housing models exposes the systemic nature of the crisis.

6.3.2.6 *Transportation and Mobility*

Bengaluru's metro network is expanding rapidly, with Phase 2 and suburban rail projects under implementation. The city has also introduced electric buses, promoted shared mobility platforms, and proposed non-motorized transport corridors. RMP 2031 is structured around TOD, with land use incentives around metro stations and major intersections (BDA 2017).

However, the private vehicle population has grown to over 8 million, leading to severe congestion and pollution. Pedestrian infrastructure is inadequate, and public transport integration remains weak, particularly in last-mile connectivity and fare interoperability. Despite alignment with NUPF's sustainability and compact city principles in planning intent, behavioural shifts and infrastructure retrofitting have not kept pace with growth.

6.3.2.7 *Urban Finance*

The city faces significant fiscal limitations. BBMP's revenue base is narrow and underexploited, with property tax compliance still low and user charges not adjusted for service costs. Municipal bonds are not yet widely used, and land value capture tools—although identified in RMP 2031—lack operational frameworks (Knight Frank 2020).

Without robust local financial autonomy, Bengaluru's plans remain dependent on external grants and state-level schemes. This fails to meet NUPF's vision of commercial financing, fiscal decentralization, and empowered local governments. The absence of a dedicated city finance dashboard or performance-linked budgeting further constrains transparency and accountability.

6.3.2.8 *Urban Governance*

Urban governance in Bengaluru suffers from extreme fragmentation. Planning and implementation powers are split among BDA, BBMP, BMRDA, BMTC, BWSSB, and several state agencies. There is no empowered metropolitan authority to coordinate across jurisdictions. Even within BBMP, ward committees remain largely symbolic, lacking budgeting powers or planning responsibilities (Lakshmisha and Nagendra 2025).

This weakens NUPF's principles of decentralized, collaborative governance and participatory planning. Institutional silos prevent the city from adopting systems-thinking approaches to interconnected challenges such as land use, mobility, and environment.

6.3.2.9 *Environmental Sustainability*

Bengaluru's once-celebrated lake system—once numbering over 1,000 lakes—is now reduced to a few hundred, many of which are encroached, polluted, or fragmented. Studies have shown that urbanization has led to loss of commons, reduced groundwater recharge, and increased disaster risk in low-lying areas (Sen and Nagendra 2021). RMP 2031 proposes ecological corridors, green buffers, and stormwater networks, but enforcement is inconsistent.

The absence of clear jurisdictional authority over lakes, wetlands, and ridge-valley systems results in bureaucratic inertia. This dilutes the operationalization of NUPF's principles of resilience, climate sensitivity, and nature-based planning.

6.3.2.10 *Urban Information Systems*

Bengaluru has made strides in digital governance, with GIS-based land management, grievance redressal systems, and dashboards like the Bengaluru Smart City portal. RMP 2031 proposes an Urban Observatory, data-sharing protocols, and a unified spatial platform.

However, data systems remain siloed across departments. There is no consolidated metropolitan database accessible to citizens, planners, and researchers. The lack of open data policies and inter-departmental integration hinders NUPF's vision of transparent, data-driven, and adaptive urban management.

6.3.3 Synthesis and Analysis

The Bengaluru Metropolitan Area represents one of India's most dynamic yet conflicted examples of metropolitan development. It is a city of paradoxes: globally recognized for its innovation economy, yet chronically underprepared in terms of infrastructure, ecological resilience, and institutional coherence. The city's rapid transformation from a postcolonial administrative town to a sprawling tech metropolis has triggered a series of cascading challenges—ranging from spatial fragmentation and resource scarcity to governance breakdown and widening socio-economic disparities.

Across the ten functional areas of the NUPF, Bengaluru shows strong alignment in planning vision but considerably weaker alignment in execution and enforcement. Strategic frameworks like the Revised Master Plan 2031 and the Urban Infrastructure Report reflect high awareness of contemporary planning imperatives—compact city development, integrated transport systems, ecological sensitivity, and diversified housing models (BDA 2017; Knight Frank 2020). However, implementation is frequently undermined by jurisdictional fragmentation, delayed project delivery, and limited citizen engagement.

The city's economic profile strongly supports NUPF's principles of demand-driven and innovation-based urban growth. Bengaluru's rise as a global technology and start-up hub has spurred new employment models, investment flows, and infrastructure demand. However, the economic benefits are highly uneven, spatially and socially. The exclusion of informal sector actors from planning frameworks, combined with poor infrastructure in peripheral areas, has created pronounced spatial inequities in access to opportunity (Knight Frank 2020).

The most significant bottlenecks lie in governance and environmental sustainability. The multiplicity of urban institutions—with overlapping mandates and no metropolitan authority—renders coordination almost impossible, especially in cross-cutting areas like housing, infrastructure, and lake management (Lakshmisha and Nagendra 2025). Participatory governance mechanisms such as ward committees exist largely in name, with little actual devolution of power or decision-making capacity. This remains a major deviation from NUPF's principles of decentralized and accountable governance.

In environmental terms, the degradation of Bengaluru's historic lake systems and ridge-valley ecology is emblematic of systemic neglect. While statutory documents propose green corridors and lake rejuvenation, enforcement is weak, and encroachment continues. Studies show that these ecological losses disproportionately affect low-income and peri-urban communities, widening the resilience gap (Sen and Nagendra 2021).

The city has initiated a number of digital governance reforms and proposes to institutionalise an Urban Observatory in RMP 2031. These efforts are aligned with NUPF's emphasis on data-driven decision-making, but the lack of interoperable platforms and institutionalized open data policies restricts their transformative potential. Meanwhile, urban finance remains heavily dependent on grants and transfers, with weak local revenue generation and limited fiscal autonomy.

In sum, Bengaluru displays a modern, forward-looking urban vision that is largely in tune with the philosophical and structural orientation of the NUPF. However, the real challenge lies in institutionalising this vision within the day-to-day functioning of government departments, civil society, and markets. Without strong governance reforms, improved regulatory capacity, and a culture of inclusive urbanism, the city's trajectory may continue to reflect growth without resilience, innovation without inclusion, and planning without delivery.

6.3.4 Conclusion

The Bengaluru Metropolitan Area illustrates the complexities of managing rapid metropolitan growth in a post-liberalization Indian context. While the city has positioned itself as a national leader in technology and innovation, its planning and governance systems have struggled to keep pace with the scale and intensity of its transformation. The vision articulated in the Revised Master

Plan 2031 and supporting infrastructure reports demonstrates an encouraging alignment with the National Urban Policy Framework's (NUPF) emphasis on sustainability, integration, and adaptability. However, the translation of this vision into practice remains deeply constrained by fragmented governance, institutional inertia, and socio-ecological disparities.

Bengaluru's experience underscores the importance of integrating spatial planning with economic development, social inclusion, and environmental resilience. The city's current form reflects not only the dynamism of a globalising economy but also the uneven impacts of unregulated growth—manifested in informal housing, ecological degradation, and unequal infrastructure access across its expanding periphery. Despite proposals for Transit-Oriented Development, compact growth, and ecological buffers, enforcement and inter-agency coordination remain weak. This limits the transformative potential of planning interventions and reduces their alignment with NUPF's end-result orientation.

At the same time, Bengaluru's growing investment in metro systems, electric mobility, and digital governance tools shows potential for leading national experimentation in mobility, data systems, and climate-sensitive infrastructure. However, the full benefits of these innovations can only be realized through enhanced institutional capacity, decentralized decision-making, and stronger fiscal autonomy for urban local bodies.

The case of Bengaluru holds important lessons for India's other rapidly urbanising metropolitan regions. First, metropolitan planning must move beyond vision documents toward enforceable and regularly monitored action frameworks. Second, governance structures need to be rationalized—preferably through empowered metropolitan authorities—to enable cohesive planning across jurisdictional boundaries. Third, ecological systems must be treated as core urban infrastructure, deserving protection on par with mobility and housing networks.

As one of the most globally connected cities in India, Bengaluru is uniquely placed to pilot integrated, data-informed, and citizen-responsive metropolitan planning models. Realising this potential will require deliberate policy shifts, long-term institutional reform, and a strong commitment to the inclusive and sustainable principles of the NUPF.

6.4 Hyderabad Metropolitan Area (HMA)

6.4.1 Introduction

The Hyderabad Metropolitan Area (HMA), the capital region of Telangana, is one of India's fastest-growing and most strategically significant metropolitan zones. It combines historical legacy, economic ambition, and demographic dynamism within a rapidly urbanising landscape. Spread over 7,257 square kilometres and encompassing 70 mandals across five districts, the region is governed by the Hyderabad Metropolitan Development Authority (HMDA), established under the HMDA Act of 2008. The city's core, Greater Hyderabad Municipal Corporation (GHMC), forms the primary urban agglomeration, while satellite towns and peripheral municipalities anchor the metropolitan fringes.

As per Census 2011, the GHMC had a population of approximately 6.8 million, while the broader HMA was estimated to have over 7.7 million. The Metropolitan Development Plan 2031 (MDP 2031) projects this number to cross 12.5 million by 2031, driven by economic growth, regional migration, and an expanding real estate market (HMDA, 2013). The city's post-liberalization transformation—accelerated by the growth of IT/ITES sectors, infrastructure investments, and policy incentives—has led to widespread urban expansion, redefined spatial dynamics, and an evolving socio-economic fabric (Hussain, 2024).

Hyderabad holds considerable geostrategic significance as a central node in southern India, with national and international connectivity via road, rail, and air. Its economic geography has been shaped by planned industrial corridors, the development of HITEC City and Gachibowli, and the expansion of knowledge-based and pharmaceutical industries. While it ranks among the top five Indian cities in terms of GDP contribution, the city is also home to a large informal workforce, complex land tenures, and a deep-rooted history of spatial inequality.

Institutionally, Hyderabad is administered through a relatively centralized framework. The HMDA functions as the apex planning and coordination body for the metropolitan region, while GHMC governs municipal-level services. However, multiple agencies—including the Telangana State Industrial Infrastructure Corporation (TSIIC), Hyderabad Growth Corridor Ltd. (HGCL), Hyderabad Road Development Corporation Ltd. (HRDCL), and various Special Purpose Vehicles (SPVs)—oversee infrastructure, transport, and housing projects. This has led to overlapping responsibilities, fragmentation in decision-making, and occasional implementation bottlenecks.

The city's historical development has transitioned through distinct phases—from the Qutb Shahi and Asaf Jahi dynasties, through British-era dual administration (Hyderabad and Secunderabad), to post-independence planned growth under state-led industrialization and recent private sector-driven real estate expansion. The growth corridors along the Outer Ring Road (ORR), Hyderabad-Warangal highway, and Shamshabad Airport zone exemplify the city's evolving polycentricity and expansion beyond traditional municipal boundaries (Neelima, Reddy, and Siddhartha 2021).

Environmental and social pressures, however, are mounting. The region's lake systems and green belts are increasingly under threat from encroachment and pollution. Informal settlements continue to grow, especially in peri-urban areas with limited service provisioning. The MDP 2031 acknowledges these challenges and proposes a multi-nodal, environmentally sensitive, and infrastructure-led urban model—but realising this vision requires stronger coordination, governance reforms, and community participation.

The following sections evaluate Hyderabad's development through the ten functional areas outlined in the National Urban Policy Framework (NUPF). Using planning documents, zoning regulations, and academic analyses, each functional area is assessed in terms of its alignment with the NUPF's fourteen core principles—including integration, sustainability, inclusivity, and decentralization.

6.4.2 Alignment with NUPF Principles: Functional Area–Wise Analysis

The Hyderabad Metropolitan Area's urban transition has been shaped by a confluence of economic ambition, infrastructure-led planning, and evolving land dynamics. This section examines Hyderabad's alignment with the ten functional areas outlined in the National Urban Policy Framework (NUPF), assessing how closely each aligns with its core principles such as integration, inclusivity, resilience, decentralization, and end-result orientation.

6.4.2.1 Urban Planning

Urban planning in Hyderabad is anchored in the Metropolitan Development Plan 2031 (MDP 2031), prepared by the Hyderabad Metropolitan Development Authority (HMDA). The plan adopts a multi-nodal urban structure, distributing growth across identified urban nodes, investment corridors, and satellite townships (HMDA, 2013). It integrates growth management strategies with transport, green zones, and zoning guidelines, representing strong conceptual alignment with NUPF's principles of compact, connected, and coordinated development.

The plan also establishes land-use zoning for the entire 7,257 sq. km metropolitan region, including Residential Use Zones (RUZ), Urban Use Zones (UUZ), Conservation Zones, and Special Development Zones. However, implementation challenges persist due to overlapping jurisdictions and rapid, market-driven real estate development—particularly along the Outer Ring Road and Shamshabad corridors (Neelima, Reddy, and Siddhartha 2021). Participatory mechanisms are limited, and spatial governance remains largely centralized.

6.4.2.2 *Urban Economy*

Hyderabad's economic growth has been driven by its IT/ITES, biotechnology, pharma, and logistics sectors. The city has emerged as a major economic node, attracting both domestic and global investment. MDP 2031 identifies strategic economic corridors and special development zones (such as the IT corridor and Pharma City) as engines of employment and innovation (HMDA 2013).

The economy, however, remains spatially polarized. Peripheral areas lack economic infrastructure and employment hubs. Informal sector participation—comprising street vendors, daily-wage workers, and migrant labourers—is largely unaccounted for in planning frameworks, reflecting weak operational alignment with the NUPF principle of equity in economic participation (Hussain 2024). While the city performs well on demand-driven innovation, economic planning remains less inclusive.

6.4.2.3 *Physical Infrastructure*

Hyderabad's physical infrastructure network includes piped water supply, underground sewerage, and road-based mobility infrastructure in core areas. However, infrastructure coverage is inconsistent across urban and peri-urban zones. According to MDP 2031, service levels are high in GHMC limits but reduce significantly toward outer municipalities and village settlements (HMDA 2013).

Zoning regulations mandate infrastructure provisioning in all new layouts, and major corridors are supported by radial road expansion, stormwater management, and grid-based energy planning (HMDA 2010). However, infrastructure in informal settlements and unplanned colonies remains poor. End-result orientation, a core NUPF principle, is often undermined by weak coordination between agencies and service duplication.

6.4.2.4 *Social Infrastructure*

The provision of education, healthcare, and community services is concentrated in central urban zones. Satellite municipalities and peripheral gram panchayats have limited access to government-run social infrastructure, particularly in fast-developing areas like Ibrahimpatnam, Medchal, and Keesara (Neelima, Reddy, and Siddhartha 2021).

The zoning guidelines encourage multi-use community facilities and social infrastructure integration into layout designs, but implementation lags persist. Planning does not systematically address vulnerable groups, including women, children, the elderly, and informal workers. This reflects partial alignment with the NUPF's principles of inclusivity and accessibility.

6.4.2.5 Housing and Affordability

Hyderabad is known for relatively affordable housing compared to other Tier-1 metros. However, informal settlements and low-income housing continue to dominate in peri-urban belts and former rural areas. Unauthorized layouts and unregulated apartments are common in the south-west and north-eastern growth corridors.

MDP 2031 promotes in-situ slum redevelopment, affordable housing zones, and mixed-use residential layouts. However, formal rental housing remains underdeveloped, and many resettlement schemes lack livelihood access and service connections (Hussain 2024). Planning mechanisms are yet to institutionalize tenure diversity and support for marginal renters. While aligned in principle, NUPF's inclusive housing framework is not fully operationalized.

6.4.2.6 Transportation and Mobility

Hyderabad has made substantial investments in mass transit systems. The Hyderabad Metro Rail, Outer Ring Road (ORR), radial roads, and multi-level flyovers represent a comprehensive effort to build a multi-modal transport network. MDP 2031 encourages Transit-Oriented Development (TOD) along metro corridors and radial growth areas (HMDA 2013).

However, last-mile connectivity remains a major issue, particularly in low-income and peri-urban areas. The city lacks an integrated fare system across modes and has minimal infrastructure for non-motorized transport (NMT). Traffic congestion and rising vehicle ownership also undermine sustainability. While planning vision aligns well with NUPF's compact and sustainable mobility principles, behavioural and spatial transformation is still in process.

6.4.2.7 Urban Finance

Like most Indian metros, Hyderabad's urban finance system is dependent on state allocations, development charges, and limited property tax revenues. While Special Purpose Vehicles (SPVs) have been used for project financing, there is limited fiscal autonomy for urban local bodies (Neelima, Reddy, and Siddhartha 2021).

Land monetization, lease models, and infrastructure bonds remain underutilized. Although the city's economic base is strong, its municipal revenue mechanisms do not reflect the scale or complexity of its planning ambitions. The lack of performance-based budgeting and inter-agency fiscal integration remains a barrier to NUPF-aligned financial sustainability.

6.4.2.8 Urban Governance

The governance of HMA is institutionally complex. HMDA serves as the apex planning body, while GHMC is the largest urban local body responsible for service delivery. Multiple parastatal agencies such as TSIIC, HRDCL, and HGCL operate in the same jurisdiction, often without coordinated mandates (HMDA 2013).

Zoning enforcement is inconsistent, and inter-agency coordination remains weak. Participatory planning tools such as ward sabhas or decentralized consultations are rarely institutionalized. This indicates a structural misalignment with NUPF's principles of decentralized, accountable, and participatory metropolitan governance.

6.4.2.9 *Environmental Sustainability*

Hyderabad's environmental degradation has accelerated in recent years. The **loss of lake systems**, depletion of groundwater, and rising air pollution reflect poor ecological planning. The city's green buffers and conservation zones, although marked in the MDP 2031, are routinely encroached upon by real estate and infrastructure projects (Neelima, Reddy, and Siddhartha 2021).

Studies show significant biodiversity loss and urban heat island effects, particularly in the fast-urbanising western corridor. While policies for lake protection, afforestation, and stormwater management exist, enforcement mechanisms remain weak. This highlights partial alignment with NUPF's climate sensitivity, ecological resilience, and green urbanism principles.

6.4.2.10 *Urban Information Systems*

Hyderabad has initiated GIS-based land records, property tax systems, and limited digital service delivery platforms. The MDP 2031 proposes spatial data infrastructure, monitoring frameworks, and e-governance models. However, integration across departments is lacking, and data remains inaccessible to citizens and researchers (HMDA 2013).

Open data policies and real-time observatories are yet to be institutionalized. NUPF's vision of data-informed urban planning and transparent governance requires stronger regulatory and institutional backing in the Hyderabad context.

6.4.3 Synthesis and Analysis

The Hyderabad Metropolitan Area exemplifies the duality of India's urban development—where ambitious planning frameworks coexist with deeply embedded governance and implementation challenges. The city's transformation into a major economic and infrastructure hub reflects the strengths of a vision-driven approach, yet it also reveals the fragilities of planning systems that are institutionally fragmented and unevenly enforced.

Hyderabad's statutory planning framework, particularly the Metropolitan Development Plan 2031, demonstrates a strong alignment with several NUPF core principles, such as integrated urban planning, compact development, economic clustering, and transit-oriented growth. The emphasis on multi-nodal development, special economic zones, and infrastructure-led corridors signals an understanding of regional polycentricity and the need for coordinated growth (HMDA 2013).

However, this conceptual alignment is undercut by gaps in operationalization—particularly in terms of equity, decentralization, and citizen participation. The planning and economic logic of Hyderabad remains highly top-down and technocratic, often marginalising informal economies, peripheral settlements, and vulnerable communities. For example, while land use zoning exists across the metropolitan region, actual enforcement remains limited in peri-urban belts where unauthorized layouts and unregulated housing continue to proliferate (Hussain 2024).

The city's economic success is concentrated in select corridors such as HITEC City and Gachibowli, while peripheral regions struggle with poor connectivity, inadequate social infrastructure, and weak economic integration. Informal sector participation in both housing and livelihoods is scarcely acknowledged in policy frameworks—revealing a disconnect between planning discourse and lived urban experience (Neelima, Reddy, and Siddhartha 2021).

Governance fragmentation is a significant challenge. While HMDA provides regional oversight, municipal bodies like GHMC, along with numerous parastatals and SPVs, operate with limited coordination. The absence of a unified metropolitan governance model weakens accountability and undermines cross-sectoral integration. Planning decisions often bypass local participation, and ward-level platforms remain largely symbolic. This contradicts the NUPF's emphasis on decentralized and participatory governance.

Environmentally, Hyderabad faces serious concerns. Lake shrinkage, groundwater depletion, and encroachments in conservation zones reflect the weak enforcement of ecological planning regulations. While MDP 2031 outlines green buffers and stormwater frameworks, these provisions have had limited success in curbing ecological degradation. This represents a major gap in the city's alignment with NUPF's resilience and climate-adaptive planning principles (Neelima, Reddy, and Siddhartha 2021).

Digital and data infrastructure in the city is emerging, but it lacks interoperability and citizen accessibility. Planning decisions are not systematically monitored through real-time dashboards or urban observatories. The absence of open urban data systems limits transparency and restricts evidence-based policymaking—undermining the NUPF's vision of data-driven governance.

Overall, Hyderabad demonstrates a strong metropolitan vision that is aspirationally aligned with the NUPF. However, the actual implementation of these principles remains uneven—shaped by governance fragmentation, informalization of growth, and weak accountability. Unless institutional coordination is strengthened, participatory mechanisms are embedded, and ecological and fiscal systems are reimagined as central to urban futures, the city risks replicating a model of growth that is economically successful but socially exclusionary and environmentally fragile.

6.4.4 Conclusion

The Hyderabad Metropolitan Area presents a complex and instructive example of metropolitan transition in contemporary India. On one hand, the city has emerged as a powerhouse of economic growth, infrastructural innovation, and regional connectivity. On the other, it remains constrained by institutional fragmentation, informal expansion, and increasing environmental vulnerabilities. The Metropolitan Development Plan 2031 articulates a forward-looking vision aligned with many core values of the National Urban Policy Framework (NUPF), including compactness, infrastructure-led growth, and polycentric development. However, the implementation of this vision remains uneven across spatial, institutional, and social dimensions.

Hyderabad's strengths lie in its long-term spatial planning frameworks, successful promotion of economic corridors, and large-scale investments in transit and housing. Yet, these gains have not been evenly distributed. Peri-urban areas suffer from inadequate infrastructure and services, while informal workers and settlements remain outside the ambit of formal planning. The absence of tenure security, regulatory clarity, and decentralized participation mechanisms impedes the inclusive urban transformation envisioned by the NUPF.

The city's governance model—dominated by a powerful development authority and multiple parastatals—has enabled large-scale infrastructural development but weakened community engagement and downward accountability. While planning documents emphasize environmental sensitivity and resilience, enforcement is often weak, and ecological degradation continues, particularly in terms of lake systems, green buffers, and open spaces.

Hyderabad's case underscores the urgent need for metropolitan areas to move beyond blueprint planning and embrace more adaptive, participatory, and inclusive approaches. The following recommendations emerge from the analysis of the Hyderabad Metropolitan Area. First, there is a critical need for institutional coordination through the establishment of a unified metropolitan governance mechanism or an empowered coordination body that can align planning, finance, infrastructure, and service delivery across multiple agencies. Second, participatory planning must be embedded within local governance by institutionalising ward-level frameworks, especially in municipalities and peri-urban areas, to enhance responsiveness and strengthen the social legitimacy of planning processes. Third, ensuring affordable and inclusive housing should be prioritization by focusing on tenure regularization, development of rental housing models, and implementation of mixed-income redevelopment strategies, particularly for informal settlements and migrant populations. Fourth, ecological protection must be treated as core infrastructure—recognising lakes, green buffers, and stormwater systems as vital urban assets—by strengthening enforcement mechanisms, updating ecological data systems, and adopting nature-based solutions in design and planning. Finally, data and monitoring systems should be institutionalized through the creation of metropolitan-level data observatories that enable real-time monitoring of land use and infrastructure while promoting open-access data to support transparency, innovation, and evidence-based urban governance.

As Hyderabad continues its transformation into a global urban node, aligning its spatial, ecological, economic, and governance strategies with the NUPF's holistic vision will be crucial—not only for the city's resilience and inclusivity but also as a model for emerging metros across India.

6.5 Conclusion

The case studies of Delhi, Kolkata, Bengaluru, and Hyderabad offer a rich and multidimensional understanding of the complexities, innovations, and contradictions inherent in metropolitan planning in India. Each of these cities, while unique in its historical evolution, spatial structure, and institutional architecture, faces a common set of challenges that reflect the broader urban transition underway across the country. Through the lens of the National Urban Policy Framework (NUPF), these case studies reveal both the strengths of statutory planning visions and the operational gaps that persist in practice.

All four cities exhibit varying degrees of alignment with the NUPF's fourteen core principles and ten functional areas. Delhi has a well-structured planning architecture and a long tradition of statutory spatial regulation, yet its governance fragmentation and implementation delays limit inclusive urban outcomes. Kolkata demonstrates strong cultural and infrastructural legacies but continues to grapple with financial and administrative constraints that hinder policy delivery. Bengaluru presents a high-performing economy and advanced digital governance tools but is hindered by institutional fragmentation and environmental stress. Hyderabad reflects a vision-driven, infrastructure-led development model but faces exclusionary planning tendencies and ecological vulnerabilities in its peri-urban fringe.

Across these metropolitan regions, several common patterns emerge: the growing tension between centralized planning and the need for decentralized, participatory governance; the dominance of infrastructure-driven growth that often overlooks the informal sector; and the uneven spatial distribution of services and opportunities, particularly in peri-urban and informal settlements. Furthermore, environmental degradation, fiscal dependence, and data fragmentation are recurrent challenges that weaken the ability of these cities to fully realize the transformative intent of the NUPF.

While each metropolitan area has made efforts to integrate sustainability, economic dynamism, and connectivity into its planning framework, the implementation gap remains wide. Without strengthened institutional capacities, clearer jurisdictional coordination, and more inclusive planning mechanisms, the principles laid out in the NUPF risk remaining aspirational rather than actionable.

This chapter has laid the groundwork by presenting the functional profiles of four major Indian metropolitan areas and assessing their alignment with national policy visions. In the next chapter, a comparative analysis will be undertaken to critically evaluate how these cities differ in their approach to urban governance, economic planning, spatial development, social inclusion, and environmental sustainability. This comparison will help identify patterns, policy gaps, and opportunities for cross-learning among India's evolving metropolitan regions.

CHAPTER

7

Comparative Analysis and Way Forward

7.1 Introduction

India's metropolitan regions are growing at an unprecedented pace, generating new opportunities for innovation, investment, and global integration while simultaneously intensifying long-standing challenges related to housing, infrastructure, governance, and sustainability. In this context, understanding how different metropolitan areas are responding to these pressures—and how closely their strategies align with national policy objectives—becomes crucial. This chapter undertakes a comparative analysis of four major Indian metropolitan areas: Delhi, Kolkata, Bengaluru, and Hyderabad. These cities have been selected for their national importance, demographic and economic weight, spatial diversity, and representativeness of distinct regional and governance models.

The analysis draws upon the National Urban Policy Framework (NUPF), which provides a unified framework of 14 core principles and 10 functional areas for sustainable urbanization in India. Each city's development was earlier studied through these lenses, exploring dimensions such as urban planning, housing, transport, environment, finance, and governance. Now, by placing these cities side by side, this chapter aims to identify common trends, context-specific differences, and policy tensions that arise from the varied trajectories of metropolitan development.

This comparative perspective helps deepen our understanding of metropolitanization not just as a spatial or economic process, but as a multi-level governance challenge—involving decisions across institutions, jurisdictions, and scales. It highlights how cities that are aligned with the same national framework often diverge in their execution, outcomes, and innovations due to differences in institutional capacity, political will, geographic constraints, and socio-economic conditions.

Beyond summarising city-specific insights, this chapter also sets the stage for broader policy reflections and reform pathways, which are explored in the next chapter. By critically examining how Delhi, Kolkata, Bengaluru, and Hyderabad perform across key functional areas, we seek to draw out actionable lessons and cross-learnings for India's evolving metropolitan future.

7.2 Cross-City Comparative Analysis by Functional Area

This section presents a comparative evaluation of how Delhi, Kolkata, Bengaluru, and Hyderabad perform across the ten functional areas identified by the National Urban Policy Framework (NUPF). Each subsection critically examines similarities, differences, and patterns across cities, based on the planning visions, governance capacities, spatial development approaches, and institutional practices observed in their respective case studies. The analysis not only reveals city-specific challenges and innovations but also highlights the uneven implementation of NUPF principles across India's leading metropolitan regions.

7.2.1 Urban Planning

Urban planning lies at the core of metropolitan development, providing the spatial and regulatory framework within which infrastructure, housing, and economic activities evolve. Across all four cities, statutory master plans exist—Delhi's Master Plan 2041, Kolkata's Vision 2025 and LUDCP, Bengaluru's RMP 2031, and Hyderabad's MDP 2031—each outlining structured visions of growth and land use. In theory, all four reflect core NUPF principles of integrated, compact, and future-ready planning. However, the degree of implementation, participatory engagement, and institutional coherence varies significantly.

Delhi has a robust tradition of master planning, with statutory approval under the Delhi Development Act and planning anchored by the Delhi Development Authority (DDA). The Master Plan 2041 focuses on sustainability, mixed land use, and participatory development. Yet, actual spatial growth often bypasses plan guidelines, especially in peri-urban and unauthorized areas, where implementation gaps persist due to governance fragmentation.

Kolkata, through the KMDA's Perspective Plan 2025 and LUDCP, presents a decentralized urban vision. However, outdated land use data, weak enforcement, and overlapping jurisdictional control have limited its planning effectiveness. The core city remains congested, while the peri-urban fringe experiences unregulated sprawl. Planning is often reactive, with limited integration of informality or environmental concerns.

Bengaluru's Revised Master Plan 2031 demonstrates a more contemporary planning approach—focusing on Transit-Oriented Development (TOD), economic clustering, and integration with infrastructure planning. Yet, the absence of coordination between BDA, BBMP, and BMRDA weakens planning coherence. Peri-urban growth often occurs outside the zoning framework, and Local Area Planning remains underdeveloped.

Hyderabad's MDP 2031 takes an infrastructure-led, corridor-based approach, emphasising satellite towns, investment zones, and multi-nodal urban growth. The HMDA provides metropolitan-level coordination, offering a relatively unified planning structure. However, the city's planning remains top-down and technocratic, with weak engagement of local communities and informal sector realities.

In all four cities, participatory planning, plan enforcement, and peri-urban regulation remain critical challenges. The integration of informal settlements, ecological zones, and dynamic land markets into formal planning processes is still evolving. While statutory documents often echo NUPF's planning principles, the translation of these frameworks into on-ground spatial equity and coherence is partial at best.

7.2.2 Urban Economy

The economic profile of India's metropolitan regions varies widely, shaped by their historic specializations, state policies, land market dynamics, and levels of infrastructure investment. Under the NUPF, urban economies are expected to be demand-driven, employment-intensive, and inclusive, enabling both formal and informal actors to thrive. While all four metropolitan areas—Delhi, Kolkata, Bengaluru, and Hyderabad—play vital roles in their respective state and national economies, they exhibit distinct trajectories in economic diversification, spatial integration, and support for marginalized livelihoods.

Delhi's economy is marked by a combination of governance and administrative functions, service industries, and a thriving informal sector. As India's capital, it attracts a vast migrant workforce and offers significant employment across formal and informal domains. However, its master planning framework has historically under-recognized the informal economy, limiting the spatial inclusion of vendors, unorganised service providers, and micro-enterprises in zoning and economic strategies. The NCR regionalization model attempts to distribute economic activities, but gaps remain in integrating employment zones with housing and transport planning.

Kolkata, once a leading industrial centre, has undergone de-industrialization and now relies heavily on the service sector, small-scale industries, logistics, and informal employment. While Vision 2025 identifies economic clusters, the plan does not clearly define land allocations for diverse employment typologies, especially those in the unorganized sector. Much of the city's economy remains concentrated in congested core areas with limited economic diversification, and economic planning has not kept pace with demographic and spatial changes.

Bengaluru represents the most dynamic of the four economies. It is India's technology capital, with major IT, biotech, aerospace, and startup ecosystems. The Revised Master Plan 2031 incorporates land use policies supporting commercial corridors, innovation hubs, and economic clustering near transport nodes. However, this growth is spatially skewed, concentrated in the east and southeast, and the city struggles to integrate its large informal workforce into mainstream planning. Informal vendors and service workers often operate on the margins of the formal economy, with minimal planning support or legal protections.

Hyderabad's economy has followed a corridor-based development strategy, with special economic zones, knowledge corridors, and strategic investments in IT, pharma, and logistics. The MDP 2031 identifies employment zones, infrastructure support, and economic nodes beyond the core urban area. While this infrastructure-driven model has attracted substantial private investment, it has also led to the marginalization of traditional economies and a growing disconnect between employment hubs and low-income housing. The informal sector remains spatially excluded from economic planning.

Across all four cities, the integration of economic planning with land use, support for informal livelihoods, and regional economic linkages remain underdeveloped. While formal sector growth is encouraged, informal economies continue to operate outside the planning regime. The NUPF's vision of a people-centric, inclusive, and productivity-oriented urban economy is acknowledged in principle but only partially realized in practice.

7.2.3 Physical Infrastructure

Physical infrastructure is fundamental to the realization of spatial equity, resilience, and outcome-oriented development—core principles emphasized by the National Urban Policy Framework (NUPF). While Delhi, Kolkata, Bengaluru, and Hyderabad have all invested significantly in expanding their infrastructure networks, gaps in coverage, decentralized provisioning, and service integration remain persistent challenges. Each metropolitan region shows uneven infrastructure access, particularly in peripheral areas and informal settlements, where infrastructure provisioning often lags behind population growth.

In Delhi, physical infrastructure systems such as water supply, sanitation, electricity, and roads are relatively well developed in core urban zones. However, the outer areas of the National Capital Region, especially in parts of Uttar Pradesh and Haryana, exhibit significant disparities. The multiplicity of providers and regulatory bodies—such as the Delhi Jal Board, multiple municipal corporations, and the NCR Planning Board—complicates integrated infrastructure planning. Though the Master Plan 2041 articulates infrastructure goals aligned with end-result orientation and sustainability, fragmented implementation remains a bottleneck.

Kolkata's core infrastructure, such as water supply and underground sewerage, dates back to the colonial era and remains functional in older zones. Yet, the city struggles with service quality, low investment in peripheral towns, and infrastructure overuse in congested areas. The Planning Authority acknowledges the need for decentralized systems and integrated service networks, but weak municipal capacities and financial constraints limit scalability. Resilience in infrastructure—particularly flood preparedness, stormwater drainage, and solid waste management—remains limited, especially under high urban density pressures.

Bengaluru has made significant advances in digital infrastructure and decentralized energy solutions, but faces acute pressure on water supply, sewerage, and waste systems. The Revised Master Plan 2031 proposes integration of land use with infrastructure through corridor-based planning and calls for decentralized systems such as local wastewater treatment and rainwater harvesting. However, ground realities remain marked by fragmented governance, as BWSSB, BBMP, and parastatal bodies function with limited coordination. Infrastructure provisioning often follows rather than anticipates urban expansion, leading to outcome deficits contrary to NUPF's anticipatory governance principle.

Hyderabad's approach, as laid out in the Metropolitan Development Plan 2031, is strongly infrastructure-led. The city has invested in radial road networks, dedicated stormwater channels, and piped water coverage in growth corridors. While this supports the NUPF principle of compact and coordinated development, equitable infrastructure access across income groups and settlement types remains weak. Informal settlements and unplanned colonies, especially on the urban fringe, lack access to basic infrastructure. Moreover, service expansion has often prioritized large-scale private investment zones, raising concerns about spatial justice and inclusive development.

Across all four metropolitan regions, the NUPF's core infrastructure principles—especially universality, resilience, decentralization, and outcome orientation—are present in vision documents but inconsistently implemented. Infrastructure often follows land market expansion rather than guiding it, resulting in fragmented growth patterns and infrastructure stress. Future infrastructure strategies must address this disconnect by prioritising universal access, integrating service delivery, and adapting infrastructure to both climatic and demographic vulnerabilities.

7.2.4 Social Infrastructure

Social infrastructure—comprising education, healthcare, cultural facilities, recreational spaces, and community services—is a key enabler of inclusive, equitable, and people-centric urban development. The National Urban Policy Framework (NUPF) emphasizes the universality of access to social infrastructure as foundational to ensuring spatial justice, health equity, and human capital development. While the statutory plans in Delhi, Kolkata, Bengaluru, and Hyderabad recognize the importance of integrating social infrastructure into urban layouts, their actual provisioning and spatial distribution reveal persistent disparities across socio-economic and geographic lines.

In Delhi, the master plan envisions integrated neighbourhoods with embedded educational, healthcare, and recreational amenities. While core areas enjoy relatively good access, unauthorized colonies, slums, and peri-urban regions—especially in the outer districts—remain underserved. Despite policy frameworks promoting equitable provisioning, the delivery of public services continues to be fragmented across multiple urban local bodies and departments. Moreover, private healthcare and education have increasingly filled the gap, reducing affordability and accessibility for lower-income groups.

Kolkata's social infrastructure reflects its historical development pattern, with high concentrations of public facilities in the core city and a gradual thinning out toward the periphery. Legacy institutions like public hospitals and universities continue to serve large populations, but they are overburdened and unevenly distributed. The planning vision in Vision 2025 and LUDCP advocates for greater spatial decentralization of services, but implementation remains constrained by limited municipal capacities and declining public investment. The inability to fully deliver inclusive and accessible social infrastructure weakens the operationalization of the NUPF's principle of spatial equity.

In Bengaluru, the Revised Master Plan 2031 proposes a distributed social infrastructure model with an emphasis on local-level planning, urban health centres, and educational catchments. However, access to public services remains highly unequal. Affluent areas enjoy premium private facilities, while outer zones—particularly in the north and southwest—lack even basic public healthcare and schools. Despite the city's leadership in digital infrastructure, the provision of essential human development services has not kept pace with population growth. The gap between planning intent and service provisioning outcomes highlights limitations in achieving the NUPF's end-result orientation.

Hyderabad's planning framework acknowledges the need for co-located social amenities in new urban layouts and townships. The Metropolitan Development Plan 2031 includes standards for the spatial integration of educational, health, and community infrastructure. However, access to quality services in the urban periphery, where rapid expansion is occurring, remains limited. The emphasis on large-scale infrastructure corridors and economic zones has often overshadowed the prioritization of human-centred infrastructure. This undercuts the NUPF principles of people-centric development and inclusivity.

Across all four cities, there is a visible disconnect between statutory social infrastructure norms and ground realities, especially in fast-urbanising and informalized zones. Social infrastructure is still largely treated as an adjunct to physical planning rather than as a central driver of inclusive urbanization. A more proactive, decentralized, and participatory approach to provisioning is necessary to align with the NUPF's principles of universal access, spatial equity, and human-centric planning.

7.2.5 Housing and Affordability

Housing and affordability remain among the most pressing challenges in India's metropolitan regions. The National Urban Policy Framework (NUPF) places housing at the heart of its inclusive urban development agenda, emphasising affordability, diversity of tenure, in-situ rehabilitation, and integration of informal housing into formal planning systems. Despite these policy ideals, all four cities—Delhi, Kolkata, Bengaluru, and Hyderabad—exhibit deep housing inequalities, with a large segment of the urban population residing in slums, informal settlements, or insecure rental arrangements.

Delhi faces acute pressure on housing due to continuous in-migration, rising land prices, and limited availability of planned affordable housing. A substantial proportion of the population resides in unauthorized colonies, resettlement areas, and rental accommodations in congested neighbourhoods. While the Master Plan 2041 identifies in-situ upgradation, rental housing, and mixed-use models as core strategies, on-ground progress remains limited. Legal complexities around land tenure, coupled with overlapping governance structures, hinder large-scale implementation. The lack of a city-wide rental housing framework and the slow pace of regularization contradict the NUPF's goals of tenure diversity and housing equity.

Kolkata's housing scenario is shaped by its colonial legacy and post-independence rent control regime. While the city still offers relatively low rental costs in central areas, many structures are dilapidated and overcrowded. Informal housing dominates peri-urban regions, particularly in the east and south. Although Vision 2025 promotes public-private partnerships for affordable housing and slum redevelopment, the slow pace of implementation and weak institutional capacity have constrained impact. Most housing strategies remain focused on core zones, with minimal attention to growing informal clusters in fringe municipalities.

Bengaluru, despite being a high-growth city, exhibits a significant housing affordability gap. The real estate market is largely supply-driven, catering to the upper-middle class and IT professionals, while low-income groups are pushed to the periphery or into informal housing. The Revised Master Plan 2031 advocates for slum rehabilitation, vertical redevelopment, and inclusionary zoning, but these tools remain underutilized. Informal housing continues to expand in gram panchayat-approved layouts without basic services. The absence of regulatory frameworks for rental housing and inadequate integration of informal settlements into formal planning weakens the city's alignment with the NUPF's principles of inclusivity and spatial justice.

Hyderabad offers comparatively more affordable housing due to lower land values in several corridors, but affordability does not necessarily equate to habitability or tenure security. Large numbers of informal settlements exist in the periphery and near economic corridors, often in vulnerable ecological zones. While the Metropolitan Development Plan 2031 supports in-situ redevelopment and inclusionary approaches, housing remains mostly market-led. The informal sector's housing needs are largely unaddressed in formal policies, and there is minimal innovation in creating affordable rental options.

In all four cities, the housing market continues to be shaped by speculative real estate dynamics, regulatory rigidity, and limited public investment in affordable and rental housing. While planning documents increasingly reference in-situ redevelopment, tenure regularization, and inclusive housing, their institutionalization is slow and uneven. Achieving the NUPF's vision for housing will require cities to rethink land use strategies, integrate informality into the formal planning domain, and prioritize housing as both a spatial and social justice imperative.

7.2.6 Transportation and Mobility

Mobility is a defining aspect of metropolitan life, shaping access to employment, education, healthcare, and leisure. The National Urban Policy Framework (NUPF) promotes mobility systems that are compact, integrated, sustainable, and equitable—encouraging multimodal transit, last-mile connectivity, non-motorized transport, and transit-oriented development (TOD). The four cities under review—Delhi, Kolkata, Bengaluru, and Hyderabad—exhibit substantial investment in mobility infrastructure, yet continue to face critical challenges in terms of congestion, accessibility, affordability, and modal integration.

Delhi has one of the most extensive mass transit networks in India, led by the Delhi Metro, supplemented by buses, suburban rail, and a growing fleet of electric vehicles. The city has adopted the TOD policy to integrate land use and transit planning along metro corridors. However, congestion remains high due to rising private vehicle ownership and inadequate last-mile connectivity in many areas. Peripheral areas, especially those in adjoining NCR districts, have limited access to reliable and affordable public transport. Moreover, pedestrian and cycling infrastructure remains inadequate. While the city aligns well with NUPF's compact and connected development vision, its mobility system remains socio-spatially uneven.

Kolkata's public transport system is historically layered, with the metro, suburban rail, trams, buses, and ferries forming a multimodal network. The city's dense urban form and relatively low private vehicle ownership support walkability and transit use. However, ageing infrastructure, service quality issues, and limited expansion of metro lines restrict the system's effectiveness. Informal transport modes such as autos and shared taxis fill critical gaps but are not integrated into planning. Although the system conceptually supports the NUPF's sustainability principle, limited investment in infrastructure upgrades and poor connectivity in fringe areas restrict its inclusiveness.

Bengaluru faces some of the most severe traffic congestion among Indian metros. While the Namma Metro is expanding and plans for suburban rail are under way, public transport mode share remains low. The city has made efforts to promote electric buses and dedicated cycling lanes, but these are limited in scale. The Revised Master Plan 2031 envisions a TOD framework, yet car-centric growth patterns, dispersed employment nodes, and inadequate last-mile services hinder its implementation. Non-motorized transport remains marginalized in both infrastructure design and public investment. Thus, while planning documents align with the NUPF's multimodal and sustainable mobility goals, behavioural and infrastructural shifts remain insufficient.

Hyderabad has adopted a corridor-based infrastructure model, with radial roads, the Hyderabad Metro, and Bus Rapid Transit (BRT) plans playing central roles. The metro system has improved north-south connectivity, and the Outer Ring Road (ORR) facilitates inter-city and logistics movement. However, the system remains primarily designed for major investment zones and middle-class neighbourhoods, with informal and low-income areas often underserved. Last-mile connectivity is weak, and pedestrian infrastructure remains fragmented. The focus on infrastructure corridors, while aligned with compactness and connectivity, is not yet complemented by policies that promote universal access or transport equity.

Across all four cities, metropolitan mobility systems are in transition. While infrastructure-led planning has expanded networks and capacities, most cities have yet to fully operationalize the NUPF's vision of mobility that is universally accessible, environmentally sustainable, and spatially integrated. Informal transport modes, pedestrians, and cyclists remain marginal in planning priorities, and the integration of fare systems, service coordination, and data platforms is still evolving. Future mobility strategies must rebalance physical infrastructure expansion with inclusive, multimodal, and people-centric transport systems.

7.2.7 Urban Finance

Urban finance forms the backbone of metropolitan planning and service delivery. The National Urban Policy Framework (NUPF) stresses the need for financially empowered local bodies, diversified revenue streams, transparency in expenditure, and outcome-based budgeting. Despite the critical importance of financial sustainability in urban governance, Delhi, Kolkata, Bengaluru, and Hyderabad continue to rely heavily on intergovernmental transfers and face significant challenges in mobilising internal revenues, managing debt, and implementing innovative financial tools.

Delhi's municipal finances are characterized by high dependency on central and state government grants. The trifurcation of the erstwhile Municipal Corporation of Delhi (MCD) led to administrative and fiscal fragmentation, which was only recently reversed. Property tax remains a major revenue source but suffers from low compliance and outdated assessment systems. While the city has access to large-scale infrastructure funding, mechanisms such as land value capture, user charges, and municipal bonds are underutilized. The absence of unified financial planning across the National Capital Region weakens the city's alignment with NUPF's principles of decentralized and coordinated resource mobilization.

Kolkata exhibits a similar dependence on state transfers, with the Kolkata Municipal Corporation (KMC) generating limited own-source revenues. Although reforms in property taxation and e-governance have improved administrative efficiency, the city's ability to fund large-scale urban infrastructure remains constrained. Financial decentralization to municipalities in the metropolitan region is weak, and small ULBs often lack the capacity to prepare and execute budgets aligned with city plans. Fiscal frameworks remain input-oriented rather than linked to performance outcomes, which challenges the NUPF principle of end-result-oriented planning.

Bengaluru's financial ecosystem reflects both innovation and fragility. While BBMP collects substantial revenues from property tax and development charges, it continues to face a fiscal shortfall relative to its growing infrastructure needs. The city has explored tools such as premium FAR (Floor Area Ratio), impact fees, and land pooling, but their implementation remains ad hoc and poorly institutionalized. The Revised Master Plan 2031 includes proposals for land-based financing mechanisms, yet coordination among multiple parastatal agencies dilutes financial accountability. The lack of an integrated urban finance strategy undermines the potential for financially sustainable and performance-linked planning.

Hyderabad has experimented with innovative financing models such as development impact bonds, pooled infrastructure funds, and monetization of public lands. The Hyderabad Metropolitan Development Authority (HMDA) and Greater Hyderabad Municipal Corporation (GHMC) have mobilized significant capital for infrastructure projects through both grants and land sales. However, fiscal dependence on land monetization introduces long-term risk, particularly when land markets fluctuate. Moreover, the uneven fiscal capacity of municipalities in the outer periphery reflects a lack of spatial equity in resource distribution. Transparency in expenditure remains limited, with few participatory budgeting mechanisms.

Across all four metropolitan areas, core challenges include weak own-source revenue mobilization, limited fiscal autonomy at the local level, fragmented budgetary processes, and lack of financial accountability. The potential of financial tools such as land value capture, municipal bonds, and impact-based budgeting remains largely untapped or poorly operationalized. Strengthening urban finance requires institutionalising fiscal decentralization, building municipal financial management capacities, and aligning budgets with inclusive and transparent development outcomes as envisioned in the NUPF.

7.2.8 Urban Governance

Effective metropolitan governance is a prerequisite for achieving sustainable and inclusive urban development. The National Urban Policy Framework (NUPF) strongly emphasizes the principles of decentralization, citizen engagement, multi-level coordination, and accountable institutions. Despite the presence of multiple statutory bodies and governance reforms across Indian cities, Delhi, Kolkata, Bengaluru, and Hyderabad continue to face significant governance fragmentation, institutional overlaps, and weak community participation.

Delhi's governance structure is marked by a complex web of authorities, including the Delhi Development Authority (DDA), Municipal Corporation of Delhi (MCD), Delhi Jal Board, and various state and central government agencies. Jurisdictional overlaps and administrative duality between the Government of NCT Delhi and the Union Government lead to frequent coordination breakdowns, especially in infrastructure delivery, land management, and public services. Although ward committees and mohalla sabhas have been discussed in policy circles, participatory mechanisms remain largely non-functional. This weakens the operationalization of decentralized and citizen-centric governance as envisioned by the NUPF.

Kolkata presents a more historically rooted and unified urban governance system through the Kolkata Municipal Corporation (KMC), which oversees a large part of the core city. However, the surrounding municipalities in the Kolkata Metropolitan Area operate under separate jurisdictions, with limited integration and planning coordination through the Kolkata Metropolitan Development Authority (KMDA). While administrative clarity exists within KMC, fiscal and functional decentralization to boroughs and wards is limited. Public participation is constrained by the lack of formal platforms and capacity at the grassroots level, undermining accountability and transparency.

Bengaluru is governed by a fragmented institutional structure, with the Bruhat Bengaluru Mahanagara Palike (BBMP) managing municipal functions, while agencies like BDA, BWSSB, BESCOM, and BMRCL operate independently on core infrastructure and services. The Revised Master Plan 2031 acknowledges the need for coordinated governance but fails to propose a concrete framework for institutional integration. Ward committees exist in name, but their effectiveness is limited due to poor devolution of powers and budgetary control. This reflects a serious gap in aligning with NUPF's principle of collaborative and multi-level governance.

Hyderabad's planning and service delivery is largely centralized under the Greater Hyderabad Municipal Corporation (GHMC) and the Hyderabad Metropolitan Development Authority (HMDA). While this offers a certain level of planning coherence, it also reinforces a top-down governance model with limited space for participatory or bottom-up decision-making. The metropolitan region includes a vast number of peripheral municipalities and gram panchayats, most of which lack institutional capacity and voice in regional planning. Citizen engagement platforms are weak, and inter-departmental coordination is still driven by project-based rather than systemic frameworks.

Across the four cities, a common challenge is the disconnect between planning institutions and implementing agencies, resulting in governance that is fragmented, reactive, and often unaccountable. There is limited evidence of institutionalized participatory governance, despite constitutional mandates under the 74th Amendment.

7.2.9 Environmental Sustainability

Environmental sustainability is a critical dimension of metropolitan development, particularly as Indian cities grapple with rising pollution, resource depletion, and climate-related risks. The National Urban Policy Framework (NUPF) calls for integrating ecological considerations into the core of urban planning through principles such as climate sensitivity, ecological integrity, sustainability, and resilience. Despite these ideals, Delhi, Kolkata, Bengaluru, and Hyderabad face significant environmental challenges, and responses often remain fragmented or reactive.

Delhi continues to experience some of the worst air pollution levels globally, compounded by vehicular emissions, construction dust, seasonal crop burning in neighbouring states, and a lack of robust green buffers. The city's ridge ecosystems, Yamuna floodplains, and urban forests are under immense pressure due to encroachments and infrastructure expansion. Although Master Plan 2041 outlines riverfront revitalization, ridge protection, and increased green cover, actual implementation remains slow and inconsistent. The ecological health of Delhi reflects a deep misalignment with the NUPF principle of anticipatory and climate-resilient planning.

Kolkata is situated in a low-lying, flood-prone region with a sensitive estuarine ecosystem. Historically, the city benefitted from wetlands, canals, and green belts, but rapid urbanization has led to the encroachment and degradation of these ecological buffers. The East Kolkata Wetlands, a Ramsar site, are under increasing threat from informal housing and real estate speculation. Although the city's planning documents acknowledge environmental risks, institutional mechanisms for enforcement and community-led conservation are weak. This undermines the principles of environmental justice and sustainability central to the NUPF.

Bengaluru has faced drastic ecological transformation over the past three decades. Once known for its interconnected lake systems and green landscape, the city now struggles with lake pollution, wetland encroachment, and urban heat island effects. Fragmented jurisdiction over environmental assets—shared between BBMP, BDA, KSPCB, and other bodies—results in limited accountability for degradation. The Revised Master Plan 2031 proposes the restoration of ecological corridors and integration of stormwater management, but these remain largely aspirational. Resilience planning is not yet mainstreamed into infrastructure or land use strategies, despite clear vulnerabilities.

Hyderabad's environmental landscape has also experienced rapid degradation, particularly in terms of shrinking lakes, declining green cover, and increasing surface runoff in urbanising corridors. The city has invested in stormwater drains and afforestation drives, but enforcement of ecological zoning remains weak. The development of economic corridors and real estate zones around the Outer Ring Road has often come at the expense of natural ecosystems. The Metropolitan Development Plan 2031 includes conservation zones, but lacks robust monitoring and enforcement mechanisms. Climate-sensitive design and nature-based solutions are not yet institutionalized across departments.

A common trend across all four cities is the prioritization of physical infrastructure and economic growth over ecological protection. While planning frameworks increasingly reference sustainability, actual environmental governance remains fragmented, under-resourced, and poorly integrated with spatial and sectoral plans. The principles of resilience, ecological integrity, and anticipatory planning, although embedded in the NUPF, have not been effectively translated into enforceable urban strategies. Going forward, metropolitan areas must treat environmental assets as core infrastructure and institutionalize ecological planning at all levels of decision-making.

7.2.10 Urban Information Systems

Robust urban information systems are essential for transparent, efficient, and adaptive metropolitan governance. The National Urban Policy Framework (NUPF) recognizes the transformative potential of data in enabling anticipatory planning, real-time monitoring, and citizen engagement. It promotes principles such as transparency, interoperability, open access, and digital accountability. While digital governance initiatives have emerged across India's metros, the degree of system integration, data availability, and institutional usage remains highly uneven in Delhi, Kolkata, Bengaluru, and Hyderabad.

Delhi has made considerable progress in digitising land records, citizen services, and grievance redressal platforms across various departments. However, these systems often operate in silos, with limited interoperability between institutions like the DDA, MCD, DJB, and GNCTD departments. Real-time monitoring of urban services, environmental data, or infrastructure rollout is still fragmented. The Master Plan 2041 proposes an Urban Observatory and data-driven planning processes, but the absence of a unified metropolitan data platform limits decision-making and inter-agency coordination, impeding the NUPF vision of informed and transparent governance.

Kolkata has adopted e-governance modules for tax collection, trade licensing, and basic service delivery, especially within the Kolkata Municipal Corporation (KMC). However, data management remains largely static and administrative in nature. There is limited use of geospatial tools, predictive analytics, or open data platforms for planning or citizen engagement. Smaller municipalities in the Kolkata Metropolitan Area often lack technical infrastructure and skilled personnel to manage digital systems. As a result, the benefits of digital inclusion and data equity—central to NUPF's governance reform agenda—remain unrealized.

Bengaluru has made significant strides in digital infrastructure. The city uses GIS-based mapping for property taxation, layout approvals, and mobility planning. Several departments maintain dashboards for service delivery and environmental compliance. The Smart City initiative has contributed to a growing ecosystem of data tools. Yet, like Delhi, data remains fragmented across departments and parastatals. There is no single metropolitan-level platform that integrates land use, infrastructure, environment, and socio-economic indicators. Public access to data is still limited, constraining participatory planning and the NUPF principle of transparency.

Hyderabad has developed several smart city and e-governance initiatives, including online building approval systems, grievance portals, and spatial data layers within the planning authority. The Metropolitan Development Plan 2031 envisions digital integration for plan monitoring and compliance. However, urban data remains largely inaccessible to the public, and institutional capacity for using data in planning decisions is weak outside major agencies like HMDA and GHMC. Data use in peripheral municipalities is minimal, creating an imbalance in planning quality across the metropolitan region.

Across all four cities, there is growing awareness of the role of data in modern urban management. However, urban information systems continue to function in isolation, with limited interoperability, uneven access, and weak institutionalization. To realize the NUPF's vision, metropolitan regions must move toward integrated, real-time, and citizen-centric data ecosystems that inform planning, monitor outcomes, and empower communities.

7.3 Emerging Patterns and Policy Tensions

The comparative analysis of Delhi, Kolkata, Bengaluru, and Hyderabad reveals both recurring patterns and distinctive trajectories in the evolution of India's metropolitan regions. While all four cities exhibit formal alignment with the National Urban Policy Framework (NUPF) through master plans, infrastructure investments, and institutional reforms, their practical outcomes expose critical tensions between planning ideals and implementation realities. These tensions reflect a complex interplay of political economy, administrative structures, land dynamics, and capacity limitations that shape how NUPF principles are realized—or bypassed—on the ground.

A dominant pattern observed across cities is the widening gap between statutory planning and actual urban growth. All four metropolitan areas have adopted forward-looking plans that incorporate elements of compact development, transit-oriented growth, environmental sustainability, and economic clustering. However, informal settlements, unauthorized layouts, and peri-urban sprawl continue to expand beyond planned boundaries. This undermines the NUPF's emphasis on spatial coherence, resilience, and anticipatory governance, revealing a systemic inability to regulate land use in rapidly urbanising contexts.

Another shared feature is the persistence of fragmented governance, with overlapping jurisdictions, limited vertical and horizontal coordination, and weak decentralization. While each city has a planning authority and local

Table 7.1 Comparative Table of Four Metropolitan Areas

Aspect	*Delhi Metropolitan Area (DMA)*	*Kolkata Metropolitan Area (KMA)*	*Bengaluru Metropolitan Area (BMA)*	*Hyderabad Metropolitan Area (HMA)*
Metropolitan Establishment	Union Territory since 1956; NCR designated in 1985.	KMDA established in 1980 as a metropolitan area.	BDA formed in 1976; metro area recognized in 1980s.	HMDA established in 2008 for metropolitan development.
Geographical Scope	Includes NCT Delhi + parts of Haryana, UP, Rajasthan (1,484 km^2).	Covers Kolkata + surrounding municipalities (1,851 km^2).	Bengaluru + adjoining regions in Karnataka (8,005 km^2).	Covers Hyderabad + 37 municipalities (7,257 km^2).
Population (2021)	Approx. 70 million (NCR region).	Approx. 15 million.	Approx. 12 million.	Approx. 10 million.
Urban Planning Authority	Delhi Development Authority (DDA).	Kolkata Metropolitan Development Authority (KMDA).	Bangalore Development Authority (BDA).	Hyderabad Metropolitan Development Authority (HMDA).
Master Plan History	Multiple plans since 1962; latest: MPD-2021.	Master Plan 2009–2021 revised for sustainability.	Revised Master Plan (2015) promoting integrated development.	Master Plan 2016 focused on sustainable growth.
Transport Infrastructure	Extensive metro, yet severe congestion.	Congested roads; limited metro.	Efficient metro; still suffers traffic congestion.	Expanding metro; traffic still a concern.
Housing	Severe shortage; large slum population.	Slum housing and old infrastructure challenges.	High real estate prices; low-income housing shortage.	Demand in middle-class & informal housing; slum redevelopment ongoing.
Environmental Challenges	Severe air & water pollution, water scarcity, green cover loss.	Poor drainage, flooding, air/water pollution.	Water scarcity, pollution, deforestation, heat island effect.	Lake loss, pollution, rapid urbanization.
Social Infrastructure	Unequal access; core areas better served.	Gaps in education and healthcare infrastructure.	Well-developed but under pressure from rapid growth.	Unequal peripheral access; expanding facilities.

Contd.

Table 7.1 *Contd.*

Aspect	*Delhi Metropolitan Area (DMA)*	*Kolkata Metropolitan Area (KMA)*	*Bengaluru Metropolitan Area (BMA)*	*Hyderabad Metropolitan Area (HMA)*
Governance Structure	Complex: Central + State + Local bodies.	Fragmented between state and municipal agencies.	BBMP + BMRC; overlapping roles create delays.	Coordinated by HMDA; low public participation.
Economic Focus	Trade, commerce, services, IT, and government.	Port trade, jute industry, IT, financial services.	IT, startups, manufacturing hub.	IT, pharma, biotech.
Urban Expansion	Rapid expansion in NCR; unregulated peri-urban growth.	Urban sprawl stressing services and infrastructure.	Rapid urbanization encroaching green areas.	IT parks driving peripheral growth and sprawl.
Key Challenges	Overcrowding, pollution, governance gaps, sprawl.	Flooding, outdated infrastructure, inequality.	Traffic congestion, water issues, ecological degradation.	Sprawl, infrastructure stress, social inequality.
Innovative/Smart Policies	Green Delhi App, Smart City initiatives, urban greening.	Smart City mobility and heritage initiatives.	Namma Metro, Smart City plans for urban sustainability.	Tech-driven Smart City projects.
Sustainability Initiatives	Urban greening, waste management, air quality focus.	Flood resilience, transport improvements.	EV promotion, urban forestry, water conservation.	Lake restoration, green space development.
NUPF Alignment Priorities	Compact growth, air quality, streamlined governance.	Resilient infrastructure, flood control, affordable housing.	Green infra, sustainable mobility, housing for all.	Controlling sprawl, lake restoration, inclusive housing.

Source: Analysis

governance institutions, effective decision-making often remains centralized or distributed among multiple parastatals without a unified metropolitan platform. Participatory governance mechanisms—though constitutionally mandated—are inconsistently implemented or non-functional. This erodes the NUPF's core commitment to transparency, accountability, and citizen-centric urban development.

Despite economic diversification in all four metros, there is a lack of integration between economic planning and social equity. Formal planning continues to prioritize elite-driven sectors such as IT, finance, and real estate, while informal economies, low-income workers, and traditional livelihoods remain excluded from spatial and economic strategies. Housing and service provisioning for migrant workers, renters, and the urban poor remain peripheral concerns, reflecting a disconnect from NUPF's principles of inclusivity and people-centric development.

Environmental degradation is another common concern. Lake systems, green buffers, wetlands, and ridge ecosystems are under consistent threat across cities. While ecological protection features in statutory documents, actual governance remains weak, enforcement fragmented, and ecological systems treated as expendable rather than integral to the urban fabric. This stands in contrast to NUPF's ecological integrity and sustainability goals.

The emergence of infrastructure-led, corridor-based development models in cities like Hyderabad and Bengaluru, and to a lesser extent in Delhi and Kolkata, points to a policy tension between market-driven growth and inclusive urbanization. These models prioritize capital-intensive infrastructure projects, often oriented toward private investment and middle-class consumption. While they align with NUPF's emphasis on connectivity and compactness, they also risk bypassing vulnerable populations and peripheral areas, leading to spatial inequality.

Finally, across all four cities, urban data systems remain fragmented, non-interoperable, and inaccessible to the public. Despite the rise of e-governance and smart city initiatives, metropolitan regions have yet to institutionalize open data platforms, performance dashboards, or integrated observatories. This limits real-time monitoring, evidence-based planning, and civic empowerment, thereby constraining the NUPF principle of informed and adaptive governance.

Taken together, these emerging patterns underscore the need for India's metropolitan regions to evolve beyond static planning documents and adopt institutional cultures that are responsive, inclusive, and systems-oriented. The next section reflects on how closely these patterns align—or diverge—from the NUPF's vision, and what this means for urban policy at large.

7.4 Reflections on NUPF Alignment

The National Urban Policy Framework (NUPF) lays out a progressive and holistic vision for India's urban future, grounded in 14 core principles that advocate for inclusive, compact, resilient, transparent, participatory, and sustainable development. Through the lens of this framework, the comparative analysis of Delhi, Kolkata, Bengaluru, and Hyderabad reveals that while the cities have adopted the language and logic of the NUPF within their statutory plans and policy statements, the practical application of these principles remains inconsistent, fragmented, and often aspirational.

Across all four cities, the principle of compact and connected urban form is reflected in visions of transit-oriented development, mixed-use corridors, and polycentric growth. However, real estate market forces, weak enforcement mechanisms, and land-use informality dilute these spatial intentions. Urban expansion often occurs in a dispersed and unregulated fashion, particularly in peri-urban zones, leading to the opposite of the compact, service-efficient, and infrastructure-aligned urbanism that the NUPF promotes.

The principle of inclusivity finds widespread acknowledgement in planning documents, particularly in terms of housing, service delivery, and access to public infrastructure. Yet, implementation remains limited in scope and scale. Informal workers, tenants, migrants, and slum dwellers continue to live on the margins of formal urban systems, with inadequate recognition in zoning frameworks, economic policies, or public services. Despite initiatives for in-situ rehabilitation and affordable housing, few cities have succeeded in institutionalising a socially inclusive urban model.

The principle of decentralization and participatory governance emerges as one of the most unevenly implemented across all four metros. Ward committees, citizen charters, and participatory platforms exist on paper but are rarely operationalized in ways that meaningfully engage residents in decision-making. Planning remains highly centralized, dominated by a few institutions with limited mechanisms for bottom-up inputs. This erodes both democratic accountability and the responsiveness needed for equitable urban development.

The principle of environmental sustainability is acknowledged across plans and policies, yet actual performance is weak. Cities continue to expand into ecologically sensitive areas, green cover is declining, lakes and wetlands are deteriorating, and climate-sensitive design remains the exception rather than the norm. Institutional fragmentation in the management of environmental assets leads to poor enforcement and minimal inter-agency coordination, weakening the impact of well-intentioned ecological provisions.

The principle of data-driven governance—critical to informed, adaptive, and transparent urban management—is the most nascent across all cases. Though

e-governance platforms and digital tools are growing, there is no institutionalized culture of open data, real-time monitoring, or integrated urban observatories in any of the four cities. Without such systems, the ability to assess outcomes, evaluate policy impact, or engage citizens meaningfully remains constrained.

Despite these gaps, it is evident that all four cities have made notable strides in aligning their urban visions with NUPF principles, particularly in their statutory plans and policy discourse. The gap lies not in the intent, but in institutionalization, enforcement, capacity, and coherence. Translating the NUPF into lived urban experience requires bridging these operational deficits, ensuring that principles are not just referenced in documents but embedded in everyday governance, planning, and service delivery systems.

The reflections in this section reaffirm the importance of NUPF as a normative and guiding framework. However, they also suggest that national urban policy must go beyond prescription and actively support cities through technical capacity-building, financial decentralization, regulatory reform, and intergovernmental coordination. The final section concludes the chapter with a summary of insights and sets the stage for policy recommendations in the next chapter.

7.5 Conclusion

This comparative analysis of Delhi, Kolkata, Bengaluru, and Hyderabad illustrates the dynamic yet uneven pathways of metropolitan development in India. Each of these cities represents a unique constellation of historical legacies, institutional capacities, and policy priorities, yet they also share common challenges that reflect broader national trends. While the cities have embraced the core principles of the National Urban Policy Framework (NUPF) in varying degrees—through planning instruments, sectoral strategies, and institutional reforms—their practical implementation remains limited by structural, financial, and governance-related constraints.

Across the ten functional areas assessed, it is evident that most metropolitan regions have adopted modern planning vocabulary, prioritized infrastructure expansion, and experimented with new forms of spatial and economic organization. However, the mismatch between plan and practice persists. Informality, exclusion, ecological degradation, and governance fragmentation continue to shape urban realities in ways that deviate from the NUPF's vision of inclusive, sustainable, and well-governed cities. While infrastructure-led growth and economic competitiveness have gained policy traction, spatial justice, environmental integrity, and participatory governance remain underdeveloped.

Despite this, there are also important lessons and innovations emerging from each city. Delhi's institutional planning framework, Kolkata's multimodal

mobility network, Bengaluru's experiments with digital infrastructure, and Hyderabad's corridor-based spatial strategy all offer valuable entry points for policy refinement and inter-city learning. What becomes clear is that achieving the transformative potential of the NUPF requires not just technical planning tools but deeper institutional reform, decentralized capacity, inter-agency coordination, and robust civic engagement.

This chapter has provided a cross-sectional understanding of where metropolitan India stands in relation to the ideals set out in the NUPF. The next chapter builds on these findings to offer concrete policy recommendations and reform strategies. These are not only meant to address the gaps identified here but to guide India's metropolitan regions toward more inclusive, integrated, and resilient urban futures.

CHAPTER

8

Building Sustainable and Inclusive Metropolitan Futures

8.1 Introduction

India's metropolitan regions stand at a critical crossroads. As engines of national economic growth, sites of complex social dynamics, and landscapes of intense ecological stress, they represent both the promise and peril of urban transformation in the 21st century. The scale and speed of metropolitanization have brought unprecedented challenges—ranging from informality and infrastructure deficits to climate risks, institutional fragmentation, and rising inequalities. Yet, they also present an opportunity to reimagine the future of urban India through a more inclusive, sustainable, and adaptive planning paradigm.

This chapter seeks to explore the contours of future-oriented metropolitan planning, guided by the principles of spatial justice, climate resilience, collaborative governance, and technological enablement. It draws upon the analytical insights of earlier chapters—from the historical evolution of city systems and regional linkages to the national policy landscape and case-based evaluations—to build a comprehensive vision for India's metropolitan futures.

At the heart of this vision lies the question: *How can India's metropolitan regions be governed and planned in a way that is both equitable and forward-looking?* Answering this requires rethinking planning instruments, strengthening institutional capacity, ensuring participatory frameworks, and embedding sustainability at every level of governance. The integration of theories such as Urban Political Ecology, Ecological Urbanism, the Just City, and Resilience Thinking helps us conceptualize these futures not as technocratic solutions, but as deeply embedded in the socio-political, cultural, and ecological contexts of Indian cities.

The Government of India's efforts—such as the URDPFI Guidelines, Smart Cities Mission, and the National Urban Policy Framework—have laid the groundwork for such transitions. However, evidence from multiple reports and case studies suggests that metropolitan governance in India continues to

be hampered by fragmented jurisdictions, inadequate financing, and lack of long-term visioning (NITI Aayog 2021; UN-Habitat 2023). Many cities still function under legacy master plans that fail to reflect the real-time dynamism and diversity of urban life.

As we move into the post-pandemic urban era, marked by digital disruption, climate anxiety, and demographic shifts, the need for adaptive, polycentric, and people-centric metropolitan planning becomes more urgent than ever. This chapter will, therefore, map out both the challenges and possibilities of metropolitan transitions in India—grounded in theory, informed by practice, and guided by a normative commitment to inclusion and sustainability.

In doing so, it envisions not just the physical and economic form of future metropolitan India, but also its governance frameworks, institutional cultures, and everyday lived realities.

8.2 Key Challenges Ahead

The pathway to building sustainable and inclusive metropolitan futures in India is fraught with complex, multi-dimensional challenges. These challenges arise not only from physical and spatial pressures but also from deep-rooted structural issues embedded in governance, socio-economic dynamics, ecological fragility, and institutional inertia. Understanding these constraints is essential for formulating transformative urban strategies that are grounded in local realities and aligned with national development aspirations.

8.2.1 Demographic Pressures and Migratory Influx

Metropolitan regions have become magnets for economic opportunities, drawing large-scale migration from rural and smaller urban areas. While migration fuels labour markets and contributes to urban productivity, it also places overwhelming stress on infrastructure, basic services, and housing systems (NITI Aayog 2021). Informal settlements proliferate along urban peripheries, often without access to water, sanitation, and public transport, reinforcing cycles of exclusion and urban poverty (UN-Habitat 2023; NIUA 2022).

8.2.2 Institutional Fragmentation and Weak Planning Capacities

One of the most persistent challenges in metropolitan governance is the fragmented institutional structure that disperses responsibilities across multiple agencies with overlapping jurisdictions. The absence of empowered Metropolitan Planning Committees (MPCs)—as mandated under the 74th Constitutional Amendment—remains a significant gap in decentralized planning (MoHUA

2015; UN-Habitat 2016b). Even where MPCs exist, such as in Kolkata or Mumbai, their functional authority and integration into state planning processes remain weak (NIUA, 2015; TCPO, 2014).

This governance fragmentation leads to siloed decision-making and a lack of coordinated spatial development. According to Sharma, Goel, and Singh (2022), even the preparation of development plans in megacities like Delhi, Ahmedabad, and Chennai largely excludes meaningful citizen participation and fails to reflect the needs of diverse social groups, further weakening urban accountability.

8.2.3 Spatial Inequality and Exclusion

The unequal distribution of urban infrastructure, amenities, and economic opportunities continues to marginalize large sections of the metropolitan population. Gender, caste, class, and disability-based exclusions are deeply embedded in how cities are planned and experienced. The CITIES INSIGHTS Report (NIUA and DFID 2020) highlights how built environments in Indian cities often fail to accommodate the needs of persons with disabilities and other marginalized communities, both in terms of design and policy frameworks.

These spatial injustices are compounded by land speculation, gentrification through area-based urban renewal, and unaffordable housing (Praharaj 2021). Urban Political Ecology theory helps contextualize these patterns as outcomes of unequal power dynamics in access to urban resources, where ecological burdens and infrastructural deficits disproportionately fall upon the urban poor (Heynen, Kaika, and Swyngedouw 2006).

8.2.4 Environmental Degradation and Climate Vulnerabilities

Indian metropolitan regions are increasingly exposed to climate risks such as flooding, heatwaves, air pollution, and water scarcity. Urban expansion often occurs at the cost of wetlands, riverbanks, and forests, diminishing natural resilience (UN-Habitat 2023). This ecological disruption, coupled with rising emissions and shrinking green cover, undermines long-term sustainability.

The concept of Ecological Urbanism urges planners to embed environmental logic into the design of cities—not as an afterthought but as the structuring principle of urban form and metabolism (Mostafavi and Doherty, 2010). Yet in practice, spatial planning often disregards such ecological thresholds. The Habitat III India Report (2016) acknowledges the growing environmental stress but points to weak enforcement of environmental protection policies, especially in metropolitan peripheries.

8.2.5 Data Deficits and Technological Gaps

While smart city initiatives have increased the availability of urban data, significant gaps remain in spatially disaggregated, real-time, and open-access information systems, especially for metropolitan-scale planning (NIUA 2022a). The digital divide further compounds this challenge, excluding smaller municipalities and citizen groups from leveraging data for planning or participation.

Moreover, the technological emphasis in many smart city projects is skewed toward infrastructure rather than inclusivity or governance innovation. Without proper institutional integration and capacity-building, digital tools risk becoming technocratic layers over structurally unequal systems (Praharaj 2021).

8.2.6 Synthesis of Challenges

These challenges are not isolated—they intersect and reinforce one another. For example, weak metropolitan governance structures exacerbate spatial inequality; fragmented planning contributes to ecological vulnerability; and lack of public participation undermines inclusive visioning. The cumulative effect is a metropolitan system that is misaligned with both the constitutional mandate for decentralization and the global imperative of sustainable urbanization.

8.3 Vision for Metropolitan Futures

India's metropolitan regions must shift from reactive, piecemeal urbanism to a proactive, inclusive, and future-ready metropolitan strategy. This vision must not only address the current challenges of fragmented governance, spatial inequality, and environmental degradation but also embed long-term adaptability, justice, and resilience at the core of planning. Building on lessons from theory, policy, and practice, this section outlines five key pillars for reimagining India's metropolitan futures.

8.3.1 Smart, Inclusive, and Resilient Metropolitanism

The future of metropolitan regions lies in the integration of technological intelligence with social inclusion. Smartness cannot be reduced to ICT-based interventions but must embrace the principles of *adaptive governance*, *real-time responsiveness*, and *human-centric infrastructure* (UN-Habitat 2013). Inclusivity must be operationalized through targeted interventions that prioritize vulnerable groups, as emphasized in the CITIES INSIGHTS Report (NIUA, 2020), ensuring that the urban future works for children, women, the elderly, and people with disabilities.

Table 8.1 Pillars of Metropolitan Vision for the Future

Pillar No.	*Vision Pillar*	*Description*	*Source(s) / Frameworks*
1	Smart, Inclusive, and Resilient Urbanism	Integration of technology, equity, and resilience in planning and service delivery	UN-Habitat (2013), NIUA (2022), Resilience Theory (Holling 1973)
2	Ecological Urbanism and Nature-Based Planning	Urban development grounded in ecological balance, landscape preservation, and regeneration	Mostafavi and Doherty (2010), UN-Habitat (2023)
3	Circular Economy and Regenerative Infrastructure	Resource-efficient urbanism focused on reuse, energy balance, and sustainable mobility	NIUA (2022), NITI Aayog (2021), SDG 11
4	Liveable and Healthy City-Regions	Prioritization of urban health, accessibility, walkability, and rights-based development	Harari (2019), Lefebvre (1968), NIUA (2020)
5	Polycentric and Interconnected Systems	Functional metropolitan regions with multiple urban nodes linked by integrated planning	Mohan and Dasgupta (2004), Glocal Urbanism (Brenner and Schmid 2005)

Source: Analysis

Resilience Thinking (Holling 1973; Meerow, Newell, and Stults 2016) supports this shift by promoting the capacity of metropolitan systems to absorb shocks—be they ecological, economic, or health-related—while retaining their core functionality. In Indian cities prone to climate risk, such as Mumbai or Chennai, resilience must be embedded through urban design, nature-based solutions, and robust risk governance frameworks (UN-Habitat 2023).

8.3.2 Ecological Urbanism and Nature-Based Solutions

The logic of ecological urbanism calls for planning approaches that consider ecological systems not as peripheral but as integral to urban life and form (Mostafavi and Doherty 2010). This includes restoring blue-green networks, conserving wetlands, embedding urban forests, and promoting decentralized wastewater systems. Metropolitan India's future must prioritize ecological metabolism—recognising the city as a living ecosystem that requires regeneration, not just infrastructure expansion.

As the Habitat III National Report (MoHUA 2016) points out, environmental degradation is now a metropolitan issue, not just a peripheral one. Cities must embrace policies that move beyond greenwashing and actively restructure land use and transport systems to promote ecological balance.

8.3.3 Circular Economy and Regenerative Infrastructure

Conventional models of linear consumption—build, use, discard—are no longer viable in the context of resource depletion and climate stress. The circular economy offers an alternative framework where urban systems are designed for reuse, recycling, and regeneration. Regenerative infrastructure—such as net-zero buildings, decentralized energy systems, and low-impact mobility—must become the cornerstone of metropolitan investments (NITI Aayog, 2021; NIUA 2022a).

This shift aligns with India's commitment to SDG 11 and requires systemic changes in procurement policies, urban finance, and public-private partnerships.

8.3.4 Liveable and Healthy City-Regions

A liveable metropolitan future must guarantee health, safety, accessibility, and dignity to all residents. This involves designing for walkability, mixed-use neighbourhoods, affordable housing, and universal access to services. The Right to the City (Lefebvre 1968) serves as a theoretical anchor, advocating that all urban residents—regardless of status—must have the right to shape, use, and access their city.

Studies such as Harari (2019) underline how spatial form affects health, mobility, and economic performance. Compact, well-connected urban geometries tend to perform better on both environmental and social indicators. India's metropolitan areas must, therefore, move away from uncontrolled urban sprawl and instead promote polycentric, transit-oriented development that reinforces equity and accessibility.

8.3.5 Polycentric and Interconnected Urban Systems

Metropolitan India is increasingly becoming a system of cities, not a single dominant urban core. As highlighted in the Stanford–World Bank paper (Mohan and Dasgupta 2004), polycentric structures enable balanced growth, reduce congestion, and enhance regional equity. Interconnected nodes within metropolitan regions—supported by integrated transport networks, digital connectivity, and spatial planning—can promote economic diversification and reduce dependency on the primary urban core.

The Glocal Urbanism framework (Brenner and Schmid 2005a) supports this idea by linking local specificity with global integration. Indian metropolitan futures must embrace this paradigm to remain competitive, inclusive, and resilient in an increasingly networked world.

This vision of metropolitan futures integrates spatial, social, ecological, economic, and institutional dimensions. It proposes a shift from fragmented governance to metropolitan coordination, from infrastructure-centric models to human-centric planning, and from short-term project thinking to long-term systemic transformation.

8.4 Strategic Planning Approaches

Realising sustainable and inclusive metropolitan futures in India requires a fundamental shift in the way metropolitan regions are planned, governed, and managed. Traditional master planning approaches—characterized by rigidity, exclusion, and outdated data—are increasingly unable to respond to the complexity, uncertainty, and diversity of urban realities. Instead, strategic metropolitan planning must embrace adaptive, participatory, and multi-scalar approaches that respond to rapid socio-spatial transformation, ecological risks, and the evolving needs of metropolitan citizens.

8.4.1 Long-Term and Adaptive Metropolitan Planning

Metropolitan planning in India often lacks long-term coherence. While many cities prepare development plans or smart city proposals, these are usually short- to medium-term and sectorally siloed. The NITI Aayog report (2021) and NIUA Annual Report (2022) both highlight the need for regional and metropolitan scale visioning that spans 20–30 years and adapts to dynamic socio-economic and environmental shifts.

Adaptive planning draws from Resilience Theory (Holling 1973) and views the metropolitan region as a complex, evolving system. Rather than fixating on static end-states, it promotes iterative planning, continuous monitoring, and the ability to revise strategies in response to emerging risks and opportunities. This includes scenario-building, stress-testing of urban systems, and flexible regulatory frameworks that allow cities to pivot under pressure.

8.4.2 Mainstreaming SDGs and Climate Goals into Metropolitan Planning

Strategic metropolitan planning must also align with global frameworks such as the Sustainable Development Goals (SDG 11) and India's climate commitments under the Paris Agreement. The UN-Habitat Country Report (2023) stresses the role of intermediary and metropolitan cities in achieving inclusive, safe, resilient, and sustainable urban futures. Incorporating climate-sensitive zoning, emission inventories, vulnerability assessments, and blue-green infrastructure into metropolitan plans is now a necessity rather than an option.

Table 8.2 Theory-to-Practice Map in Metropolitan Planning

Theory / Framework	*Core Concept*	*Application in Metropolitan Planning*
Future Studies (Bell, 2003)	Anticipating preferred futures	Visioning long-term urban growth and transformation scenarios
Urban Political Ecology	Urban inequalities linked to ecological injustice	Planning to redistribute environmental and infrastructural benefits equitably
Ecological Urbanism	Nature as a structuring element of cities	Integrating blue-green infrastructure, wetlands, and natural buffers
Just City (Fainstein, 2010)	Equity and justice in urban outcomes	Inclusive zoning, affordable housing, social infrastructure
Resilience Theory (Holling, 1973)	Adaptability in complex systems	Climate-responsive planning, scenario-based strategies
Right to the City (Lefebvre, 1996)	Collective urban citizenship and access	Participatory planning, gender-responsive and accessible public spaces
Collaborative Planning (Healey, 1997)	Stakeholder engagement and negotiation	Metropolitan-level participatory mechanisms and citizen inclusion
Glocal Urbanism	Local-global interplay in urban change	Contextualising global models to suit Indian metropolitan realities

Source: Analysis

Moreover, planning must focus on low-carbon transport, resource-efficient buildings, and nature-based solutions—elements critical for metropolitan resilience in an era of increasing climate volatility.

8.4.3 Integrating Digital Tools and Open Data in Governance

The future of planning lies in the intelligent use of real-time, spatially disaggregated data to inform decision-making and citizen engagement. Many smart city initiatives have introduced digital dashboards, GIS platforms, and IoT-based systems, but their use in metropolitan planning remains underdeveloped. Praharaj (2021) points out that data infrastructure must go beyond centralized control and become more participatory, open, and usable across departments and jurisdictions.

Urban data ecosystems can help identify planning gaps, track inclusion indicators, support predictive modelling, and enable real-time response mechanisms. For example, Delhi's Open Data Portal and Kochi's Integrated

Command Control Centre are pioneering efforts in linking technology to inclusive planning.

8.4.4 Participatory and Collaborative Planning Models

A strategic approach cannot succeed without engaging the very people it aims to serve. The URDPFI Guidelines (2014) and Habitat III National Report (2016) emphasize the constitutional mandate for citizen participation through Ward Committees, Metropolitan Planning Committees (MPCs), and public consultations. However, in practice, these mechanisms remain underutilized or symbolic in many Indian cities.

Drawing from Collaborative Planning Theory (Healey 1997), metropolitan planning must promote multi-stakeholder dialogues, community-led visioning, and iterative feedback mechanisms. Such approaches are especially vital in multi-jurisdictional metropolitan regions where planning must align across municipal, regional, and state-level actors.

Inclusion also means enabling youth, women, informal workers, slum dwellers, and persons with disabilities to shape metropolitan futures. This aligns with the Right to the City perspective, which frames urban planning not just as a technical process but as a democratic right.

8.4.5 Innovation in Planning Tools and Institutional Coordination

India's planning tools need systemic upgrades. Development Plans, Zonal Plans, and City Sanitation Plans must be complemented with Metropolitan Strategic Frameworks, Spatial Development Strategies, and Integrated Investment Plans that work across departments. Institutional coordination is critical for this, especially in polycentric regions where multiple municipalities coexist.

The URDPFI Guidelines (Volume IIA, 2014) propose a more integrated model involving the Town and Country Planning Organisation, State Planning Boards, and local planning authorities, with an emphasis on vertical and horizontal integration. States like Tamil Nadu and Maharashtra have demonstrated some success in this through mechanisms like metropolitan transport authorities and climate cells.

Together, these strategic planning approaches signal a shift away from reactive, sectoral, and technocratic planning to a more resilient, inclusive, and systemic metropolitan governance model. They aim to institutionalize future-readiness while remaining rooted in the everyday needs and rights of citizens.

8.5 Institutional Reforms and Governance Innovation

Institutional structures in India's metropolitan regions have historically been shaped by colonial legacies, post-independence planning regimes, and fragmented jurisdictional boundaries. While constitutional reforms such as the 74th Amendment aimed to decentralize urban governance, their implementation has been uneven, and in many cases, superficial. The lack of empowered and coordinated metropolitan governance has resulted in a planning vacuum, limiting cities' ability to respond effectively to rapid urbanization, ecological risks, and growing social inequalities.

Reforms in metropolitan governance are, therefore, not simply administrative requirements—they are foundational to realising the inclusive and sustainable futures outlined in earlier sections. Effective metropolitan futures demand governance that is multi-level, participatory, transparent, and aligned with the socio-spatial complexity of large urban regions.

One of the most critical institutional gaps in Indian metropolitan regions is the delayed and diluted implementation of the Metropolitan Planning Committees (MPCs). Despite being constitutionally mandated under Article 243ZE of the 74th Amendment, MPCs have been established in only a few cities and are often relegated to advisory roles without substantial authority. The URDPFI Guidelines (2014) and the Habitat III National Report (2016) highlight how this has limited the capacity for integrated spatial planning and investment coordination across jurisdictions. In many states, pre-existing development authorities continue to function parallel to MPCs, leading to duplication, conflict, and bureaucratic inertia.

The National Institute of Urban Affairs (2022) identifies the absence of inter-jurisdictional coordination as a major bottleneck in metropolitan planning. Fragmentation of responsibilities across municipalities, parastatal agencies, and state departments impedes the formulation of cohesive development strategies. The NIUA Annual Report (2022) further emphasizes the importance of coordinated frameworks that bring together transportation, housing, environment, and economic planning under unified governance mechanisms.

Reforms must also address the financial architecture of metropolitan planning. Most Urban Local Bodies (ULBs) in India operate with limited fiscal autonomy and rely heavily on state or central transfers. Without fiscal empowerment, decentralized planning remains an unfunded mandate. Instruments such as land value capture, green bonds, municipal borrowing, and participatory budgeting need to be scaled up and institutionalized across metropolitan regions. The Stanford–World Bank paper (Mohan & Dasgupta, 2004) stressed the importance of fiscal devolution to empower cities in managing their spatial and economic transitions effectively.

Digital governance innovation presents another frontier for reform. As shown in recent urban initiatives under the Smart Cities Mission, digital platforms can enable real-time service delivery, citizen participation, and performance monitoring. However, as Praharaj (2021) warns, without inclusive design and cross-agency integration, such technologies risk becoming tools of elite capture rather than catalysts for democratic planning. Governance reform must therefore include digital literacy, interoperable systems, open data platforms, and ethics-based frameworks for algorithmic urbanism.

Additionally, metropolitan governance must be rooted in the principles of transparency, subsidiarity, and co-production. Drawing from the collaborative planning model (Healey, 1997), this implies establishing institutional mechanisms that allow for genuine negotiation between state actors, civil society, private sector stakeholders, and marginalized communities. Metropolitan planning boards or councils should include representation from all tiers of government, alongside domain experts and citizen groups, to ensure that development reflects collective aspirations.

Legal harmonization is another prerequisite. The current landscape of overlapping laws—from municipal acts to special area statutes—needs alignment under a coherent metropolitan governance framework. The URDPFI Guidelines (2014) suggest that state governments undertake legislative reviews to ensure consistency, clarity, and flexibility in metropolitan governance. Examples from Maharashtra and Tamil Nadu indicate the possibility of integrating special planning authorities with MPC functions to avoid institutional redundancy and streamline accountability.

Finally, capacity-building is indispensable. The NITI Aayog report (2021) highlights the chronic shortage of trained urban planners, data analysts, and urban economists within public planning institutions. Institutional reforms must be accompanied by investments in human capital, with specialized training for planners, elected officials, and administrators in metropolitan governance, strategic planning, and participatory methods.

Institutional reforms and governance innovation thus form the backbone of metropolitan transformation. Without restructured and responsive governance, the most visionary plans are unlikely to be realized. Metropolitan regions must be empowered with not just the mandate, but also the mechanisms, capacity, and legitimacy to govern in ways that are inclusive, transparent, and future-ready.

8.6 People-Centric and Inclusive Futures

A metropolitan future that is not inclusive is inherently unsustainable. Inclusion must go beyond rhetorical commitments and be embedded in how cities are designed, governed, financed, and experienced. For India's metropolitan regions—marked by social heterogeneity, informal economies, and deep-rooted inequalities—the imperative to centre people in planning is not only ethical, but strategic. This section focuses on key pathways to operationalising inclusive metropolitanism, drawing from both normative frameworks and grounded practices.

Inclusive planning begins with recognising the Right to the City (Lefebvre 1968) as a foundational principle. This concept asserts that all urban residents—regardless of income, identity, or tenure—must have the right to participate in and benefit from urban life. It reframes urban space not as a commodity, but as a shared social and political resource. Metropolitan governance must institutionalize this right through participatory platforms, equitable access to services, and spatial justice in land use decisions.

Gender-sensitive and youth-responsive planning is a crucial dimension of inclusion. Despite growing policy attention, cities continue to be designed from a male-centric lens, often neglecting the mobility patterns, safety concerns, and spatial needs of women, children, and the elderly. The Cities Insights Report (NIUA and DFID 2020) emphasizes the need for gender audits, inclusive design standards, and disaggregated data collection to inform planning. Public spaces, transit systems, and built environments must be reimagined through an intersectional lens that recognizes how gender interacts with caste, class, and ability.

The role of cultural identity and heritage in shaping inclusive futures is also critical. Metropolitan areas, while rapidly globalising, are also spaces of diverse cultural traditions, linguistic communities, and indigenous knowledge systems. Planning must protect and revitalize these cultural assets—not as passive monuments, but as living practices that shape belonging and well-being. This is especially important in marginalized urban areas, where cultural spaces are often displaced by speculative development or uniform redevelopment schemes.

Housing and mobility represent two of the most contested domains in metropolitan India. As highlighted in Praharaj (2021), area-based redevelopment often results in gentrification and displacement, pushing low-income residents to peripheral zones with inadequate infrastructure. Affordable housing policy must go beyond supply-side targets to include location, accessibility, tenure security, and integration with employment hubs. Similarly, mobility justice requires prioritising walking, cycling, and public transit over car-centric planning, ensuring that transport systems serve the needs of low-income, women, elderly, and disabled users.

The Right to the City framework, when operationalized through participatory planning tools such as neighbourhood assemblies, ward sabhas, and citizen report cards, can help build legitimacy and responsiveness into metropolitan governance. Yet, as Sharma, Goel, and Singh (2022) observe, such tools remain underutilized or tokenistic in many Indian cities. Deepening participation requires enabling environments, legal mandates, and sustained institutional support.

Digital inclusion is another critical frontier. Smart city platforms, while expanding service delivery, often exclude those without digital access or literacy. As Praharaj (2021) argues, a people-centric smart urbanism must embed inclusivity at the level of design, accessibility, and governance. Community Wi-Fi zones, participatory GIS platforms, and vernacular-language applications are some ways to bridge the digital divide within metropolitan regions.

Inclusivity also demands that urban transformations be guided by the lived realities of informal workers, migrants, women-headed households, transgender persons, and others at the urban margins. Urban Political Ecology helps us see how infrastructural choices, environmental burdens, and policy biases often reinforce exclusion. A genuinely inclusive future must challenge these structural dynamics by redistributing not just resources, but voice, visibility, and power.

Building people-centric metropolitan futures is not only about adding inclusion to existing models; it is about reimagining planning itself—from a top-down, technocratic exercise to a dialogic, justice-oriented process. Such a shift will enable India's metropolitan regions to function not merely as engines of economic growth, but as inclusive, dignified spaces of urban citizenship.

8.7 Global Best Practices and Indian Applications

While metropolitan governance challenges vary by region, cities around the world are navigating shared pressures of climate change, inequality, mobility transitions, and resource scarcity. Examining global best practices offers critical insights into how visionary urban strategies can be effectively translated into action. However, their relevance to India depends on how well they are adapted to local institutional realities, governance structures, and socio-spatial diversity.

Metropolitan Seoul has emerged as a leading example of integrated regional governance. The Seoul Metropolitan Government coordinates across 25 autonomous districts, employing a long-term vision supported by its own metropolitan planning institute. Projects like the Cheonggyecheon River restoration demonstrate how ecological infrastructure can simultaneously address climate vulnerability, pedestrian mobility, and urban revitalization. This aligns closely with the principles of ecological urbanism that have growing relevance for Indian cities (UN-Habitat 2023).

Amsterdam, through its 2020 Circular Strategy, has adopted the Doughnut Economics framework to restructure its urban metabolism. The city uses material flow analysis, green procurement policies, and public-private partnerships to build regenerative urban systems. This approach is particularly relevant to Indian metropolitan regions struggling with landfill overflow, construction waste, and unsustainable consumption patterns (UN-Habitat 2013).

Singapore's Urban Redevelopment Authority (URA) showcases the potential of state-led anticipatory planning. The URA updates its Concept Plans every ten years and Master Plans every five years, combining land-use strategy with transport, housing, and environmental goals. These plans are developed using scenario-based modelling and extensive public engagement. While the scale and centralization of Singapore's system may not be replicable in India, its emphasis on long-range, cross-sectoral visioning is highly applicable (UN-Habitat 2013).

In India, certain metropolitan innovations already demonstrate the potential of inclusive and future-ready planning. Pune's participatory budgeting, launched in 2006, enables citizens to propose local projects and vote on them, improving transparency and local accountability (UN-Habitat 2016). Kochi's Water Metro project integrates multi-modal transport and climate-responsive infrastructure to connect low-income island communities to the urban core (NIUA 2022a).

Delhi's Electric Vehicle Policy (2020) is another example of integrated planning, targeting 25% EV registration by 2024 and incentivising both private and public electric mobility. Its design is informed by climate action plans, health impact studies, and economic incentives (NIUA 2022). Similarly, Tamil Nadu's Gender Budgeting Framework requires each department to earmark allocations for women's development and submit gender audits, thereby institutionalising inclusion in financial planning (NITI Aayog 2021).

These Indian examples are supported by global planning principles but adapted to context. As noted by Brenner and Schmid (2005a), glocal urbanism requires local adaptation of global models—recognising cultural, institutional, and political specificities. For instance, Amsterdam's data-driven circularity is resource-intensive, whereas in India, low-tech community-based resource systems (e.g., composting, recycling collectives) may be more scalable and inclusive.

International frameworks also offer tools for structuring metropolitan boundaries. The OECD's Functional Urban Area (FUA) methodology, based on commuting zones and service flows, provides a more dynamic understanding of metropolitan extent. Applying such frameworks in India would help shift away from rigid municipal boundaries toward spatially fluid planning geographies (OECD 2021; NIUA 2022).

While global models offer inspiration, their successful localization in India hinges on building institutional capacity, policy continuity, and public trust. The key is not to replicate but to reinterpret—infusing best practices with participatory approaches, vernacular knowledge, and a rights-based ethic.

8.8 Concluding Reflections

The future of India's metropolitan regions cannot be left to inertia, fragmented governance, or market-led speculation. As urban India crosses critical demographic, ecological, and technological thresholds, the need to envision and implement sustainable, inclusive, and adaptive metropolitan futures has never been more urgent. This chapter has traced the key challenges, normative visions, strategic pathways, institutional reforms, and grounded practices that together offer a roadmap for metropolitan transformation.

A consistent theme across these discussions is the imperative to move beyond technocratic and sectoral planning models toward integrated, participatory, and justice-oriented metropolitan governance. The limitations of current institutional arrangements—most notably the under-empowered Metropolitan Planning Committees, limited fiscal autonomy of local bodies, and weak inter-jurisdictional coordination—must be addressed through legal reforms, capacity-building, and decentralized finance mechanisms (MoHUA 2015; NITI Aayog 2021; UN-Habitat, 2016).

Equally important is the integration of people-centric principles into every aspect of metropolitan planning. Concepts like the Right to the City, ecological urbanism, and resilience theory are not abstract ideals—they are grounded frameworks for reconfiguring urban systems to be more equitable, adaptive, and responsive to local realities. Ensuring gender sensitivity, mobility justice, digital inclusion, and cultural resilience are not add-ons but prerequisites for a democratic and inclusive urban future (NIUA and DFID 2020; Sharma, Goel, and Singh 2022).

Global and Indian examples—from Seoul's ecological restoration and Amsterdam's circular economy to Pune's participatory budgeting and Kochi's climate-responsive mobility—illustrate that transformative change is possible when vision, governance, and people align. However, as Brenner and Schmid (2005a) remind us, the success of these practices depends on how well they are localized, negotiated, and institutionalized within specific urban contexts.

Metropolitan futures must also embrace uncertainty as a condition of planning. This requires flexible policy instruments, real-time data ecosystems, and planning cultures that value experimentation, co-creation, and learning. The vision is not a single master plan, but an evolving set of strategies grounded in a shared commitment to inclusion, ecological balance, and long-term resilience.

Ultimately, the chapter calls for a new metropolitan ethic—one that sees urbanization not merely as an economic phenomenon, but as a social, ecological, and political project. The challenge is not simply to plan cities, but to reimagine urban life itself. If India's metropolitan regions are to become truly sustainable and inclusive, they must be guided by institutions that are accountable, planning systems that are adaptive, and citizens who are empowered to shape their own urban futures.

References

Ahrar, S., and A. Staub. "Bridging The Digital Divide: Methodological Strategies for Conducting Remote Urban Research". *Enquiry The ARCC Journal for Architectural Research*, vol. 22, no. 1, July 2025, pp. 52-63, doi:10.17831/enqarcc.v22i1.1242.

Artioli, F. and P. Le Galès. 2025. 'Metropolitan Governance as Organised Anarchy: The Case of the Paris Region', *Cities*, 158, p. 105607. Available at: https://sciencespo.hal.science/hal-04871083v1 [Accessed 24 March 2025].

Asian Development Bank (ADB) and National Capital Region Planning Board (NCRPB). 2021. *India: Delhi Urban Environment and Infrastructure Improvement Project (Report No. 55285-001).*

Banerjee, S. 2018. 'Urban Expansion of the City of Kolkata since Last 25 Years using Remote Sensing', *IJRAR*, 5(2): 361–7.

Bangalore Development Authority (BDA). 2017. *Revised Master Plan for Bengaluru – 2031 (Draft): Volume-1 (Vision Document).* Available at: https://data-opencity.sgp1.cdn.digitaloceanspaces.com/Documents/Recent/Bengaluru-BDA-RMP-2031-Volume_4_PlanningDistrictReport.pdf

Bhagat, R.B. 2014, January. 'Urban Policies and Programmes in India: Retrospect and Prospect', *Yojana*, 58, pp. 4–8.

Biswas, A. and K.K. Maurya. 2018. 'Governance and Institutional Framework for Smart Cities in India.' In *Handbook of Research on Urban Governance and Management in the Developing World*, J.M. Katusiimeh. United States of America: IGI Global.

Brenner, N. and C. Schmid. 2005a. 'Glocal Urbanism: Urban Restructuring between the Global and the Local' in *The Global Cities Reader*, edited by R. Keil. London: Routledge, pp. 224–30.

BRICS. 2019, 14 November. 'Brasília Declaration (11th BRICS Summit): Commitment to sustainable and inclusive urbanization'.

Chatterjee, A. and R.N. Chattopadhyay. 2020. 'Problems and Policies of Metropolitan Growth in India' In *Satellite Towns in Neo-metropolitan Development in India*. Singapore: Springer.

Census of India. 2011. *Provisional Population Totals – Urban Agglomerations and Cities.* New Delhi: Office of the Registrar General and Census Commissioner, Government of India.

CSCAF. 2022. *Climate Smart Cities Assessment Framework 3.0 – Technical Document.* New Delhi: Ministry of Housing and Urban Affairs, Government of India.

Delhi Development Authority (DDA). 2021. *Draft Master Plan for Delhi–2041*. Available at: https://dda.gov.in

Elliott, J.R. 1997. 'Cycles Within the System: Metropolitanisation and Internal Migration in the US, 1965–90', *Urban Studies*, 34(1): 21–41. Available at: https://www.jstor.org/stable/43083248.

Fields, D. 2009. 'The Planned City Sweeps the Poor Away: Urban Planning and Displacement in India', *Planning in Practice*, 5(3): 1–18.

Gandhi, S. and A. Pethe. 2017. 'Merging Challenges of Metropolitan Governance in India', *Environment and Urbanization ASIA*, 8(1): 62–74.

GIZ and MoHUA. 2022. *Pathways for Mainstreaming Urban Climate Actions in India*. Deutsche Gesellschaft für Internationale Zusammenarbeit (GIZ) GmbH and Ministry of Housing and Urban Affairs.

Government of India. 1976. 'The Urban Land (Ceiling and Regulation) Act, 1976.' New Delhi: Ministry of Law and Justice. Available at: https://legislative.gov.in/sites/default/files/A1976-33.pdf

———. 1992. 'The Constitution (Seventy-Fourth Amendment) Act, 1992.' New Delhi: Ministry of Law and Justice. Available at: https://legislative.gov.in/sites/default/files/74th%20Amendment.pdf.

———. 2016. *Habitat III National Report*. New Delhi: Ministry of Housing and Urban Affairs. Available at: https://habitat3.org/wp-content/uploads/Habitat-III_India-National-Report.pdf.

Guénard, C. and P.N. Giraud. 2014. 'Urbanization and Development'. In *Climate Change and Development Series*, edited by M. Hallegatte, A. Vogt-Schilb, J. Rozenberg, M. Bangalore, and C. Beaudet. The World Bank.

Habitat III National Report – India. 2016. *Urban Challenges and Policy Responses*. New Delhi: Ministry of Housing and Urban Poverty Alleviation, Government of India.

Harari, M. 2019. 'Cities in Bad Shape: Urban Geometry in India', University of Pennsylvania. Available at: https://faculty.wharton.upenn.edu/wp-content/uploads/1970/01/CityShapeSept2019-1.pdf.

Healey, P. 1997. *Collaborative Planning: Shaping Places in Fragmented Societies*. Vancouver: UBC Press.

Heynen, N., M. Kaika, and E. Swyngedouw. 2006. *In the Nature of Cities: Urban Political Ecology and the Politics of Urban Metabolism*. Routledge.

Holling, C.S. 1973. 'Resilience and Stability of Ecological Systems'. *Annual Review of Ecology and Systematics*, Vol 4. Canada: University of British Columbia

Hussain, L. 2024. 'Urban Expansion and Changing Settlement Patterns of Hyderabad City After 1990s', *International Journal for Multidisciplinary Research*, 6(5): 53–9.

Hyderabad Metropolitan Development Authority (HMDA). 2010. 'Zoning Regulations and Master Plan Guidelines—Hyderabad Metropolitan Region'. Available at: https://www.hmda.gov.in

———. 2013. 'Metropolitan Development Plan–2031 for Hyderabad Metropolitan Region'. Available at: https://assetyogi.b-cdn.net/wp-content/uploads/2014/09/Notification-hmda-master-plan-2031.pdf

International Water Management Institute (IWMI). 2021. 'Peri-Urban Interface of Indian Cities: A Scoping Study of Challenges and Opportunities'. Colombo, Sri

Lanka: IWMI. Available at: https://www.iwmi.cgiar.org/publications/iwmi-research-reports/rr-peri-urban-interface.

Kebza, M. 2024. *Urban Transitions in the Global South: Dynamics of Indian Metropolitanisation.* Oxford University Press.

Kim, S.M. 2012. 'Governance Challenges in Regional Planning: India's NCR Experience', *ISOCARP Congress Proceedings 2012*, pp. 1–12.

Knight Frank. 2020. 'Bengaluru Urban Infrastructure Report – India Urban Infrastructure Series.' Available at: https://content.knightfrank.com/research/2142/documents/en/bengaluru-urban-infrastructure-report-2020-india-urban-infrastructure-report-7671.pdf

Kolkata Metropolitan Development Authority (KMDA). 1998. *Land Use and Development Control Plan (LUDCP), West Bank Area.*

———. 2005. *Perspective Plan for Kolkata Metropolitan Area: Vision 2025.*

Kundu, D., A. Pandey, and P. Sharma. 2019a. *Making Cities Work: Policies and Programmes in India.* New Delhi: National Institute of Urban Affairs.

Land (2022) *Special Issue: The Governance of Land Use.* Basel: MDPI. Available at: https://www.mdpi.com/journal/land/special_issues/governance_land_use

Lakshmisha, L. and H. Nagendra. 2025. *When Urbanisation Leads to Governance Beyond the State: The Case of Commons and Lake Systems in Bengaluru.* (Unpublished manuscript)

Lefebvre, H. 1968. *Le droit à la ville* [The Right to the City]. Paris: Anthropos.

Long Range Transportation Plan (LRTP). 2021. *Sustainable Mobility Frameworks for Indian Cities.* New Delhi: Ministry of Housing and Urban Affairs.

Majumdar, S. and L. Sivaramakrishnan. 2020. 'Mapping of Urban Growth Dynamics in Kolkata Metropolitan Area: A Geospatial Approach', *Urbanization and Regional Sustainability in South Asia.* Springer, pp.27–42.

Marwaha, V., R. Gupta, and S. Bhatia. 2024. 'Institutional Fragmentation in Indian Metropolitan Governance'.

McDonald, R.I., P. Green, D. Balk, K. Weber, J. Padowski, M. Flörke, C. Scheidner, T. Gleeson, S. Eckman, B. Lehner, T. Boucher, G. Grill, and M. Montgomery. (2014) 'Cities, Pollution, and Biodiversity: Governance and Policy for the Future of Urban Nature', *Solutions*, 5(6): 60–9.

McGranahan, G., C. Tacoli, and D. Satterthwaite. 2006. *Urban Systems and the Rural–Urban Interface: Urbanization and Environmental Burdens.* London: International Institute for Environment and Development (IIED).

Meerow, S., J.P. Newell, and M. Stults. 2016. 'Defining Urban Resilience: A Review.' *Landscape and Urban Planning*, 147, pp. 38–49. Available at: https://doi.org/10.1016/j.landurbplan.2015.11.011

Mills, G. and O. Tarasova. 6–10 September 2021. 'Implementing Integrated Urban Services'. Conference presentation at European Meteorological Society (EMS) Annual Meeting 2021. Available at: https://meetingorganizer.copernicus.org/EMS2021/EMS2021-501.html

Ministry of Environment and Forests. 2011. *Coastal Regulation Zone (CRZ) Notification.* New Delhi: Government of India.

Ministry of Housing and Urban Affairs (MoHUA). 2014a. *Swachh Bharat Mission – Urban: Guidelines*. New Delhi: Government of India. Available at: https://swachhbharaturban.gov.in

———. 2014b. *Urban and Regional Development Plans Formulation and Implementation (URDPFI) Guidelines – Volume I & II*. New Delhi: Government of India. Available at: https://mohua.gov.in/upload/uploadfiles/files/URDPFI%20Guidelines%20Vol%201.pdf

Ministry of Housing and Urban Affairs (2014) *URDPFI Guidelines – Volume I*. Government of India. [Duplicate copy used for additional citations].

———. 2015a. *Smart Cities Mission: Guidelines*. New Delhi: Ministry of Housing and Urban Affairs, Government of India.

———. 2015b. *HRIDAY Scheme Guidelines*. New Delhi: Government of India.

———. 2015c. *Urban and Regional Development Plans Formulation and Implementation (URDPFI) Guidelines – Volume I & II*. New Delhi: Government of India. Available at: https://mohua.gov.in/upload/uploadfiles/files/URDPFI%20Guidelines%20Vol%201.pdf

———. 2015d. *Urban Transport Initiatives in India: Best Practices in PPP*. New Delhi: Government of India.

Ministry of Housing and Urban Affairs (MoHUA). 2016. *Outcome Budget 2016–17*. New Delhi: Government of India. Available at: https://mohua.gov.in.

———. 2017. *Smart Cities Mission Statement and Guidelines*. New Delhi: Government of India.

———. 2018. *National Urban Policy Framework: Strategic Intent Document*. New Delhi: Ministry of Housing and Urban Affairs, Government of India.

———. 2020. *National Urban Policy Framework*. New Delhi: Government of India.

———. 2023. *National Urban Policy Framework (Draft)*. New Delhi: Government of India. Available at: https://mohua.gov.in/upload/latestnews/63f729b902a64NUPF_Draft_2023.pdf.

Ministry of Housing and Urban Poverty Alleviation (MoHUPA). 2009. *National Policy on Urban Street Vendors*. New Delhi: Government of India. Available at: https://mohua.gov.in/upload/uploadfiles/files/Streetvendingpolicy2009.pdf

Ministry of Urban Development (MoUD) and Ministry of Environment and Forests (MoEF). 2010. *National Mission on Sustainable Habitat: Mission Document*. New Delhi: Government of India.

Ministry of Urban Development (MoUD). 2008. *National Urban Sanitation Policy (NUSP)*. New Delhi: Government of India.

———. 2012. *Evolving City Systems: An Institutional Framework for Metropolitan Planning in India*. New Delhi: Government of India.

———. 2014. *National Urban Transport Policy (NUTP)*. New Delhi: Government of India. Available at: https://mohua.gov.in.

———. 2015. *Operational Guidelines for HRIDAY Scheme*. New Delhi: Government of India.

———. 2016a. *Habitat III – India National Report*. New Delhi: Ministry of Urban Development, Government of India.

———. 2016b. *Outcome Budget 2016–17*. New Delhi: Ministry of Urban Development, Government of India.

———. 2022. *Integrated Urban Planning and Management: Policy Frameworks and Initiatives*. New Delhi: Government of India.

———. 2023. *Annual Report 2022–23*. New Delhi: Ministry of Housing and Urban Affairs, Government of India.

Mohapatra, P. 2024. 'Informality and the Inclusive City: Planning Challenges in Indian Metropolises'. Indian Journal of Urban Affairs.

Mohan, R. and S. Dasgupta. 2004. 'Urban Development in India in the Twenty-First Century: Policies for Accelerating Urban Growth' Stanford Center for International Development Working Paper No. 231. Stanford University.

Mostafavi, M. and G. Doherty (eds). 2010. *Ecological Urbanism*. Baden: Lars Müller Publishers.

Mumbai Metropolitan Region Development Authority (MMRDA), n.d. *Planning Division Overview*. Available at: https://mmrda.maharashtra.gov.in/division/planning/overview [Accessed 24 March 2025].

———. 2024. *Planning and GIS Tools in the Mumbai Metropolitan Region*. Mumbai Metropolitan Region Development Authority.

National Institute of Urban Affairs (NIUA) and Department for International Development (DFID). 2020. *Cities Insights Report: Inclusive Urban Development in India*. New Delhi: NIUA and Department for International Development (DFID), Government of the UK.

———. 2021a. 'Data Smart Cities Strategy: Empowering Cities through Data'. New Delhi: NIUA. Available at: https://smartnet.niua.org/dsc/pdf/DataSmart_Cities_Strategy_Book.pdf

———. 2021b. *Dynamics of Peri-Urban Areas in India: Governance, Infrastructure, and Land*. New Delhi: NIUA. https://niua.in/publication/dynamics-peri-urban-india

———. 2021c. *Handbook on Urban Governance and Metropolitan Planning*.

———. 2021d. 'Reforms and Best Practices in Urban Planning and Governance in India'. Available at: https://niua.in

———. 2022a. *Annual Report 2021–2022*. New Delhi: NIUA. Available at: https://niua.in/intranet/sites/default/files/ANNUALREPORT_21-22_english.pdf [Accessed 25 March 2025].

———. 2022b. *Pathways for Urban Climate Action in India*. NIUA and GIZ India. Available at: https://niua.in

Nazim, M. 2022. 'Urban Governance and the Crisis of Indian Cities: Policy Paralysis and Prospects'. *Journal of Urban Affairs*, 44(3): 407–26.

Neelima, A., A.S. Reddy, and A. Siddhartha. 2021. 'Socio-Environmental Perspectives of Urban Development: The Case of Hyderabad, India', *International Journal of Scientific & Engineering Research*, 12(3): 675–9.

NITI Aayog, 2021. *Reforms in Urban Planning Capacity in India*. [pdf] Available at: https://www.niti.gov.in/sites/default/files/2021-09/UrbanPlanningCapacity-in-India-16092021.pdf.

———. 2021b. *Strategy for New India @ 75*. New Delhi: Government of India.

NIUA. 2021a. *Making Cities Work: Policies and Programmes in India*. New Delhi: National Institute of Urban Affairs. Available at: https://niua.in/intranet/sites/default/files/2087.pdf

———. 2021b. *Policy Landscape for Inclusive Cities*. New Delhi: National Institute of Urban Affairs.

———. 2022. *Pathways for Urban Climate Action in India*. NIUA and GIZ India. Available at: https://niua.in

National Urban Policy Framework (NUPF). 2018. *National Urban Policy Framework: Strategic Intent Document*. New Delhi: Ministry of Housing and Urban Affairs, Government of India.

National Urban Transport Policy (NUTP). 2014. *National Urban Transport Policy—Revised 2014*. New Delhi: Ministry of Urban Development, Government of India.

Organisation for Economic Co-operation and Development (OECD). 2021. *Definition of Functional Urban Areas (FUA)*. Available at: https://www.oecd.org/en/data/datasets/oecd-definition-of-cities-and-functional-urban-areas.html .

Praharaj, S. 2021. 'Area-based Urban Renewal Approach for Smart Cities Development in India: Challenges of Inclusion and Sustainability', *Urban Planning*, 6(4): 93–103. Available at: https://www.cogitatiopress.com/urbanplanning/article/view/4484 [Accessed 25 March 2025].

Puttalingaiah, S., S. Irfan, and A.D. Hanjagi. 2020. 'Levels of Urbanization in Bangalore Urban District of Karnataka, India.', *European Proceedings of Social and Behavioural Sciences*, 84, pp. 314–22.

Revi, A. 2016. 'Afterwards: Habitat III and the Sustainable Development Goals'. *Urbanization*, 1(2).

Sustainable Development Solutions Network (SDSN). 2021. *The Seven Transformations for More Equitable and Sustainable Cities: A Guide for Policymakers and Practitioners*. SDSN & TWI2050. Available at: https://www.sdsntrends.org/research/2021/seven-transformations.

Swachh Bharat Mission (SBM). 2014. *Swachh Bharat Mission (Urban) Guidelines*. New Delhi: Ministry of Urban Development, Government of India.

Sen, A. and H. Nagendra. 2021. 'The Differentiated Impacts of Urbanisation on Lake Communities in Bengaluru, India', *International Journal of the Commons*, 15(1): 209–25.

Seshadri, S.R. 2022. 'The Covid-19 Pandemic and the Health Sector: What Have We Learned?', In *Understanding post-Covid-19 Governance Challenges in India*. Azim Premji University, pp. 45–62.

Seta, F., J. Sen, A. Biswas, and A.A. Khare. 2017. 'From Poverty, Inequality to Smart City', *Springer Transactions in Civil and Environmental Engineering*.

Sharma, A. 2019. 'Governance Gaps and the Challenge of Urban Expansion in India', *Urban Studies*, 56(2): 301–20.

Sharma, R., A. Goel, and S. Singh. 2022. 'Analysis of Urban Development Plan Formulation in India with Special Reference to Public Participation', *International Journal of Research and Analytical Reviews (IJRAR)*, 9(4): 74–88. Available at: https://www.researchgate.net/publication/364353389 [Accessed 25 March 2025].

Solecki, W. and R. Leichenko. 2006. 'Urbanization and the Metropolitan Environment: Lessons from New York and Shanghai', *Environment*, 48(4): 8–23.

United Nations. 2016. Habitat III: New Urban Agenda. UN Conference on Housing and Sustainable Urban Development. https://habitat3.org/the-new-urban-agenda/

UN-Habitat. 2013. *Urban Planning for City Leaders*. Nairobi: UN-Habitat.

———. 2016a. *Habitat III National Report: India*. New Delhi: Ministry of Housing and Urban Affairs, Government of India.

———. 2016b. *The New Urban Agenda*. United Nations. Retrieved from https://habitat3.org/the-new-urban-agenda

———. 2020. *World Cities Report: The Value of Sustainable Urbanization*. Available at: https://unhabitat.org

———. 2023. *India Country Report 2023*. Available at: https://unhabitat.org/sites/default/files/2023/06/10._india_country_report_2023.pdf [Accessed 25 March 2025].

UN-Habitat and OECD. 2024. *Global State of National Urban Policy 2024*. Nairobi: United Nations Human Settlements Programme (UN-Habitat) and Organisation for Economic Co-operation and Development (OECD).

Urban and Regional Development Plans Formulation and Implementation (URDPFI). 2015a. *Urban and Regional Development Plans Formulation and Implementation Guidelines – Volume I*. New Delhi: Ministry of Urban Development, Government of India.

———. 2015b. *Urban and Regional Development Plans Formulation and Implementation Guidelines – Volume II A and II B*. New Delhi: Ministry of Urban Development, Government of India

———. 2015c. *Urban and Regional Development Plans Formulation and Implementation Guidelines – Volume I & II A*. New Delhi: Ministry of Urban Development, Government of India.

URDPFI Guidelines, 2014. *Urban and Regional Development Plans Formulation and Implementation Guidelines Volume IIA and IIB*. New Delhi: Town and Country Planning Organisation, Ministry of Housing and Urban Affairs, Government of India.

VBVR. 2022. 'HMDA Master Plan 2031: The Future of Hyderabad', Available at: https://vbvrprojects.com/hmda-master-plan-2031-the-future-of-hyderabad/

Wang, W., F. Wu, and F. Zhang. 2024. 'Metropolitanization Through Making "New Metropolitan Plans" in China', *Habitat International*, 143, p.102987. doi: 10.1016/j.habitatint.2023.102987.

Watson, V. 2009. 'The Planned City Sweeps the Poor Away...: Urban Planning and 21st Century Irbanization'. *Progress in Planning*, 72(3): 151–193. Available at: https://doi.org/10.1016/j.progress.2009.06.002.

World Bank. 2015. *Competitive Cities for Jobs and Growth: What, Who, and How*. The World Bank. Available at: https://www.worldbank.org

World Resources Institute. 2021. *Seven Transformations for More Equitable and Sustainable Cities*. WRI Ross Center for Sustainable Cities.

Index